Efficient Building Design Series
Volume I
Electrical and Lighting

J. Trost

Prentice Hll

Upper Saddle River, New Jersey   Columbus, Ohio

Library of Congress Cataloging-in-Publication Data

Trost, J.
    Efficient building design series / J. Trost
       p.   cm.
    Includes index.
    Contents: v. 1. Electrical and lighting
    ISBN 0-13-080335-9
    1. Building   I. Title.
  TH146.T64   1999   98–35394
   690 — dc21   CIP

Cover art: © Ceri Fitzgerald
Editor: Ed Francis
Production Editor: Christine M. Harrington
Design Coordinator: Karrie M. Converse
Text Designer: Carlisle Publishers Services
Cover Designer: Ceri Fitzgerald
Production Manager: Patricia A. Tonneman
Marketing Manager: Danny Hoyt

This book was set in Cochin by Carlisle Communications, Ltd. and was printed and bound by Courier/Kendallville, Inc. The cover was printed by Phoenix Color Corp.

Printed in the United States of America

10 9 8 7 6 5 4 3 2 1

ISBN: 0-13-080335-9

Prentice-Hall International (UK) Limited, *London*
Prentice-Hall of Australia Pty. Limited, *Sydney*
Prentice-Hall of Canada, Inc., *Toronto*
Prentice-Hall Hispanoamericana, S. A., *Mexico*
Prentice-Hall of India Private Limited, *New Delhi*
Prentice-Hall of Japan, Inc., *Tokyo*
Simon & Schuster Asia Pte. Ltd., *Singapore*
Editora Prentice-Hall do Brasil, Ltda., *Rio de Janeiro*

PREFACE

The art of design can associate itself with scientific skill, and do so without an inferiority complex.

Richard Neutra, 1954

Lighting designs shape perception and can enhance architecture. Talented lighting designers "see" much more than a typical observer.

This book is a primer for students, architects, constructors, managers, occupants, and owners who wish to refine and improve their understanding of lighting opportunities and building electrical systems. Committed readers can develop a working knowledge of the design decisions, equipment options, and operating costs associated with building lighting and electrical installations.

Readers who study the text and complete the review problems should be able to:

- Design, detail, and evaluate building lighting.
- Understand building electrical services and components.
- Integrate lighting and electrical components with building, materials, finishes, assemblies and structure.
- Estimate annual lighting and electrical utility costs.

A secondary goal is to respect your time, talent, and perception by presenting material in a concise, lucid format. Illustrations are included with text to expand and reinforce the information presented, and actual building applications are emphasized. Study problems follow the chapters so that you can develop confidence in your ability to apply new knowledge and skills. Lighting chapters cover perceptions, lamps, luminaires, and design examples. Electrical chapters attempt to explain this convenient energy form that lights, heats, cools, and powers buildings.

When a Professional—doctor, lawyer, architect—speaks of his work as "practice" he is confessing that there is a lot he doesn't know. Happily, he is also expressing a commendable willingness to learn.

Eugene Raskin, 1974

ACKNOWLEDGMENTS

David Leaney encouraged, supported, and improved this work. Where text and illustrations communicate effectively his ideas and suggestions are likely causes. David is a retired founding principal of D. W. Thomson Consultants Ltd., Vancouver B. C. Before retiring he was registered as a professional engineer in British Columbia, Alberta, Washington State, Yukon, and the United Kingdom. He is an ASHRAE Fellow and a CIBSE Fellow, and he has lectured in the architecture program at the University of British Columbia, and represented Canada as a contributor to divisions G & H of the NCARB Architects Registration Examination.

Further recognition and appreciation are due to Dr. Don Barnes, Louis Erhardt, and James Needham, Ph.D. for their perceptive help with parts of the manuscript. Thanks also to Prentice Hall reviewers D. Perry Achor, Purdue University; Robert Murphy, Wentworth Institute; and Marcel Sammut, Architect and Structural Engineer.

CONTENTS

This text describes building lighting and electrical systems. Chapters 1 through 8 emphasize design intent, while Chapters 9 through 13 stress construction requirements and operating costs. Home and office building examples tie together the lighting and electrical chapters. The same example buildings are also used in companion texts that cover HVAC and plumbing topics.

PART I

LIGHTING CHAPTERS

PART II

ELECTRICAL CHAPTERS

PART

I

LIGHTING

LIGHTING TERMS

Professions develop jargon to describe the concepts and equipment they work with. This special language also protects future income. To work and communicate effectively with lighting professionals you should speak their language. Skim this list of terms before you begin Part 1 and review it after each chapter to build a language foundation that supports effective communication with the individuals who light your buildings.

Acuity   Fine detail vision.

Adaptation   Weighted average of light entering the eye.

Ballast   Device that starts and regulates current in fluorescent and HID lamps.

Beam spread   Vertex angle in degrees that defines a cone of light leaving a lamp.

Beam candlepower   Spot light rating. Beam luminous intensity.

Brightness   A comparative sensation. Ranges from dim to dazzling.

Candlepower or **Candela**   Unit of luminous intensity. One candlepower or candela = 12.57 lumens.

CBCP   Center beam candlepower.

Cd/m^2   Candela per square meter. Metric for luminance.

CIE   Center International de l'Eclairage.

Color   A comparative sensation.

Color temperature   A source color metric based on Kelvin temperature.

CR   Cavity ratio. A numerical index of space proportions used in lighting calculations.

CRF   Contrast rendition factor. A numerical index for diffuse lighting.

CRI   Color rendering index for lamps.

CU   Coefficient of utilization. The percent of lamp lumens that reach the work plane.

DF   Daylight factor. The percent of outdoor light available inside a building.

Efficacy   An efficiency index for lamps. Measured in lumens per watt.

ESI   Equivalent sphere illumination. Diffuse shadow-free light.

Fluorescent   Lamps that emit light by exciting fluorescent materials with an electric arc.

Footcandle   Unit of illuminance. Density of light incident on a plane or surface. One footcandle = 1 lumen per square foot.

Glare   Uncomfortable brightness contrast.

Halogen   An incandescent lamp in which the filament is surrounded by iodine gas.

HID lamps   High-intensity discharge. Arc discharge lamps (see *mercury, sodium,* and *metal halide*).

Highlight   Interesting brightness contrast.

Illuminance   Density of light incident on a plane or surface. Measured in footcandles or lumens per square foot.

Incandescent   Light emission caused by heating.

Lamp life   Total operating hours when 50% of a group of lamps have failed.

Lightness   A comparative sensation of reflectance or transmission. Ranges from black to white or black to clear.

LLF   Light loss factor. The percent of lamp output lost over time.

Low E   Glass coatings used to limit heat and light transmission.

Lumen   Unit of luminous flux, light quantity. Lamp output is measured in lumens.

Luminaire   A lamp or light fixture.

Luminance or **luminous**   Emitting light, giving off light.

Lux   Metric unit of illuminance. Density of light incident on a plane or surface. One lux = 1 lumen per square meter.

mA   Amperes ÷ 1,000. Unit of electric current for fluorescent lamps.

Metal halide lamp   A HID lamp that uses a mixture of several conductive vapors to carry an electric arc.

Mercury lamp   A HID lamp that uses mercury vapor to conduct an electric arc.

Munsell   A system for defining colors.

Ostwald   A system for defining colors.

Photopic vision   Cone vision, color vision, detail vision.

Scotopic vision   Rod vision. Black and white, peripheral night vision.

Sodium lamp   A HID lamp that uses sodium vapor to conduct an electric arc.

VCP   Visual comfort probability. Numerical index for fixture glare.

CHAPTER 1

Light and Perception

"What you see is what you see."

Stella

———◦———

This short chapter discusses sight, the most powerful human sense. We seek meaning in the image's light forms, and responses to light are a logical starting point for lighting-design studies. Read the text, enjoy the images, and note four visual stimuli that command attention. Don't be dismayed by words like *luminance* and *illuminance*. Luminance is visible light leaving a surface, and illuminance is the invisible radiant energy that causes luminance. Both are discussed at length in the next chapter. Light influences perception, and designers use patterns created by light, shade, and shadow to enhance surfaces and spaces.

———◦———

1.0 BRIGHTNESS CONTRAST

SIGHT

Vision is the most powerful human sense. Visual talent, the ability to use the eye-brain interface effectively, is a unique ability comparable to athletic skill or musical aptitude. Light is the essence of art and design. Artists use the phrase "understanding light" to describe their craft, and master artists refine and perfect their visual talents by creating images that amplify perception.

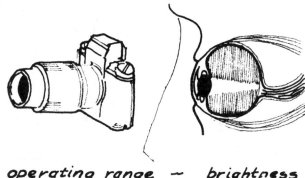

operating range ~ brightness
100:1 camera   >1,000,000:1 eye
FIGURE 1.1

Appraisal

The eye-brain interface is much more sophisticated than a fine camera (see Figure 1.1). The eye's range exceeds most camera-film combinations and the brain adds assessment and judgment to each visual image. Mental appraisals range from simple tasks like locating a missing object, to scholarly pursuits interpreting fine art or archaeological artifacts.

FIGURE 1.2

Contrasts Draw Attention

Drawings illustrate familiar examples of the evaluation and interpretation that occurs as the eye-brain interface sees. Four human responses to visual information—*brightness, pattern, motion,* and *color*—are emphasized, because they form the foundations of lighting design. Many lighting designers believe all four are actually responses to brightness and lightness* contrasts (see Figure 1.2).

Brightness contrast attracts attention. When an object in the visual field is brighter than its surroundings, eyes instinctively focus on that object. This eye-brain driven reflex is well documented in merchandising where the sales of impulse items can be directly related to brightness contrast. People are more likely to buy merchandise when it is displayed considerably brighter than the immediate surroundings.

Increasing overall brightness in a space does *not* increase brightness contrast, so lighting designers exploit the visual response to brightness contrast by varying lighting levels. The eye-brain response to a brightness contrast of 5:1 is the same as its response to a brightness contrast of 50:10, but the latter requires much more energy.

The eye adapts quickly to surrounding brightness, and the adapted eye can comfortably function in brightnesses ten times or one-tenth its adaptation level. Museums exploit both the eye's range and the brightness contrast response when illuminating delicate art. Curators keep ambient lighting dim, and use small light sources to illuminate paintings.

Highlight, sparkle, flash, radiance, gleam, and *brilliance* are terms used to describe brightness contrast. Lighting designers add words such as *punch, focus, dramatic,* and *noble,* to describe the visual impact of their work. Jargon notwithstanding, brightness contrast is usually accomplished by spotlighting surfaces or by displaying light-reflecting objects on light-absorbing backgrounds.

---

*Lightness and brightness are different sensations. This text uses "brightness" for both.

1.1 PATTERN, FORM, AND SIZE

The eye-brain looks for meaning in all visual information. When incoming images are new or incomplete, testing and analysis are typical responses. Judgments about object dimensions, form, and location are affected by experience and a desire to make sense of visual signals (see Figure 1.3).

The eye-brain attempts to interpret each visual input, but object size seems to vary with the background perspective, and straight lines appear to curve when viewed on a radial background. An array of lines on a flat surface becomes a cube, and the front and back faces of the cube exchange positions. Some patterns seem to cycle while others reveal static images. The desire to seek meaningful information from visual input seems to be perpetual, and oscillations suggest a continuing eye-brain feedback and testing loop. Pattern recognition examples confirm continual test cycles in the seeing process (see Figure 1.4).

Architectural designs exploit form and pattern to create visual impressions. Lines, planes, and volumes define spaces, and lighting can enhance space perceptions. Light can make a wall seem more distant, making a room seem more spacious (see Figure 1.5). Lighting designs use viewers' continuing search for information to make space look longer, wider, or taller. Changing the mix and intensity of light in a room changes viewer space perceptions.

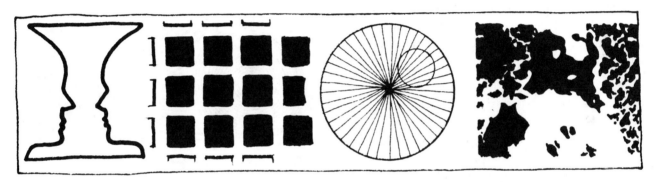

FIGURE 1.3

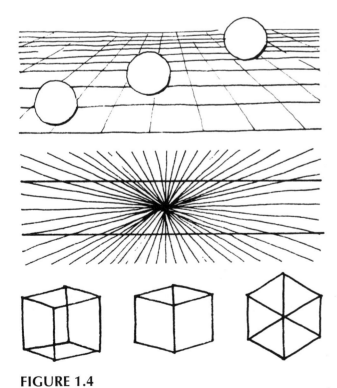

FIGURE 1.4

FIGURE 1.5

1.2 MOTION AND COLOR

MOTION

Moving objects—fluids, animals, people, or light sources—all command immediate visual attention. Motion, like brightness contrast, draws the human eye (see Figures 1.6 and 1.7). The reflex is probably defensive. It helps people avoid danger, such as speeding cars.

Designers exploit motion's attraction with all manner of signs and devices from flickering candles and throbbing lava lamps, to the rotating mirror spheres used to enhance dancing. Moving lights maximize visual attraction by combining motion and brightness contrast.

Motion, brightness contrast, pattern, and color are the essential components of Disneyland rides, video games, Las Vegas slot machines, and university visualization laboratories.

COLOR

Color is a simple word for a complex mental sensation. Color vision is a comparative process. White snow remains white when seen in deep shadow, and yellow and blue retain their identity in sunlight or shade.

Although colors maintain identity when lighting varies, the appearance of a color seems to change when viewed with other colors. Selecting colors that complement one another is an artistic opportunity built on comparative vision.

Color, like brightness contrast, pattern, and motion, has demonstrable effects on sight and perception. Blue and green are described as "cool," while red, yellow, and orange are labeled "warm." Controlled tests studying behavioral responses to color reinforce cool-warm concepts. Volunteers who performed the same tasks in identical red and blue rooms consistently overestimated air temperature, background noise levels, and time spent in the red room. Room size was overestimated in the blue room.

Warm and cool colors are further described as advancing and receding. An alignment test confirms these descriptors; when volunteers are asked to align a blue and a red sphere of equal size, a significant majority place the blue sphere nearer the eye.

Warm colors are "active and stimulating," while cool colors are "relaxing and restful." Fast-food es-

FIGURE 1.6

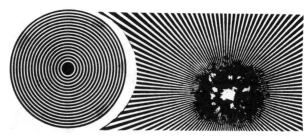

FIGURE 1.7

tablishments use warm interior colors to encourage rapid dining. At your next fast-food experience, notice the effects of brightness contrast, color, and music on the way people eat.

Color Terms

Because color vision is a comparative mental process, the terms that describe color perception are not precise. Use the following jargon only when it confirms your visual impressions.

White is a balanced mixture of all light wavelengths, black is the absence of light, and grays are blends of black and white.

Color is a perception caused by an unbalanced mixture of light wavelengths. Green light has more energy in the wavelengths we describe as green and less at other wavelengths. Green objects reflect more light in the green wavelengths.

Hue is a pure color. Blue and red are hues.

Chroma, purity, and *saturation* describe a color's freedom from white or gray.

Value is the relative lightness or darkness of a color. Yellow is lighter than blue.

Tints, tones, and *shades* are colors diluted with white, gray, and black (see Figure 1.8).

Brightness

Color vision ceases in moonlight. A blue light appears brighter than an equal red light at night but the two reverse in daylight. As brightness increases, warm colors fade or weaken before cool colors, and intense illumination weakens all colors.

Color constancy is a term used to describe the eye-brain's ability to recognize colors illuminated by unusual light sources. Color constancy is not absolute, and good designers are careful to select colors using the type of light source specified for the intended location—this means selecting exterior house paint colors outdoors, not in a paint store.

Complement seeking is an eye-brain effort to substitute the complement of a single color that dominates a scene. Evidence of complement seeking is the after-image people report following concentration on a monochromatic pattern. Red meats seem more attractive when displayed in green surroundings, on a green background.

Defining Colors

The visible spectrum spans a range of wavelengths, and several systems have been developed to define color. This black and white format is inadequate, and serious lighting-design students must commit to further reading and investigation.

C.I.E. The Center International de l'Eclairage (illumination) defines a color with three numerical values that represent percentage of red, green, and blue. C.I.E. values are also used to describe lamp output.

Ostwald The Ostwald System catalogs colors in triangles of progressive tints, tones, and shades.

Munsell The Munsell Color System classifies colors by surface reflectance in ten steps perceived as equal increments of surface lightness. Black approaches Munsell Value (MV) 1 and white approaches MV 10. Each MV step is equal to the square root of a color's reflectance. Munsell

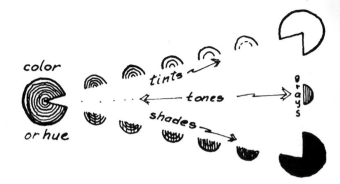

FIGURE 1.8

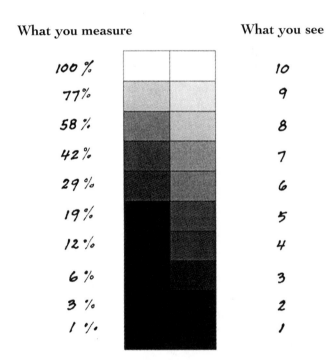

% reflectance   Munsell Values

FIGURE 1.9

Value differences are excellent indicators of lightness contrast. A difference of 4 MV is a moderate contrast. A difference of 8 MV is a strong contrast. Figure 1.9 lists Munsell reflectances on the left and approximates ten equal perception steps on the right.

1.3 RESPONSES AND DESIGN

PALETTE

Brightness contrast, pattern, motion, and color can be used to inform and influence viewers. These four variables are the lighting designer's palette.

In marketing, visual attraction is the first step toward a sale. In architecture, light is used to inform and influence viewer perception, mood, and behavior. Light informs and influences on several levels. At a building entry, light may show the route to a door, but light can also communicate sensations of safety, space, warmth, and welcome. Light in buildings defines spaces and surfaces. It enhances the shapes and forms that enclose space, and commands viewer attention. Light can stimulate, excite, and entice as it complements art and architecture. The first step in lighting design is visualizing brightness patterns that make objects or spaces attractive and interesting (see Figures 1.10A–D).

Because the eye-brain continually searches for meaning in visual information, lighting designers have an opportunity to communicate beyond just reflex reactions to brightness, pattern, motion, and color. For example, people:

- Make more purchases when merchandise displays are notably brighter than their surroundings. Increased sales suggest they may prefer the variety that brightness contrast adds to a retail environment.
- Interpret a line as longer when arrowheads reverse, and they perceive rooms or spaces as longer, wider, or taller when light is used to emphasize one dimension or plane.
- Are attracted by motion in the visual field and find some surroundings more pleasing when motion is part of the lighting scheme.

LIGHTING DESIGN

Perception is the foundation of intellectual activity, and sight is our strongest perceptive sense. Talented lighting designers know sight is an instinctive mental process that searches for information and meaning—they use light to interest, inform, and influence people.

A common thread ties the Kimbell Museum in Texas, the Seagram Building in New York, and Philip Johnson's Glass House in Connecticut. Richard Kelly designed lighting for all three. Kelly's trinity of lighting design perceptions are focal glow, ambient luminescence, and the play of brilliants.

"Focal glow is the campfire of all time, . . . the sunburst through the clouds, and the shaft of sunshine that warms the far end of the valley. Focal glow commands attention and interest. It fixes the gaze, concentrates the mind and tells people what to look at. It separates the important from the unimportant.

Ambient luminescence is a snowy morning in open country. It is underwater in the sunshine, or inside a white tent at high noon. Ambient luminescence minimizes the importance of all things and all people. It fills people with a sense of freedom of space and can suggest infinity.

Play of the brilliants is the aurora borealis, . . . the Versailles hall of mirrors with its thousands of candle flames. Play of the brilliants is Times Square at night, . . . the magic of a Christmas tree, Fourth of July skyrockets. It quickens the appetite and heightens all sensation. It can be distracting or entertaining."*

Exciting and rewarding careers await individuals who understand the eye's range and the mind's responses to light. Sight is a comparative evaluation of lightness and brightness, which designers exploit to attract attention and influence perception.

The Great Illuminator by Philip Cialdella & Clara D. Powell, *Lighting Design and Application,* May 1993, pp. 58–65.

A

B

C

D

FIGURE 1.10

1.4 PRODUCTIVITY

Lighting affects human perception, and light can stimulate behavioral responses. Customers eat more rapidly in a fast-food environment with bright lighting and warm colors, than in a candlelit, white tablecloth, gourmet restaurant. Shoppers make more impulse purchases when selected merchandise is noticeably brighter than its surroundings. People perceive space changes when a room's lighting is changed from concealed source to exposed source.

However, while light influences perception and behavior, lighting will not control a complex individual behavior like productivity. Productivity is influenced by a mix of visual inputs and mental impulses that can include pleasure, power, lust, envy, delight, love, and memories of a recent meal. Lighting is an important contributor to human perception, and light affects simple behaviors like impulse buying or circulation paths. Light may influence a complex behavior such as productivity but lighting will **not** reliably improve productivity over time.

RESEARCH

Many studies confirm severely limited relationships between lighting and behavior, but a 1975 lighting research project discovered a *10% increase* in employee productivity when illuminance values were increased from 50 to 150.* Another study found *no improvement* in visual performance when illuminance values exceeded 50, and very little improvement from 30 to 50.** Review this research and read further if lighting numbers stimulate your interest. Always check sponsors before accepting research findings. Disposable diaper manufacturers and cloth diaper makers funded separate studies to judge *the environmental impact of diapers*. Findings were contradictory, both with a 99% confidence level.

MORE

Readers finding this chapter's coverage of sight, pattern, and color too brief will enjoy: *Image Object and Illusion*, a collection of *Scientific American* articles published in 1974; and Edwin H. Land. "The Retinex Theory of Color Vision." *Scientific American*, December 1977. "Retinex" is Land's word for the retina-cortex sensation called vision.

---

* "Productivity." Electrical World, June 1977.
** Donald Ross. *The Limitations of Illumination as a Determinant of Task Performance*. IEEE annual meeting, October 1977, Los Angeles.

REVIEW QUESTIONS

1. Lamps produce luminance and illuminance. Which is visible?
2. Name the phenomena that can attract the eye.
3. Explain "color."
4. Tones are colors or hues mixed with what?
5. Name three color cataloging systems. Which one is used to describe lamp output?

ANSWERS

1. Luminance is visible.
2. Brightness contrast, pattern/form/size, motion, and color.
3. Color is an unbalanced light mixture with dominant wavelengths.
4. Gray.
5. Munsell, Ostwald, and C.I.E. C.I.E. is used to describe lamp output.

CHAPTER 2

Lighting Metrics

Light as energy is measured by photometry and follows its laws.
Light for vision has no such simple rules or procedures . . .
The eye is the only instrument that can evaluate light for vision . . .

Louis Erhardt

Develop lighting knowledge by reading and applying the photometric terms explained in the text. Luminance values broaden your lighting vocabulary, but the numbers don't represent visual impressions. Brightness is a sensation and visual impressions are comparative evaluations of lightness and brightness contrasts.

Work through the problems following the text and then use a light meter to develop an understanding of illuminance, luminance, and reflectance values.

2.0 LIGHT AND SIGHT

LIGHT

Light is:

- Radiant energy that excites the human retina and creates visual sensation.
- An energy form the human eye can see.

These definitions provide some useful information, but offer less than complete revelation. The next paragraph offers a little more, but a lucid explanation of light is difficult.

In 1900 Max Karl Ernst Ludwig Planck (1858–1947) postulated that radiant energy could be described by units called *quanta,* and that the energy content of quanta increases as wavelength decreases. Albert Einstein (1879–1955) developed the concept of wave-particle dualism, and defined the *photon* with wave and particle properties. Dual properties permit wave theory to explain color while particle theory explains transmission and absorption.

Understanding light is a worthy aspiration. Happily, lighting design is possible without complete comprehension. In this text, light is defined simply as visible electromagnetic energy.

Wavelength

The electromagnetic spectrum catalogs radiant energy by wavelength and frequency. Light occupies a small visible portion of the spectrum with wavelengths ranging from 380 to 770 nanometers. A nanometer is very small (10^{-9} meters), so the wavelengths of light fall between 15 and 30 millionths of an inch (see Figure 2.1).

Light with wavelengths longer than 610 nanometers is called "red," and light with wavelengths between 440 and 500 nanometers is "blue." As wavelength decreases, frequency and energy increase. Blue light is more energetic than red light.

Most light sources also emit longer and shorter invisible wavelengths. Longer wave *infrared* radiation is perceived as heat, but when visible wavelengths are absorbed they also degrade to heat. Shorter wave *ultraviolet* can cause photoelectric, fluorescent, and photochemical effects. Ultraviolet radiation also causes suntanning and can be used to kill germs.

Color Temperature

A colored light source has a large part of its energy concentrated around a specific wavelength. A colored object reflects most incident light in a narrow wavelength band. White light includes all visible wavelengths, but wavelength content varies for specific light sources.

A blackbody is one that absorbs all incident radiation at all temperatures, and also radiates a maximum at all wavelengths for a given temperature. The color of a light source can be quantified using *Kelvin* temperature to describe light emitted by a blackbody radiator. When blackbody temperature reaches 800 K, red light is emitted. The light becomes yellow at 3,000 K, white at 5,000 K, pale blue at 8,000 K, and bright blue at 60,000 K. Zero K is absolute zero or minus 273°C. The following table gives approximate color temperatures for a few familiar light sources.

Source	Color Temperature K
Sunlight at sunset	1,800 K
Sunlight at noon	4,800 K
Incandescent lamps	2,600–3,100 K
Fluorescent lamp (cool white)	4,200 K
Northwest sky	Up to 25,000 K

Build color knowledge by studying the C.I.E. chromaticity diagram where "good" light sources lie along a blackbody locus based on color temperature.

Velocity

In a vacuum all light wavelengths travel 300,000 kilometers per second. In glass or water, the velocity of light is reduced, and each wavelength travels at a different speed.

SIGHT

Light enters the eye through a protective cornea and aqueous humor (see Figure 2.2). Then it passes through an opening in the iris called the pupil. The size of the pupil controls the amount of light that will be passed on by the lens. Ciliary muscles change lens curvature so that light from sources at differing distances is focused on the surface of the retina. The retina is covered with sensors called *rods* that provide night vision and peripheral vision.

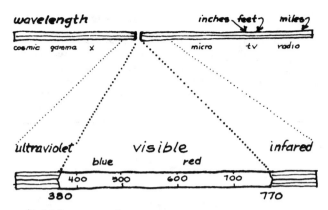

visible spectrum wavelength-nanometers

FIGURE 2.1

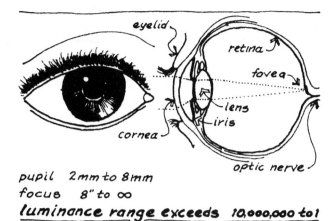

pupil   2mm to 8mm
focus   8" to ∞
luminance range exceeds 10,000,000 to 1

FIGURE 2.2

FIGURE 2.3

Detail vision and color vision occur near the center of the retina in a tiny area called the fovea. Sensors called *cones* dominate in the fovea and respond to red, green, or blue light. Cones do not respond to low light levels. Most colors are perceived as gray tones in moonlight.

The optic nerve carries electrical signals from the retina to the brain for interpretation. About 1 million optic nerve fibers serve more than 100 million rods and cones, so the retina also processes visual information.*

---

*An excellent discussion of color vision can be read in "The Retinex Theory of Color Vision" by Edwin H. Land, *Scientific American*, December 1977.

Adaptation

The range of adapted vision extends a log step above or below the adaptation level without discomfort. When moving from indoors to outdoors notice how easily and quickly your eyes adapt to large changes in visual field brightness (see Figure 2.3). Adaptation is instant for a tenfold change, 100:1 takes a second or two, and 1,000:1 can take 30 seconds or more.

Numerical luminance value changes do *not* indicate the eye's sensitivity to change; a luminance change from 1 to 2 is perceived as one-tenth the change from 1 to 1,000.

2.1 PHOTOMETRIC TERMS

Numbers used to describe visual experiences are taken from meters that cannot see. Study the following terms and numbers to develop a working lighting vocabulary, but *don't* believe the numbers represent visual sensations.

HISTORY

A *standard candle* was the historical starting point for photometric terms and measurements (see Figure 2.4). The candle was carefully constructed with detailed specifications for wax, wick, and burning rate, and was assigned a luminous intensity rating of *1 candlepower.*

Three candle-related terms were defined to describe light quantity, light density, and surface brightness:

- The *lumen* was defined as the quantity of light incident on a 1-square-foot surface 1-foot distant from a standard candle.
- The *footcandle* was defined as the density of illumination (illuminance) 1 foot distant from a standard candle (see Figure 2.5).
- The *footlambert* was defined as a surface luminance of 1 lumen per square foot.

Luminance and brightness are not equivalent because brightness is a sensation that includes contrast in the field of view and adaptation, while luminance is a photometric unit. A luminous candle seems bright on a dark night but dull on a sunny day.

HISTORICAL TERMS

Lighting terms based on the standard candle include:

Candlepower—Luminous intensity. The light source intensity of a standard candle.

Lumen—Luminous flux. Quantity of light. A standard candle emits 12.57 lumens. A sphere with a 1-foot radius has a surface area of 12.57 ($4\pi r^2$) square feet so the illuminance 1 foot distant from a standard candle is 1 lumen per square foot.

Footcandle—Illuminance. Density of illumination incident on a surface or plane. One footcandle is an illuminance of 1 lumen per square foot.

Footlambert—Luminance. A surface that emits 1 lumen per square foot, *measured in the direction being viewed,* has a luminance of 1 footlambert (see Figure 2.6).

1 candle power ~ 12.57 lumens
illuminance 1 foot away ~1fc
1 footcandle = 1 lumen per sqft.
if the surface facing the candle reflects 1 lumen per square foot its luminance is 1 footlambert

standard candle

FIGURE 2.4

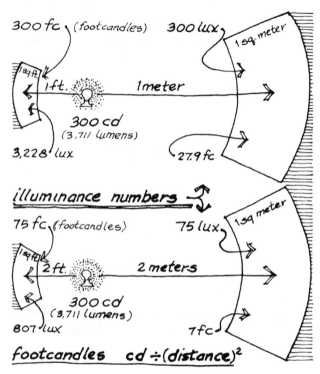

300 fc (footcandles)   300 lux
1 sq. meter
1 sq. ft.   1 ft.   1 meter
300 cd (3,711 lumens)
3,228 lux   27.9 fc

illuminance numbers

75 fc (footcandles)   75 lux
1 sq. meter
1 sq. ft.   2 ft.   2 meters
300 cd (3,711 lumens)
807 lux   7 fc

footcandles   cd ÷ (distance)^2

FIGURE 2.5

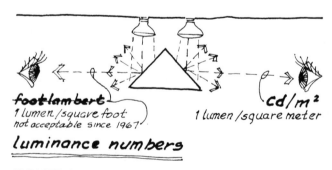

footlambert
1 lumen/square foot
not acceptable since 1967

cd/m^2
1 lumen/square meter

luminance numbers

FIGURE 2.6

CURRENT TERMS

The standard candle burns no more. It has been replaced by the *candela,* which is defined as 1/60 of the intensity of a square centimeter of a blackbody radiator at 2,045 K. Fortunately, the output of a standard candle is equal to a candela, and most historical terms are unchanged.

Candela (cd) or **candlepower**—Unit of *luminous intensity* for a light source. One candela (cd) equals 1 candlepower (cp), and 1 candela yields 12.57 lumens.

Lumen—*Luminous flux* or quantity of light.

Footcandle (fc) or **lux**—*Illuminance units*. The density of illumination incident at a point on a surface, measured in lumens per square foot. One lumen per square foot is 1 footcandle. Lux is the SI unit of illuminance. One lux is 1 lumen per square meter, so 1 fc is about 10 lux (10.76).

cd/m^2 or **nit**—Unit of luminance. Luminous intensity per unit of projected area, for a reflecting or an emitting surface. One cd/m^2 or 1 nit is a luminance of 1 lumen per square meter *in the direction being viewed*. If the reflecting or emitting surface diffuses light, 1 lumen per square meter creates a luminance of 1/π cd/m^2 (Figure 2.6).

BEAM CANDLEPOWER

Illuminance decreases as distance to a light source increases (fc or lux = cp/d^2). Manufacturers specify *beam candlepower* and beam spread for spotlights and floodlights to aid illuminance calculations (see Figure 2.7).

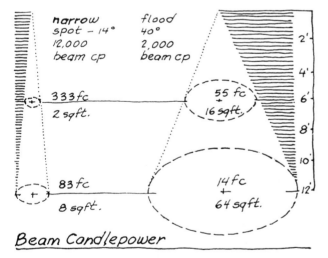

Beam Candlepower

FIGURE 2.7

Assume a 300 candela point source to verify the photometric numbers shown in Figure. 2.5 on the facing page. Then complete the end of chapter problems to ensure understanding.

NUMBERS

The following tables illustrate familiar viewing experiences quantified with approximate photometric numbers.

Intensity Values	cd
Sun (clear day)	670,000,000
75 watt spot lamp (average)	4,500
75 watt flood lamp (average)	1,800
Candle flame (1 foot distant)	1

Illuminance Values	fc
Sunlight + skylight (clear day)	10,000
Foggy day (dense fog)	1,000
Commercial offices	10–100
Residence interior (at night)	10
Candle flame (1 foot distant)	1
Moonlight (clear, full moon)	0.01

Luminance of Light Sources	cd/m^2
Sun	+/− 2,000,000,000
Incandescent lamps	
500 watt (clear)	12,000,000
100 watt (frosted)	170,000
Fluorescent lamp (40 watt cw)	7,000
Moon	5,000
Candle flame	5,000

Values are for brightest spot on each source.

Surface Luminance (estimated)	cd/m^2
Snow in sunlight	20,000–30,000
Grass in sunlight	2,000
Grass in shade	100
This page in sunlight	13,000
This page in shade	1,000
This page in library at night	150
This page in home at night	20

Converting Photometric Units

Multiply	By	To Get
Candela	1	Candlepower
Candela	12.57	Lumens
Footcandle	0.09	Lux
Lux	10.76	Footcandles
cd/m^2	0.29	Footlamberts
Footlambert	3.42	cd/m^2

2.2 VISUAL PERFORMANCE

HOW MUCH LIGHT?

Five seeing variables define visual tasks:

- Luminance
- Size
- Contrast
- Time or speed
- Accuracy

When a task is difficult, increased luminance can help maintain *speed and accuracy* (see Figure 2.8).

Professor H. R. Blackwell studied visual performance with students at Ohio State University. His laboratory tests in 1958 defined the necessary luminance, and the related illuminance, needed to correctly perform a variety of visual tasks. Reading high contrast type like this text was found to require about 2 footcandles, and tracing a blueprint required about 1,000 footcandles (see Figure 2.9).

"When reading 8 point type, to achieve 99% seeing accuracy, the minimum page illuminance falls between 1 and 2 footcandles, for a viewer under 40 years of age with a visual assimilation time of one-fifth of a second."

Age erodes acuity, and older viewers may need as much as 50% more illuminance for a given seeing task.

FIGURE 2.8

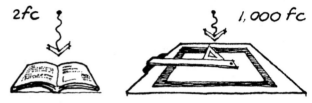

FIGURE 2.9

RECOMMENDATIONS

Visual performance research findings don't directly apply to workplace seeing tasks because the motion, contrast, and glare typical in the workplace visual field are absent in laboratory tests.

Lighting manufacturers, government agencies, and the Illuminating Engineering Society (IES) recommend illuminance for various visual tasks. The following small example is from the 1981 IES Handbook.*

Recommended Illuminance	fc
Dining	5–10
Sewing, light to medium fabrics	50–100
Jewelry and watch manufacturing	200–500

*Chapter 7 offers more illuminance recommendations and calculations.

"Logic, n. — The art of thinking and reasoning . . .

Major Premise: Sixty men can do a piece of work sixty times as quickly as one man.

Minor Premise: One man can dig a post-hole in sixty seconds; therefore —

Conclusion: Sixty men can dig a post-hole in one second.

This may be called syllogism arithmetical, in which, by combining logic and mathematics, we obtain a double certainty and are twice blessed."

Ambrose Bierce
The Devil's Dictionary

EXAMPLE PROBLEMS

Complete the following problems and activities to build your lighting vocabulary; then check the answers that follow.

1. Find the total luminous flux emitted by a lamp rated at 100 candelas.
2. Find the illuminance (lux) 1 meter distant from a point light source rated at 100 candelas.
3. Find the illuminance (lux) 2 meters distant from a point light source rated at 100 candelas.
4. Find the illuminance (fc) 1 foot distant from a point light source rated at 100 candelas.

5. Find the illuminance (fc) 6.56 feet distant from a point light source rated at 100 candelas.
6. Find the luminance of a diffusing surface that reflects 70% of incident light if the illuminance density is 25 lux.
7. Find the luminance of a diffusing surface that reflects 70% of incident light if the illuminance density is 25 fc.
8. Which two preceding problems (1–7) have visible answers?
9. Use a light meter to measure several indoor and outdoor illuminance levels. Then try to estimate illuminance without the meter.

ANSWERS

1. **1,257 lumens** 1 cd = 12.57 lumens, (100)(12.57) = 1,257 lumens.
2. **100 lux** 100 cd = 1,257 lumens = 100 lumens per square meter at 1 meter distant. One lumen per square meter = 1 lux.
3. **25 lux** Lux = cd/d^2 = $100/2^2$ = 25 lux. The density of light decreases as distance to the light source increases. For a *point source* of light each doubling of distance reduces lux or footcandles by a factor of 4. (This calculation can be used to determine illuminance under spotlights when beam candlepower is known. A method for calculating overall illuminance in buildings will be developed in Chapter 7.)
4. **100 fc** 100 cd = 1,257 lumens = 100 lumens per square foot 1 foot away. One lumen per square foot = 1 fc.
5. **2.3 fc** $100/6.56^2$ = 2.32 fc (see problem 3). 6.56 feet = 2 meters, and 2.32 fc = 25 lux.
6. **5.6 nits (cd/m^2)** Illuminance = 25 lux = 25 lumens per square meter. If reflectance is 70%, surface luminance is (25)(70%) = 17.5 lumens per square meter = 17.5/π or 5.57 cd/m^2.
7. **59.9 nits (cd/m^2)** Illuminance = 25 fc = 25 lumens per square foot. If reflectance is 70%, surface luminance is (25)(70%) = 17.5 lumens per square foot or (17.5)(10.76) = 188.3 lumens per square meter = 188.3/π or 59.9 cd/m^2.
8. Only luminance values (see problems 6 and 7) are visible, but the numbers do not describe visual sensations. The diffusing surface in problem 7 is about ten times more luminous than the surface in problem 6, but it does *not* appear ten times as bright. Luminance values can be assigned to lightness (reflectance) and brightness, but these values don't duplicate visual sensations. The eye-brain sees lightness from black to white, and brightness across a broad scale from dim to dazzling.

9. Because the eye adapts and a light meter counts, an hour spent comparing what you see with what the meter reads will build an appreciation of illuminance and luminance values. GE sells a light meter that displays illuminance values for about $45. If that price strains your budget a handheld photographic light meter can be used. Verify and/or adjust the following table by comparing photographic and light meter readings.

fc	f stop	Time	ASA
2	1.4	1/30	400
10	2.8	1/30	400
20	4	1/30	400
50	5.6–8	1/30	400
100	8–11	1/30	400
200	11–16	1/30	400

You can also use a camera's through the lens light meter, but you'll have to experiment with a bit of tracing paper taped over the lens and develop your own conversion scale.

To estimate reflectance with a light meter first measure incident footcandles and then rotate the meter 180° to measure reflected footcandles. Divide reflected fc by incident fc to estimate % reflectance.

The following chart offers some approximate reflectance values you may verify.

Surface %	Reflectance
Mirror	90–95
White paint	60–90
Concrete	10–60
Birch (clear finish)	20–40
Walnut (oil finish)	5–15
Grass	5–15
Asphalt	1–10

CHAPTER

3

Lamps

Lighthouse, n. A tall building on the seashore in which the government maintains a lamp and the friend of a politician.

Ambrose Bierce

———◆———

This chapter describes incandescent, fluorescent, and high-intensity discharge lamps—three lamp types that comprise most building lighting. As you read about each, try to develop convictions about appropriate lamps for specific applications. The text doesn't suggest "best" lamps for a restaurant, church, hospital, or school because lamp selection embraces design intent and experience. When you see an attractive lighting installation try to understand its pleasing features in terms of your impressions about brightness contrast and color. Then note lamp types and wattages used to attract your interest.

Lamp manufacturers quote "efficacy" numbers to compare lamps, and luminaire manufacturers note lighting "watts per square foot" for building installations, but there's more to lighting design than lamp lumens and electrical costs.

———◆———

3.0 LAMP EFFICACY, LIFE, AND COLOR

The human eye's sensitivity to light peaks in the yellow-green range (near 555 nanometers) and the lumen is defined by the human eye. A perfectly efficient light source would emit 680 lumens of yellow-green light. A perfectly efficient white light source might emit from 200 to 400 lumens per watt, depending on the definition of "white light."

EFFICACY

Efficacy is a lighting term for the number of lumens a lamp produces from each watt of electrical input energy. A standard 100 watt incandescent lamp with a clear glass bulb radiates about 1,750 lumens and has an efficacy of 17.5.

LIFE

Lamp life is rated in hours; a rating of 1,000 hours means that after 1,000 hours, half of a representative sample of lamps are still operable and the other half have burned out. Lamp life ratings are based on typical conditions. Abnormal supply voltage, vibration, ambient temperature, or frequent on-off cycles can reduce lamp life.

COLOR

Color temperature is a term used to describe the color of light. Standard incandescent lamps operate at color temperatures from 2,600 to 3,000 K. Higher color temperatures indicate more blue energy and lower color temperatures mean more red energy.

Color temperature is *not* an indicator of the appearance of colored objects; instead a *color rendering index* (CRI) is used to compare the appearance of colored objects illuminated by different light sources. Lamp CRIs are comparative numbers that vary with color temperature. An incandescent lamp is assigned a CRI of 100 at 2,900 K, and north sky daylight is assigned a CRI of 100 at 7,500 K. Manufacturers recommend lamps with CRIs of 90 or more when color rendition is an important consideration.

Efficacy, life, color, and operating characteristics are discussed for each of three principal lamp types.

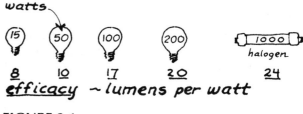

FIGURE 3.1

3.1 INCANDESCENT LAMPS

Electric arc lights were developed in the early 1800s, but Thomas Edison is credited with developing the first marketable incandescent lamp in 1879. Edison's lamp, an evacuated bulb with a filament of carbonized sewing thread, delivered 1.4 lumens per watt. Tungsten filaments were first used in 1907, and in 1913 lamps filled with inert gas replaced the evacuated bulb. Incandescents are not very efficient. A standard incandescent lamp converts most of the electrical input to heat and less than 10% to light, but low-cost lamps and fixtures make incandescent lamps a popular choice for many commercial applications and most residential lighting.

EFFICACY

The efficacy of standard incandescent lamps extends from 10 to 30 lumens per watt. Smaller lamps rate near 10 while larger lamps are more efficient because their filaments can operate at higher temperatures. Halogen-incandescent lamps offer still higher efficacy, but decorative and long-life lamps yield fewer lumens per watt (see Figure 3.1).

LIFE

Incandescent lamps usually fail when switched on. A 100 watt tungsten filament operates near 4,800°F (2,900 K) and weakens as it ages. When a cold lamp is turned on the initial current may be 10 times normal operating current, and this current surge can break a weak filament (see Figure 3.2). Incandescent lamps that are not cycled on and off may burn for many years.

Standard incandescent lamps have a rated life of 750 or 1,000 hours. Light output decays 10 to 20% by the time a lamp fails. Decorative lamps are rated from 1,500 to 4,000 hours and extended service lamps are available with 2,000 to 8,000 hour ratings. These lamps offer longer life but yield less light (see Figure 3.3).

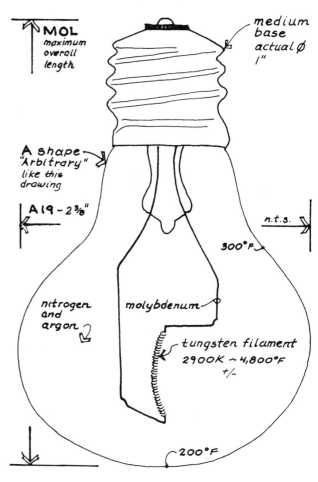

FIGURE 3.2

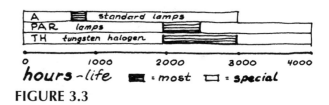

FIGURE 3.3

COLOR

The color temperature of light emitted by standard incandescent lamps ranges from 2,600 to 3,000 K, photographic lamps operate near 3,400 K, and tungsten melts at 3,665 K (Figure 3.2). Incandescent light is called "warm" because most visible energy is emitted in the yellow-orange-red wavelengths that flatter human skin tones. Incandescents, with an assigned CRI value of 100, are considered "good" color rendering light sources.

OPERATION

Reduced input *voltage* reduces incandescent lamp efficacy and color temperature, but increases lamp life. Increasing lamp voltage has the opposite effect. As the table shows a small change in input voltage can have a large impact on lamp life. See also Figure 3.4.

Voltage	% Light	% Life
Design (120 volts)	100	100
More (130 volts)	130	40
Less (110 volts)	75	300

Effects are approximate for a standard 1,000 hour, 120 volt lamp.

Dimming controls reduce lamp voltage and can be good investments because they extend lamp life.

However, dimmers are *not* used for museum lighting or spaces where color rendition is an important concern. Incandescent dimmers are inexpensive, and solid state incandescent dimmers conserve electrical energy.

SPECIAL LAMPS

Halogen incandescent lamps provide longer life (2,000 to 4,000 hours), less decay, and more light than standard lamps. Halogen lamps include a quartz tube that surrounds the lamp filament with iodine gas (see Figure 3.5). Iodine vapor in the quartz tube limits filament evaporation and minimizes light loss over time. Halogen lamps are available in MR, PAR, and T shapes.

Low-voltage incandescent lamps have compact filaments that permit improved beam control. Twelve or 24 volt lamps, can deliver a brighter (and smaller) beam of light than 120 volt lamps of equal wattage. Remote transformers can serve several lamps or a transformer can be included with each light fixture.

Low-voltage building lighting applications include spot lighting and decorative lighting; low-voltage halogen lamps combine the advantages of both types. In garden and landscape lighting, low-voltage systems offer easy installation and reduced shock risk.

Incandescent lamps designed for *high-voltage* (240 or 277 volt) operation are used to reduce wiring costs in branch lighting circuits.

Long-life lamps are actually designed for 130 or 140 volt power. Operated at 120 volts, they last a long time and cut replacement labor, but emit less light than standard lamps.

Quality colored lamps use *interference filters* on the lens that selectively transmit one color (wave-

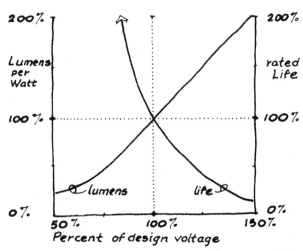

voltage   lumens (per watt) and lamp life

FIGURE 3.4

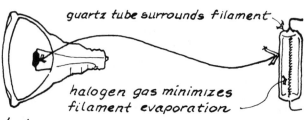

halogen PAR

FIGURE 3.5

length-band) and reflect other colors back into the lamp.

Interference filters can also be applied to the reflecting surface of incandescent lamps. Certain coatings reflect visible light but they are transparent to longer-wave infrared energy radiating from the lamp filament. These *cool beam* lamps are used to light ice cream displays and theater makeup rooms.

Infrared lamps are used for industrial heating and drying applications, and for warming residential bathrooms.

A great variety of *decorative* types, sizes, shapes, colors, and bulb coatings are available (see Figure 3.6). Globular lamps are often used to hide a low-budget porcelain socket, and silver bowl lamps, developed years ago for use in indirect fixtures, are "discovered" again by lighting designers every 10 years. There may be more lamp types than beer brands; if you cannot find the "right" lamp at your local lighting dealer try theater, auto, or electronics suppliers.

LAMP SHAPE AND SIZE

A code composed of watts plus a letter-number is used to specify lamp size and shape. The letter designates shape and the number is the lamp's largest diameter measured in eighths of an inch. For example, 50 watt R 20 describes a reflector lamp 2.5 inches in diameter (see Figure 3.7).

Several lamp base designs are used to accommodate differing lamp sizes and operating watts. A medium screw base is used for most standard lamps from 15 to 300 watts. A larger mogul screw base is used for large lamps. Other base designs are used with special purpose lamps or fixtures.

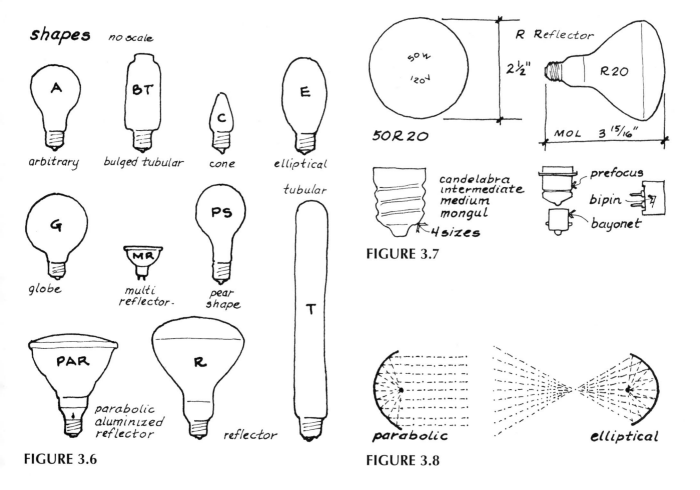

shapes no scale

arbitrary · bulged tubular · cone · elliptical

globe · multi reflector · pear shape · tubular

PAR parabolic aluminized reflector · R reflector · T

FIGURE 3.6

50 R 20 · R Reflector · R20 · 2½" · MOL 3 15/16"

candelabra intermediate medium mongul — 4 sizes

prefocus · bipin · bayonet

FIGURE 3.7

parabolic · elliptical

FIGURE 3.8

CBCP center beam candlepower

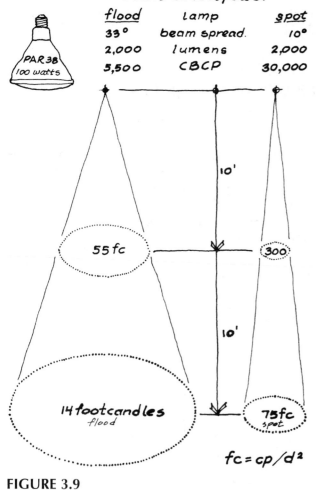

	flood	Lamp	spot
	33°	beam spread	10°
	2,000	lumens	2,000
	5,500	CBCP	30,000

PAR 38
100 watts

10'

55 fc

300

10'

14 footcandles
flood

75 fc
spot

$$fc = cp/d^2$$

FIGURE 3.9

Reflector lamps are designed to concentrate and aim light output. Their efficacy is lower than standard lamps, but reflector lamp performance is measured in beam candlepower and beam spread instead of lumens per watt. 100 watt spot and flood lamps produce equal lumens, but the spot's beam is much brighter and smaller (Figure 3.9). Reflector (R), multi-reflector (MR), and parabolic aluminized reflector (PAR) lamps are designed for spot (narrow beam) or flood (wide beam) lighting applications. R lamps are less expensive than PAR lamps, but PAR lamps offer better beam control and they can survive raindrops. Small MR lamps offer superior beam control for highlighting applications.

Elliptical reflector (ER) lamps are designed for use in pinhole fixtures because their light output converges outside the lamp (see Figures 3.8 and 3.10). Recently they have been touted as energy-conserving lamps, but incandescent lamps are a poor choice when energy conservation is a primary goal.

 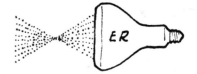

ER

FIGURE 3.10

3.2 FLUORESCENT LAMPS

Thomas Edison entered a fluorescent lamp patent in 1896 but production of practical commercial fluorescent lamps began in the mid-1930s.

Fluorescent lamps are arc discharge light sources. An electric current flows through mercury vapor inside an evacuated glass tube. The arc radiates energy, and this radiation excites fluorescent materials which convert arc radiation to visible light. Arc current in standard 4-foot lamps is about 430 mA (milli-amperes), less than half an ampere. A phosphor mixture coats the tube and sets light color. Fluorescent lamps are controlled by a *ballast* that starts the arc and limits arc current (see Figure 3.11).

EFFICACY

Fluorescent lamp-ballast efficacy ranges from 60 to nearly 100 lumens per watt. New lamp output depreciates before stabilizing after 100 hours of operation so "initial" lumens are measured after a 100 hour burn-in. Efficacy is initial lumens divided by input watts. Electronic ballasts increase efficacy by increasing the electrical power supply frequency from 60 Hz to 25,000 Hz.

Ambient temperature affects efficacy. As temperature drops, mercury vapor condenses and lamps flicker and dim. Outdoor winter operation of fluorescent lamps requires special low-temperature ballasts, and glass lamp enclosures are also required in cold climates.

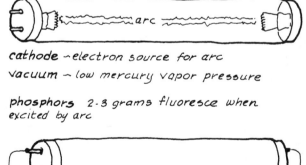

cathode ~ electron source for arc

vacuum ~ low mercury vapor pressure

phosphors 2-3 grams fluoresce when excited by arc

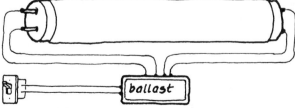

FIGURE 3.11

LIFE

Compact fluorescent lamps have life expectancies around 10,000 hours. Larger standard lamps have rated lives near 20,000 hours.

Because fluorescent lamps are long-lived, their light output is significantly reduced as they approach failure. Manufacturers quote "mean lumens" at 40% of life when light output has dropped about 15% below the initial lumen rating of a new lamp. Lamp life estimates assume 3 hours of operation per start. If lamps operate 12 hours per start their life expectancy increases by about 20%. Years ago a cunning advertisement advocating 24-hour-a-day lighting, touted: *"they're never turned off so they last longer"* thinking readers grasp the trick in this apparent truth, but many less thoughtful designers embraced 24-hour lighting for buildings constructed in the 1950s and 1960s.

Recall that at rated life half of a group of lamps have failed. Some building operators replace individual lamps when they fail, but others prefer group replacement at 70% of rated life when few failures have occurred.

After 20,000+ hours lamp cathodes are worn, tube ends are blackened, mercury may be contaminated, phosphors take less pleasure in arc stimulation, and lamps fail. Lamp disposal is an environmental concern because a 1995 vintage 4-foot lamp contains about 23 milligrams of mercury. In 1989 discarded lamps accounted for about 5%* of the total mercury found in municipal solid waste.

CRI

As mentioned earlier, the CRI is a number index used to compare the color of surfaces illuminated by a lamp to the color of the same surfaces illuminated by incandescent light or daylight; a CRI value of 100 is assigned to daylight and incandescent light. Fluorescent lamps with CRI values above 70 approximate daylight or incandescent light (at the color temperature of the lamp being tested).

---

*A. T. Kearney and Franklin Associates Inc. "Characterization of Products Containing Mercury in Municipal Solid Waste in the United States," January 1991.

Color Rendering Index

Source (Kelvin Temperature)	CRI
Incandescent (2,900 K)	100
CW fluorescent (4,400 K)	66
WW fluorescent (3,100 K)	55
WWX fluorescent (3,020 K)	77
Improved color fluorescent (3,000 to 4,000 K)	To 90
North sky daylight (7,500 K)	100

COLOR

Careful fluorescent lamp selection can create a lighting environment that complements any interior color scheme. Most fluorescent lamps emit light with higher color temperature than incandescent lamps—they produce more blue-green energy and less red-orange-yellow energy. However, a great variety of "white" fluorescent lamps are available; "triphosphor" improved color lamps use a mix of three phosphors to produce spikes of blue, green, and red spectral energy that imitate incandescent light.

OPERATION
Voltage

The operating voltage of a fluorescent lamp is controlled by a ballast. In large buildings fluorescent lighting circuits are usually served at 277 volts (347 volts in Canada) to reduce wiring costs.

Dimming

Dimming fluorescent lamps is more expensive than dimming incandescent lighting. Extra dimming ballasts and/or electronic ballasts and special controls are required. An alternate approach is to switch half of the lamps in a fluorescent installation, permitting two illuminance choices.

LAMP TYPES AND BASES

Four fluorescent lamp types are used for most building lighting applications (see Figure 3.12).

Preheat lamps require starters and take a few seconds to light. Preheat applications include some compact lamps and residential under-cabinet fixtures. Preheat lamps have bipin bases. Older preheat fixtures had replaceable starters.

Instant start or "slimline" lamps light immediately. They have single-pin bases.

Rapid start lamps light after a slight delay; most use bipin bases.

High-output and *very-high-output* lamps have recessed contact bases. These lamps use increased arc current to produce more light, but they have lower efficacy than standard lamps. High-output lamps are rated at 800 mA and very-high-output lamps operate at 1,500 mA.

LAMP DESIGNATIONS

Compact fluorescent lamps use small tubes, but standard fluorescent lighting installations use 1.5-inch (T12) and 1-inch (T8) lamps. T indicates tubular shape and the following number is the tube diameter in eighths of an inch. T8 lamps offer "better" color and higher efficacy than T12 lamps.

Fluorescent lamps are manufactured in a great variety of shapes and lengths but 4-foot and 8-foot tubes offer more light per lamp dollar. Actual tube length is slightly less than the nominal dimension. Fluorescent fixtures accommodate 4-foot lamps in a total fixture length of 48 inches. Square fluorescent ceiling fixtures use bent "U" tubes or "compact" lamps instead of straight lamps.

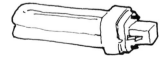

FIGURE 3.12

Most fluorescent lamp designations begin with the letter F. Review the following generic examples to understand the code, but use *only* current manufacturers' catalogs for lamp selection. See also Figure 3.13.

F20T12/CW/RS is a 20 watt, 2′ long, 1.5″ diameter, cool white, rapid start lamp.

F40T12/WW/RS is a 40 watt, 4′ long, 1.5″ diameter, warm white, rapid start lamp.

F40T12/WWX/U is a 40 watt, 1.5″ diameter, deluxe warm white, "U" shaped lamp. *This lamp fits a 2′ square fixture. It is a 4′ lamp bent into a "U" shape.*

Instant start (slimline) lamps use lamp length descriptors instead of watts.

F42T6/CW is a 42″ long, 3/4″ diameter, cool white (slimline) instant start, 25 watt lamp.

F48T12/W is a 48″ long, 1.5″ diameter, white (slimline) instant start, 40 watt lamp.

F96T12/CW is a 96″ long, 1.5″ diameter, cool white (slimline) instant start, 75 watt lamp.

F96T12/W/HO is a 96″ long, 1.5″ diameter, white (800 mA) high output, 110 watt lamp.

F96T6/D/VHO is a 96″ long, 3/4″ diameter, "daylight" color (1,500 mA) very high output, 215 watt lamp.

Danger! The preceding descriptors are generic. The following four lamps from two recent manufacturers' catalogs illustrate variations.

FO96T8 is a 96″ long, 1″ diameter, "Octron" (265 mA) 59 watt lamp manufactured by Osram/Sylvania.

CF5DS/827 is a 1/2″ diameter, 4″ long, 5 watt, compact fluorescent lamp, with a CRI of 82, a color temperature of 2,700 K, manufactured by Osram/Sylvania.

F40T12SP30/RS/WMP is a 48″ long, 1.5″ diameter, 3,000 K, rapid start, "Watt-Mizer Plus," 32 watt lamp, manufactured by General Electric.

F30T12SP41/RS/WM is a 36″ long, 1.5″ diameter, 4,100 K, rapid start, "Watt-Mizer," 25 watt lamp, manufactured by General Electric.

Older standard fluorescent lamps used about 10 watts per foot of length, but new lamp watts are best found in manufacturer catalogs.

Newer energy-efficient fluorescent lamps are advertised for their color and watts saved, but the lamp codes *don't* indicate efficacy. The following examples for 48-inch GE lamps illustrate:

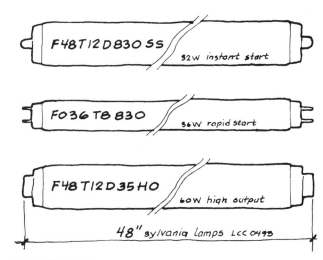

FIGURE 3.13

Description	CRI	Efficacy
F40T12CWX	89	53
F40T12CW/RS/WM	62	78
F32T8SPX30	84	92

Note: F32 above indicates watts for a 48″ lamp. This makes lamp identification even more challenging.

BALLASTS

Fluorescent and HID lamps must be connected through ballasts that start the arc and limit operating current (see Figure 3.14). Actual lighting watts are determined by the lamp-ballast combination.

An aged 40 watt lamp controlled by an obsolete magnetic ballast will use nearly 50 watts, but a new 32 watt lamp served by an electronic ballast can consume *less than* 32 watts. Three types of fluorescent ballasts—*preheat, rapid start,* and *instant start*—serve corresponding lamp types. Some T8 high-efficacy lamps operate on rapid start or instant start ballasts but instant start lamps and ballasts are most efficient.

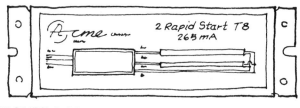

FIGURE 3.14

FIGURE 3.15

Magnetic or Electronic?

Magnetic ballasts offer low initial cost but they are noisy and less efficient than electronic ballasts. Ballasts are rated A through F for noise output. An A rated ballast is least noisy when two standard 4-foot lamps are served by each ballast. Longer lamps, or one lamp per ballast, will make more noise.

In renovation work you may find older fixtures that use preheat lamps and ballasts. Some rapid start lamps will work on preheat ballasts, but matched lamp-ballast combinations will be more efficient.

Electronic ballasts are selected for many new lighting installations because they produce more light, less heat, and less noise than magnetic ballasts. They offer power factors approaching 1, dimming capability, and low harmonic distortion.* Manufacturers quote "ballast factor"—lamp lumen output as a percent of rated lumens compared to an ANSI "reference ballast."

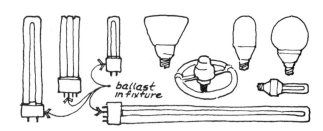

FIGURE 3.16

SPECIAL FLUORESCENT LAMPS
Rapid Start or Instant Start

Rapid start (RS) fluorescent lamps dominate the market but they start poorly in cold weather. Instant start (slimline) lamps are more expensive and have less life expectancy, but they start at lower ambient temperatures than RS and are frequently used in outdoor applications.

HO and VHO

Standard loading for a 4-foot fluorescent lamp is a bit less than half an ampere (see Figure 3.15). High-output (800 mA) and very-high-output (1,500 mA) rapid start lamps are available. HO/VHO lamps produce more light, but their efficacy is lower than standard lamps. When high illuminance is required, HO and VHO lamps offer lower first costs than standard lamps because fewer fixtures are required.

Compact

Compact fluorescent lamps' wattages range from 5 to 50 and lengths from 5 to 24 inches. Compact circular lamps have been available for many years but recent compact lamps are small "U" shape tubes or clusters of tubes. The smaller (4 to 8 inches) compact lamps were developed to replace incandescents. Some include attached ballasts and screw bases to permit installation in incandescent sockets; others use detached ballasts (see Figure 3.16).

Compact fluorescents can provide real electrical cost savings, but they are not very effective in spot lighting applications. With life ratings up to 10,000 hours these lamps can cut incandescent energy costs by as much as 70%.

Larger (up to 24 inches) compact fluorescent lamps rated up to 50 watts compete with standard and "U" lamps in 2-foot square fixtures.

Energy-Efficient Fluorescent Lamps

Manufacturers have developed a number of new lamp-ballast combinations that offer energy savings when compared to standard lamps and ballasts. Note that *both* lamps and ballasts must be used to realize the advertised savings. Installing an energy-efficient lamp in an old fixture with an antique ballast will not produce great savings (and some lamps will not light).

---

*Harmonic distortion caused by magnetic ballasts on three-phase lighting circuits can overload the common neutral conductor.

One efficient lamp-ballast combination uses tri-phosphor lamps with electronic ballasts to achieve efficacies as high as 100 lumens per watt. 48-inch lamps operate at 265 mA and offer good color rendering characteristics.

Cold Cathode

Cold cathode fluorescent lamps use an internal soft iron cylinder as a source of arc electrons. While cold cathode lamps are less efficient than standard fluorescents, they last for many *years*. Cold cathode lamp tubes can be shaped to fit curves or angles, so they are often used in decorative light coves.

Neon

Cold cathodes are also used as an electron source in neon lamps. Neon emits an orange-red light when excited by a high-voltage arc. Neon lamps operate at high voltage with currents near 30 mA and consume about 7 watts per foot of length. Krypton and argon emit other colors. Phosphors or tinted glass are used to modify color.*

---

*For more information, read *Neon: Argon to Xenon* by Michael Cohen Lighting Design and Application April 1995.

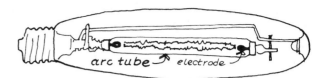

FIGURE 3.17

3.3 HIGH-INTENSITY DISCHARGE LAMPS

HID lamps are intense light sources that produce light by passing an electric arc through a conducting vapor. The arc radiates visible light, and most HID arcs operate at high temperature and pressure. Light color is determined by the elements used in the conducting vapor.

It takes time to start, heat, vaporize, and stabilize HID arcs, and warm-up times as long as 5 minutes are not unusual. Ceramic or quartz arc tubes are used to withstand temperatures that can exceed 1,000°C, and an outer glass bulb is designed to retain lamp materials in the event of a violent failure (see Figure 3.17).

All HID lamps require ballasts to strike the arc and to limit arc current. Magnetic ballasts add about 15% to lamp watts; electronic ballasts permit dimming but they don't increase light output.

Most lamps will *not* light for some minutes after a power interruption because temperatures and pressures in the arc tube exceed ballast capacity. Restart time can vary from 1 to more than 10 minutes and supplementary lighting or special hot-start lamps are required when HID sources are used for sports or assembly lighting.

HID lamps have average lives as long as 40,000 hours. Manufacturers use a great variety of lamp descriptors: ANSI codes H for mercury, S for sodium, and M for multiple arc metals. Although other shapes are available, E (elliptical), B (bulged), and T (tubular) shapes are used extensively for these lamps (see Figure 3.18). Medium and mogul bases are typical, and available wattages range from 35 to more than 2,000. Arc tubes are designed to operate in a specific burning position. Tilting lamps reduces efficiency and life.

HID EFFICACY AND LIFE

Mercury and sodium HID lamps were developed in the 1930s and significantly improved by the mid-1960s. Sodium lamps are available in low-pressure (SOX) and high-pressure (HPS) versions. Vaporized metals carry the visible arc, mercury lamps produce green light, and sodium lamps yield yellow light. Metal halide lamps use mercury, sodium, scandium, and other halide conductors to produce "white" light.

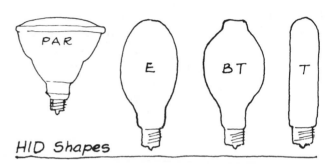

HID Shapes

FIGURE 3.18

Mercury

Clear mercury lamps produce green-blue light (5,710 K). "Deluxe" mercury lamps add a phosphor coating on the outer bulb to "whiten" light output.

Efficacy of mercury lamps ranges from 30 to 60 lumens per watt, starting time is 3 to 7 minutes, and life can exceed 24,000 hours with considerable decay as lamps age. Mercury sources are being replaced with more efficient metal halide or sodium lamps, but some landscape lighting designers prefer clear mercury to enhance foliage.

Sodium

Sodium lamps are very efficient sources of yellow-orange light. Low-pressure sodium looks slightly orange (1,740 K), and high-pressure sodium appears yellow (2,100 K) or "golden" in advertising descriptions.

Low-pressure sodium (SOX) lamps produce monochromatic light near the human eye's peak sensitivity. Initial efficacy can be as high as 180 but color rendering is dreadful. Lamp life ranges from 10,000 to 20,000 hours and light output drops less than 10% as lamps age. Low-pressure sodium is often used for roadway lighting where economical operation is more important than color rendition.

High-pressure sodium lamps have initial efficacy values as high as 140 and life ratings from 16,000 to 40,000 hours. Light output decays about 20% as lamps age. Improved color lamps are available, but CRI increases come at the expense of lamp life and efficacy.

Metal Halide

Metal halide HID lamps use mixtures of mercury, sodium, thallium, scandium, and additional conducting materials in the arc tube to obtain "white" light output. Efficacy approaches 100 lumens per watt and life ratings range from 10,000 to 20,000 hours. MH lamps are extensively used for sports lighting and increasingly in commercial and industrial applications where an intense light source is desired.

Color Rendering Index

Source (Kelvin Temperature)	CRI
Mercury (5,710 K)	15
"Improved" mercury (3,900 K)	To 50
MH (3,600 K)	To 70
Sodium—low psi (1,740 K)	–
Sodium—high psi (2,100 K)	22
"Improved" sodium (2,200 K)	To 70

Source: GE Lamp Catalog #9200/21.

COMPARISONS

See Figure 3.19 for comparisons between incandescent, fluorescent, and HID lamps.

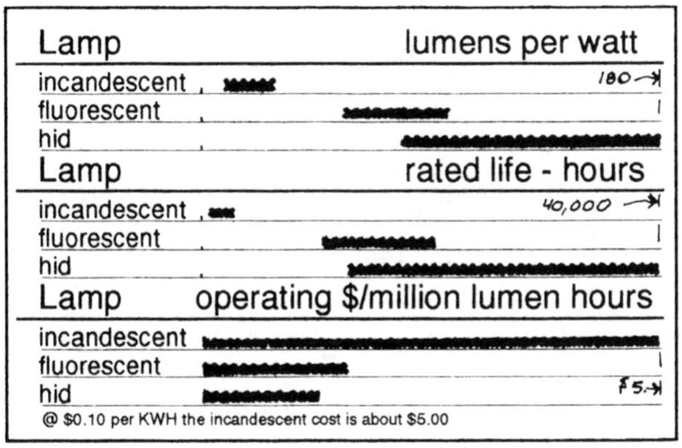

Lamp	lumens per watt
incandescent	180 →
fluorescent	
hid	
Lamp	rated life - hours
incandescent	40,000 →
fluorescent	
hid	
Lamp	operating $/million lumen hours
incandescent	
fluorescent	
hid	5. →

@ $0.10 per KWH the incandescent cost is about $5.00

FIGURE 3.19

Other Lamps

The *"E" lamp* is an inductive lamp which uses radio waves to excite a light-emitting plasma. Development has been well publicized. Two manufacturers now offer lamps and a third is scheduled for 1998.

Electroluminescence is a term for light emitted by certain materials when exposed to an alternating electric field. An example is the small night light that plugs into a duplex outlet. Attempts to develop large marketable electroluminescent sources have not been successful.

Lasers, light pipes, liquid crystals, and light-emitting diodes begin just the *"L" list* of other available lamps.

REVIEW QUESTIONS

1. Efficacy is measured in ____.
2. An ideal light source would produce about ____ lumens from each watt of input energy.
3. Low-pressure sodium HID lamps have efficacies as high as ____.
4. Which lamp type—incandescent, fluorescent, or HID—has the best CRI?
5. Rated lamp life is the number of operating hours until ____.
6. Are tungsten-halogen lamps ballasted?
7. An easy way to double the life of an incandescent lamp is ____.
8. Which fluorescent lamp-ballast type offers the highest efficacy?
9. What is the length and diameter of an F42T8 fluorescent lamp?
10. The arc inside a fluorescent lamp tube is conducted by ____.
11. Arc current for a standard 48-inch fluorescent lamp is about ____.
12. Name four advantages of electronic ballasts over magnetic ballasts.
13. Rated life for a standard fluorescent lamp is about ____.
14. Fluorescent lamp light output will drop about ____% after 8,000 hours of operation.
15. A spotlight is rated 100,000 beam candlepower. How many footcandles in the center of the beam 100 feet distant?
16. A lamp designated H400E28 is ____.
17. How many watts should be allowed on the electrical circuit that serves the H400 lamp in question 16?
18. Which HID lamp offers the highest efficacy?
19. Which HID lamp offers longest life?
20. Which HID lamp offers the highest CRI?
21. Why do large buildings serve fluorescent and HID lighting at 277 volts?
22. Name two functions of a ballast.

ANSWERS

1. lumens per watt
2. 680
3. 180
4. incandescent, CRI = 100
5. 50% of a representative lamp group fail
6. No. They are incandescent lamps.
7. reduce supply voltage slightly with a dimmer
8. instant start (slimline)
9. 42 inches long and 1-inch diameter
10. mercury vapor
11. half an ampere—actually 425 or 430 mA (energy-conserving lamps operate at 265 mA or less)
12. higher power factor, reduced harmonic distortion, higher efficacy, and less noise
13. 20,000 hours
14. 15
15. 10
16. a 400 watt, elliptical, mercury lamp, 3.5 inches in diameter
17. 460 watts—ballast adds 15%
18. low-pressure sodium (SOX)
19. high-pressure sodium
20. Metal halide. Manufacturers claim CRI values of 90 for "improved" MH and sodium lamps, but the sodium CRI is at a very low color temperature.
21. Higher voltage allows more lamps on each 20 ampere circuit. This reduces electrical system costs.
22. start the arc and limit arc current

CHAPTER 4

Lighting Design

Hobbes — *How's your snow art progressing?*
Calvin — *I've moved into abstraction.*
Hobbes — *Ah!*
Calvin — *This piece is about the inadequacy of traditional imagery and symbols to convey meaning in today's world.*
By abandoning representationalism, I'm free to express myself with pure form, specific interpretation gives way to a more visceral response.
Hobbes — *I notice your oeuvre is monochromatic.*
Calvin — *Well C'mon, it's just snow.*

Bill Watterson 94

Lighting design is a two-step process. Designers, visualize desired brightness contrasts and patterns, and then select lamps and luminaires to fulfill their visual intentions.

This chapter begins with a design-oriented discussion of luminaires that illuminate and/or decorate. Read to develop convictions about brightness, shade, and shadow patterns that enhance rooms or spaces by emphasizing architectural features or by adding bright focal points.

Lighting shapes viewer perceptions, and the palette of artistic lighting design includes brightness contrast, pattern, and color.

Three luminaire types using concealed lamps are described as cone, band, or uniform light sources. Each luminaire is discussed emphasizing design possibilities, and opinions are offered concerning appropriate applications.

Decorative luminaires that illuminate and add visual interest are briefly discussed; the chapter ending review pages include design sketch templates.

4.0 SELECT LUMINAIRES

Luminaire is the proper word for a lighting assembly that connects one or more lamps to a power source and distributes their light. Luminaire components can include diffusers, reflectors, lenses, prisms, shields, louvers, airways, transformers, ballasts, and electrical wiring. *Fixture* is a less descriptive word, often substituted for luminaire in common usage, and occasionally in this text.

Because brightness contrast attracts viewer attention, lighting designers emphasize objects or surfaces when they select luminaires with concealed lamps. Selecting luminaires with visible lamps or diffusers emphasizes the luminaire.

Two simple observations are the basis of luminaire selection. Beyond providing comfortable lighting that accommodates activities expected to take place in the room or space, **luminaires are selected (1) to emphasize objects or surfaces, or (2) to provide decorative focal points in a space.**

Decorative luminaires illuminate surfaces, and concealed source luminaires draw viewer attention to bright surfaces near lamps. Talented lighting professionals select luminaires only after choosing decoration *or* surface illumination as the primary design intent.

A plaster sculpture is illustrated in diffuse and directional light (see Figure 4.1 A and B). Designers prefer directional luminaires when shade and shadow patterns enhance the illuminated object.

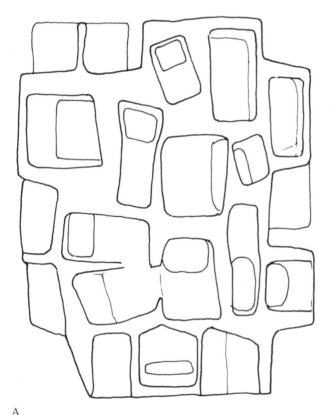

A

B

FIGURE 4.1

4.1 ILLUMINATE OR DECORATE

A luminaire recessed in the ceiling can be an excellent choice when the design intent is illuminating a beautiful table. A crystal chandelier can be an equally fine choice above the same table when design intent is an added focal point. Fixtures with concealed lamps emphasize architectural features, objects, openings, surfaces, and details. Decorative fixtures add focal points, variety, pattern, and interest.

Two dining room scenes compare a concealed source fixture recessed in the ceiling with a decorative chandelier (see Figures 4.2 and 4.3). Both provide adequate light for dining and conversation, and both can be examples of "good" lighting design.

Admirers of the concealed fixture claim that it better illuminates gourmet dishes, and its bright specular reflections in china, crystal, and silverware provide variety and interest. They allege the soft light reflected from the table to the diners stimulates intimate dinner conversation.

Chandelier admirers believe a stepped cone of flashing prisms is the perfect complement for a sumptuous table. They allege dinner conversation is more spirited when diners see each other covered with a lace of specular reflections.

Intimate conversation is usually associated with less light, and spirited conversation with bright light, so a dimmer can mitigate the conversation contentions. Perceptive readers will agree, however, that each fixture creates a very different dining ambience.

FIGURE 4.2

FIGURE 4.3

4.2 DESIGNS

Design is the creative visualization that precedes fixture selection. Accomplished designers first visualize the space, surfaces, and objects to be illuminated. Then they invent and evaluate mental images of brightness contrast and patterns that can make the space visually inviting, comfortable, and interesting. Finally designers choose from their mental images the brightness patterns that best enhance the space. Intelligent fixture selection happens only after designers mentally *invent, visualize,* and *evaluate* brightness patterns.

Comparative room sketches illustrate a variety of design approaches using fixtures with concealed lamps that illuminate objects or surfaces. Creative lighting designers visualize such scenes *before* selecting fixtures. As you study the sketches think about the fixture type and location that could produce the brightness patterns shown; then review each sketch a second time and pick a favorite design. Finally, discuss the design elements that attracted your attention.

Figure 4.4A compares designs that "wash" walls with light. Illuminating a wall can make it seem more distant so one room should appear "longer" and the other "wider." The left scene increases apparent ceiling height by illuminating beams, and it adds contrast by spotlighting the vase and the tabletop. The right scene uses a dark window and tabletop to provide variety and contrast in the field of view.

Figure 4.4B is very similar, but it shows a two-way valence light source. Uplight coves make the ceiling appear higher, and downlight wall washers make the wall seem more distant. The dark valence face yields dramatic contrast. A lighter face or a perforated face will soften this effect. Installing or constructing valences or coves demands true edges and careful joining because the lamps highlight all faults.

Figure 4.4C paints walls with arches of light. The brightness patterns are more dramatic and can be more interesting than uniform surface luminance. Careful spacing is important when using brightness patterns. Fixtures too close together yield an expensive wall "wash," and fixtures too far apart can create trivial patterns. Manufacturers offer graphic data on arch shape and dimensions for specific lamp-fixture combinations.

A

B

C

D

FIGURE 4.4

A designer's palette just begins with bright arches on walls. The heart shape in Figure 4.5 is just a spotlight aimed into a corner. What sources and surfaces will produce the other shapes?

Figure 4.4D compares illuminated ceiling beams with illuminated flags seen against a dark ceiling. The flags serve as decorative luminaires. The light they reflect adds focal points and modifies room ambience. Visualize the fixture type, location, and mounting details that you would use to best illuminate the beams or the flags.

Figure 4.4E illustrates a low light source with dim and bright intensity. The low line of light suggests the horizon at sea; some designers claim a floating effect. Compare this figure with Figures 4.4A through 4.4D and notice how different the room appears when light is introduced below eye level.

Visualize a concealed vertical fluorescent in the corner of a room. Do you think you'll like the visual effect? If so, build and test one behind an opaque cove.

Figure 4.4F is included as an example of uniform lighting, an approach that spreads lumens equally throughout a space. Why is uniform lighting used in many schools and offices, but in few homes, restaurants, or retail stores?

Proponents claim uniform lighting provides an ideal environment for performing visual tasks, but critics contend it creates dull and boring spaces that fail to recognize the eye's range and the stimulation brightness contrast can offer. Figure 4.4F illustrates a typical uniform lighting scheme in large rooms with dark or light interior surfaces. Luminaires in the lower view include diffusers designed to minimize ceiling brightness contrast.

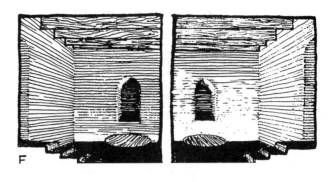

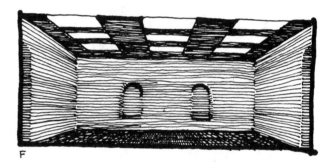

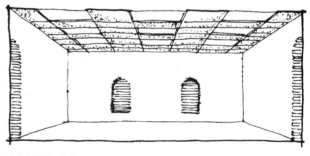

FIGURE 4.4

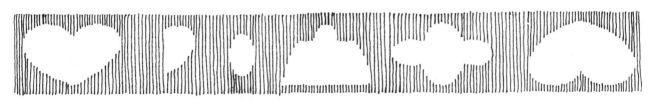

FIGURE 4.5

4.3 RECESSED DOWNLIGHTS

ARCHITECTURAL LIGHTING?

The next few pages emphasize fixtures with shielded lamps used to illuminate surfaces (see Figure 4.6). "Architectural lighting" is a possible descriptor for these built-in luminaires. Three fixture types provide *cones* of light, *bands* of light, or *uniform* lighting.

CONES OF LIGHT

Recessed can downlights can be effective luminaires when used to emphasize objects or surfaces. Manufacturers detail these fixtures to project a cone of illumination, and designers locate and aim them to accent or silhouette. Lamps or reflectors designed to produce a narrow cone provide dramatic brightness patterns that can enhance a painting, a plant, or a table; however, using these fixtures to illuminate large surfaces or an entire room is an aesthetic null that wastes money and energy.

Clearance

Recessed fixtures typically include a housing, support arms, and visible trim. If fluorescent or HID lamps are used they'll also include a ballast. When installed in insulated ceilings, an extra housing is required.

Recessed can luminaires shield the lamp to minimize glare, so considerable space above the ceiling is required. Where space is limited specify smaller cans with R-20 or MR-16 lamps.

Trims

A black step baffle cuts glare, but reduces light output. Quality reflective cone trim allows you to specify an economical A lamp, but the housing requires more vertical clearance to conceal the source. The pinhole must use an ER lamp, so check the light distribution profile to determine the most effective mounting height.

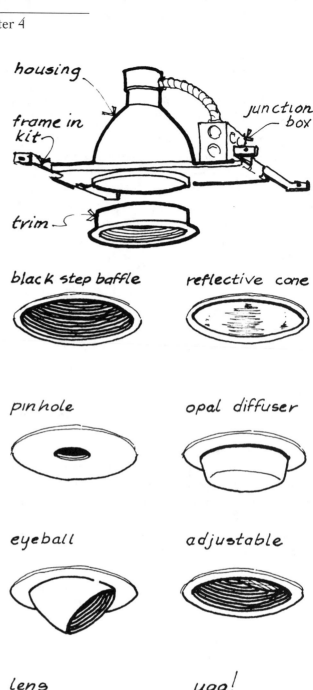

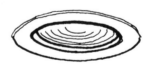

FIGURE 4.6

The opal diffuser is not an effective accent light because the opal is a bright spot on the ceiling and it provides a wider (and less intense) cone of illumination.

Wall washers can increase visual interest where their brightness patterns complement arches in an arcade (see Figure 4.7). However, unless you sell fixtures for a living, there are better ways to illuminate wall surfaces. Compact fluorescent wall washers or fluorescent coves are an effective alternative where scallop patterns are not essential design features.

A single luminaire yields a more dramatic brightness contrast pattern than a group of closely spaced fixtures, and it will do a better job accenting an object or emphasizing a surface.

Framing spots use reflectors and a mask to outline a painting or sculpture with an exact brightness envelope. A wall washer or a small luminaire mounted on the picture frame can provide almost the same dramatic effect because the eye is drawn by brightness, but responds to the painting's contrast instead of brightness pattern (see Figure 4.8).

OPINIONS

Recessed cans will be elements of quality lighting design when they are used to accent, emphasize, focus, or direct viewer attention to a specific object or surface. They are a poor choice for illuminating large surfaces or areas.

Since recessed cans are not efficient area lights, don't specify them with compact fluorescent lamps. Compact fluorescents save energy but they won't deliver a tight beam of accent light. If you need intense brightness contrast try DC or HID lamps (see Figure 4.9). Translucent colored trims add a decorative edge to recessed cans, but this bright accent rim can compete with the illuminated object for viewer attention. Develop your opinions about such fixtures by careful study of installations you find appealing.

lighting a painting

FIGURE 4.8

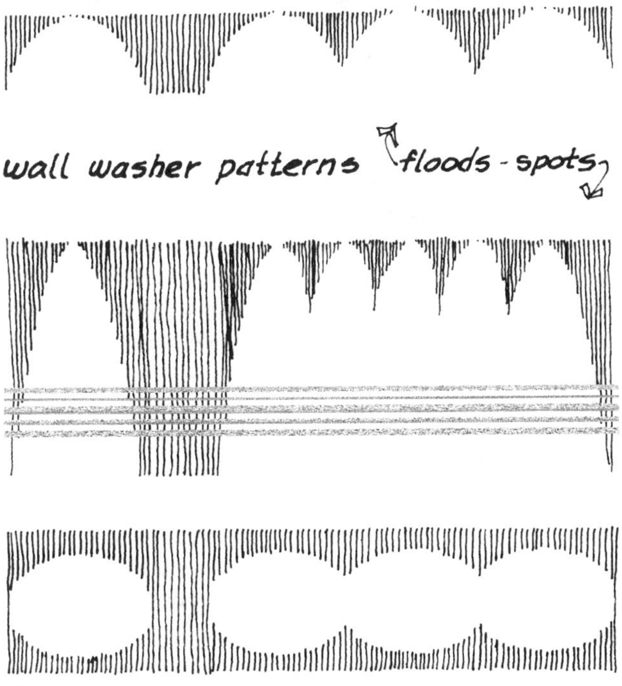

wall washer patterns floods - spots

horizontal surface patterns

FIGURE 4.7

FIGURE 4.9

4.4 COVE LIGHTING

BANDS OF LIGHT

Coves are appropriate fixtures where the brightness patterns they produce makes a room more interesting or inviting. Here *cove*[*] refers to a linear luminaire with hidden lamps. Concealed lamps and a long axis make cove fixtures ideal for surface illumination. They can be used to increase apparent ceiling height, expand room proportions, or dramatize surface textures. Talented designers use coves to create focal planes, embellish architectural lines, define circulation paths, or enhance attractive surfaces or objects. The bands of brightness contrast they create can grace an appealing space or make a bland interior more inviting (see Figure 4.10).

The following are recommended **details** for built-in cove luminaires:

- Use economical 48-inch or 96-inch fluorescent strip fixtures. Specify electronic ballasts or "A" rated magnetic ballasts where quiet operation is important.
- Strip fixtures must be mounted on noncombustible surfaces. "Greenfield" (flexible conduit) is used between the box and the fixture to limit ballast noise.
- Mounting brackets and lamp sockets create minor shadow lines. Overlap lamp ends and revise bracket details if shadows are objectionable.
- Set cove dimensions so lamps and fixtures are *not* visible and check sight lines to be sure lamps are *not* mirrored in windows. Allow adequate clearance for re-lamping.
- In up and down coves try a cool lamp on top and a warm lamp below. Also try switching top and bottom lamps separately. If an installation is too bright paint the back of the cove black—if too dark, add a reflector. If the visible cove face looks too dark, consider perforations.
- Cove edges and joints must be true and level because the bright background will emphasize any tilt or defect.

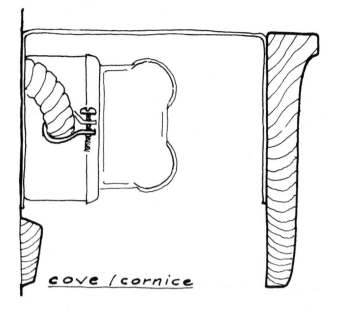

cove / cornice

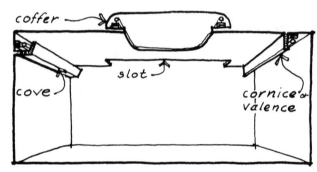

coffer —
slot —
cove —
cornice or valence

FIGURE 4.10

- Ducts or structural members can be used to conceal lamps instead of coves *only* when careful erection, painting, and finishing procedures are followed.
- Consider coves suspended with wire or chain if you like sailing. They sway gently when the air conditioning system operates.
- Where curves and long life are required, specify cold cathode lamps.
- When planning a cove installation, check architectural, structural, and mechanical drawings and details carefully. Interference between luminaires, finishes, structure, ductwork, and piping should be resolved before construction.

---

[*]A cove luminaire is a shielded uplight, mounted high on a wall, to illuminate upper wall and ceiling. Here *cove* describes any linear fixture with concealed lamps regardless of illuminance direction or fixture location. Coffer, valence, cornice, and slot luminaires are described as coves on these pages.

The eye "sees" bands of brightness and accommodates gradual brightness change. The sketches in Figure 4.11 illustrate some cove lighting effects.

Study the sketches in Figures 4.11A and 4.11B *before* reading on. Imagine people, furnishings, color, and activity in each space. Which lighting scheme would you prefer if the room was used as an office, a church, or a restaurant? Why?

When ceilings and walls are white, coves (uplight) increase apparent ceiling height. Cornice luminaries (downlight) appear to increase room size and lower the ceiling. What happens when dark finishes or strong advancing colors replace white surfaces?

Cornice lighting on the side walls can make a room seem wider (Figure 4.11C); slot or cornice luminaires on the far wall increase apparent room length (Figure 4.11D). Would either lighting installation be better for church use than the two shown in Figures 4.11A and 4.11B?

Indirect lighting describes an installation with concealed lamps where general room illumination is first reflected by ceilings or walls. *Direct* lighting aims lamp light at objects or work surfaces.

The coffered ceiling shown in Figures 4.11E and 4.11F can increase apparent room height. Coffers are used extensively on cruise ships to make spaces with low ceilings appear more spacious.

Because only surfaces receive direct light, "architectural lighting" might describe the sketches in Figure 4.11. Look at each sketch again and develop your design opinions. Which lighting scheme would you prefer if the room was used as a restaurant, an office, a retail store, or a church? Why?

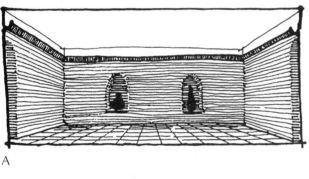

A

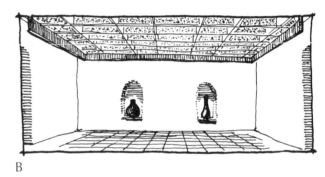

B

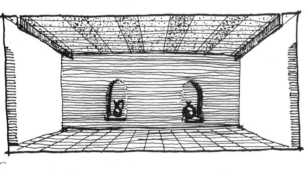

C

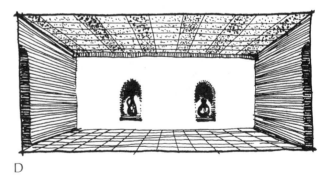

D

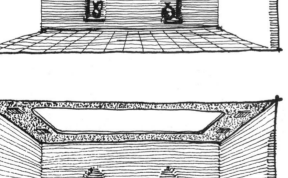

E

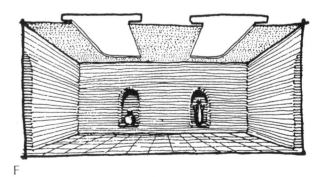

F

FIGURE 4.11

COVES AND DESIGN

Study each cove lighting illustration and then draw in your own lighting design for a restaurant, church, or office using the top view in Figure 4.12. Add furnishings, people, and at least *two* bright focal points illuminated with recessed cans. Experiment with color to add visual interest.

Surface brightness decreases as the distance from a cove increases, but the eye "sees" just a bright surface. Cove lighting can be especially effective when the illuminated surface is interesting. Interior designers use art, carving, color, and ornament to grace the ceiling surface.

Coves draw attention to the ceiling because brightness contrast attracts the eye. If the ceiling is just an unadorned white plane it will seem higher when cove lighting is used, but lighting design can offer more than an increase in perceived ceiling height.

Talented lighting professionals view the ceiling plane as a design opportunity.* Cove lighting emphasizes the ceiling surface. Texture, line, or depth can make a ceiling more interesting. The illustrations in Figure 4.12 suggest brightness contrast effects using texture, shade, and shadow. The bottom sketch repeats the far wall arches and adds light to silhouette vases and flowers; it is the beginning of a three-dimensional lighting design.

Visual perceptions change as brightness, textures, shades, shadows, and colors change. Lighting is the essence of design. Study the illustrations again after completing the top view. Notice how your perception of the room changes as you consider each sketch. Categorize each view using the following words:

Strong
Weak
Interesting
Dull
Inviting
Attractive
Best

Then select three or four other adjectives that further describe the "best" illustration.

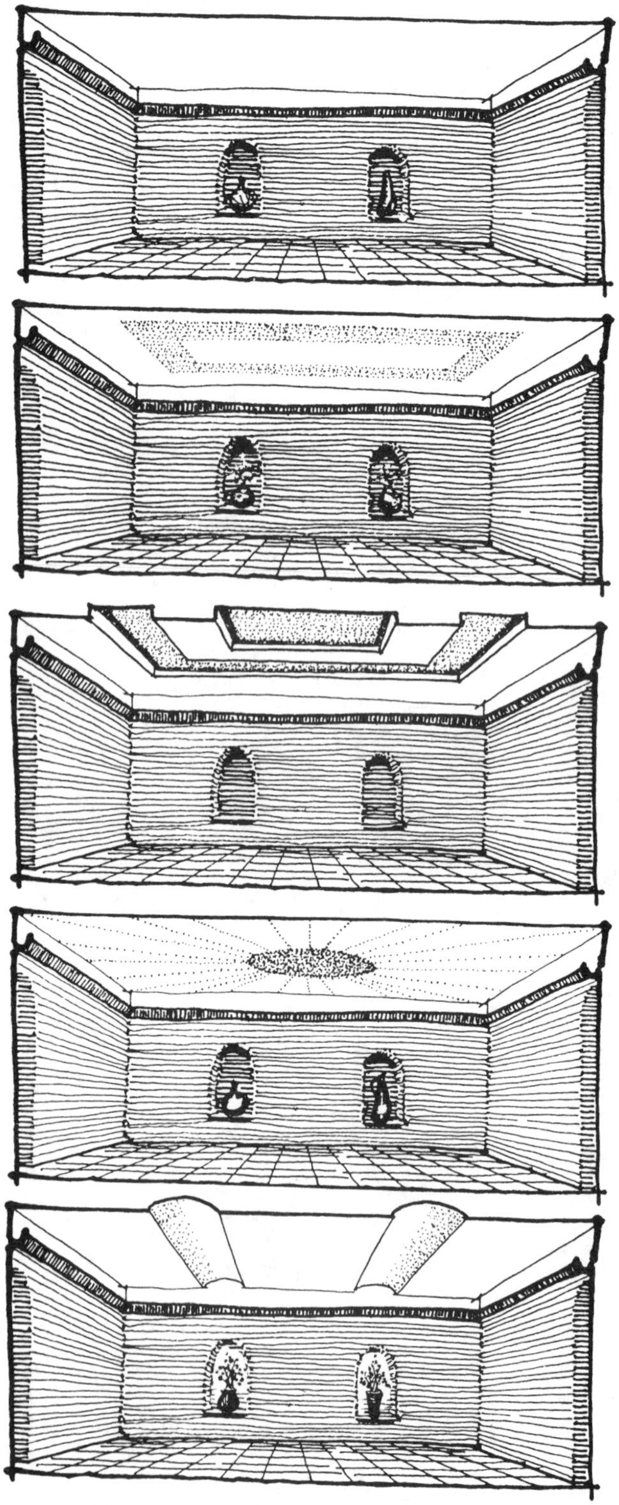

FIGURE 4.12

---

*When working with residential ceilings (sheet rock on wood joists), curved patterns or color accents are more successful than straight line patterns because ceilings are rarely true and level.

4.5 UNIFORM LIGHTING

Almost any group of luminaires can be spaced to obtain uniform lighting, but fluorescent troffers in a lay in ceiling grid are an economical option. In high-bay applications, HID lamps compete with fluorescents; incandescent sources are seldom used because of high operating costs. Illumination decreases near walls because they absorb light, so spacing luminaires for uniformity requires a centered symmetrical fixture layout (see Figure 4.13).

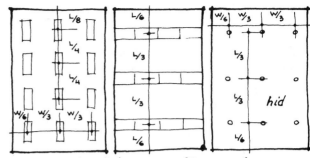

reflected ceilings · uniform schemes

FIGURE 4.13

SPACING

S/MH (spacing to mounting height) is a number used to determine fixture spacing for uniform illumination (see Figure 4.14). Spacing is the center-to-center distance between small fixtures, or the edge to edge spacing for 24" fluorescents and mounting height is the fixture-to-desktop distance (or the fixture-to-lane distance in a bowling alley).

Luminaire manufacturers provide S/MH values and photometric diagrams showing candlepower distribution for each fixture. Luminaires with wide light distribution patterns can be spaced further apart, saving fixtures and dollars, but wider light distribution means less shielding and more glare.

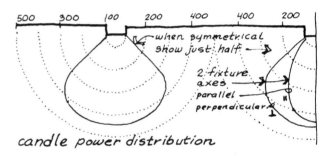

S/MH spacing / mounting height

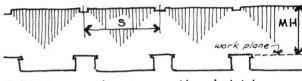

candle power distribution

FIGURE 4.14

GLARE

Luminaires with wide distribution patterns can produce uncomfortable glare. Glare is defined as uncomfortable brightness contrast. A classic glare example is approaching auto headlights at night. Headlights don't glare in daylight and lighting designers minimize glare problems by increasing background brightness, reducing source brightness, or shielding the source.

The eyebrow shields light sources above a 45-degree angle, so bright lamps overhead are not usually glare sources. As the fixture shielding angle decreases, fixture spacing increases, but glare problems are likely (see Figures 4.15 and 4.16).

Chapter 7 includes a glare index and a calculation method used to determine the number of fixtures required for a given illumination level.

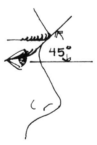

FIGURE 4.15

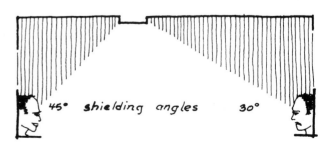

45° shielding angles 30°

FIGURE 4.16

FIXTURES

Suspended ceiling systems with lay in fluorescent troffers rule the school and office lighting market. Many sizes and shapes are available, but when initial cost drives selection, 24" x48" troffers are usually the economical choice (see Figure 4.17).

Shallow troffers are desirable because the space above suspended ceilings is usually crowded with piping, conduit, and ducts. However, troffer depth increases when deep parabolic diffusers are used. Where fire rated ceilings are required, an insulated fixture enclosure takes more space (see Figure 4.18).

Troffer Options

Troffers include ballasts, reflectors, and diffusers; some also have duct connections and dampers for air conditioning. Parabolic diffusers minimize light in the glare zone, and specular reflectors can maximize light output and reduce lighting costs (see Figure 4.19). Removing lamps and installing specular reflectors in existing fixtures *may* be a good investment.

Other Luminaires

In high-bay or high ceiling retail installations, fixture glare is not usually a problem. HID fixtures or 8-foot fluorescent strips are used extensively because they can deliver uniform illumination economically. Fixture selection is usually based on estimated life cycle costs, and talented designers add brightness contrast with color and spotlights to stimulate sales. Indirect fixtures minimize glare, but direct fixtures deliver more illumination per watt of electrical input (see Figure 4.20).

CU

CU (coefficient of utilization) is an index of fixture efficiency. It is the percent of lamp lumens that reach the work plane. A fixture's CU varies with the size, proportions, and reflectance of the illuminated room (see Figure 4.21). Fixtures in a large room will have a higher CU than the same fixtures in a small room because walls absorb light. Large rooms have proportionally less wall area. White surfaces reflect more light than black surfaces so fixture CU will be higher in a white room.

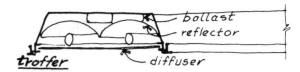

FIGURE 4.17

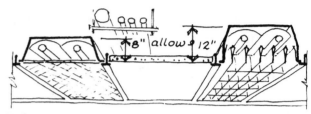

FIGURE 4.18

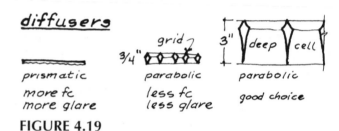

FIGURE 4.19

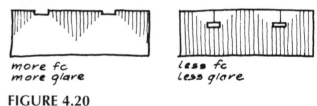

FIGURE 4.20

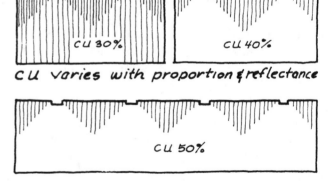

FIGURE 4.21

UNIFORM LIGHTING DESIGN

Many building lighting installations are planned and detailed to provide a constant level of interior illumination. Advocates of uniform lighting believe "good" lighting is assured when equal footcandles are provided in similar rooms and spaces. Uniform lighting "design" is a three-step process:

1. Determine an appropriate illuminance for the intended occupant activity.
2. Select fixtures and calculate the number required.
3. Space the fixtures for uniformity.

The resulting scheme is a grid or rows of evenly spaced luminaires; a calculation method is covered in Chapter 7.

The sketches in Figure 4.22 illustrate the worst uniform lighting installations. Rows of wraparound fixtures glare and the luminous ceiling is uncomfortably bright. The sketches in Figure 4.23 show better uniform lighting using recessed or shielded fixtures to minimize glare.

OPINIONS

Critics describe uniform lighting schemes as boring at best and wasteful at worst. Uniform schemes are boring because they minimize the brightness patterns and contrasts that people rely on for visual reference and information. The fixture rows paint a meaningless, repetitive glare pattern on the ceiling that degrades visual comfort. Uniform schemes waste electrical energy by spreading light like fertilizer on a lawn, instead aiming *less* illumination at specific objects, surfaces, or activity areas.

Interior designers visualize materials, fabrics, and color selections in a given room or space. Talented lighting professionals complement interior colors, textures, and surfaces with light. They use brightness contrast to define and grace attractive objects, details, surfaces, and activity areas. Because uniform schemes minimize brightness patterns and contrasts they are used infrequently, and only in conjunction with brighter accent areas or surfaces that create visual interest.

Danger! Fixture rows in uniform lighting schemes should reinforce the structural grid. *Don't* layout fluorescent fixtures in patterns that cross or conflict with the pattern of beams, columns, and walls that define a room.

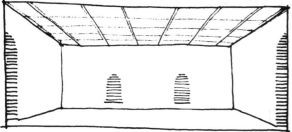

FIGURE 4.22

FIGURE 4.23

4.6 DECORATIVE LUMINAIRES

ILLUMINATE AND DECORATE?

Richard Kelly's trinity of lighting-driven perceptions is repeated as an introduction to decorative luminaires.

"Focal glow is the campfire of all time, . . . the sunburst through the clouds, and the shaft of sunshine that warms the far end of the valley. Focal glow commands attention and interest. It fixes the gaze, concentrates the mind and tells people what to look at. It separates the important from the unimportant.

Ambient luminescence is a snowy morning in open country. It is underwater in the sunshine, or inside a white tent at high noon. Ambient luminescence minimizes the importance of all things and all people. It fills people with a sense of freedom of space and can suggest infinity.

Play of the brilliants is the aurora borealis, . . . the Versailles hall of mirrors with its thousands of candle flames. Play of the brilliants is Times Square at night, . . . the magic of a Christmas tree, Fourth of July skyrockets. It quickens the appetite and heightens all sensation. It can be distracting or entertaining."

Artistic lighting begins when designers visualize the brightness patterns that make rooms or objects attractive and interesting. The sketches in Figure 4.24 picture two elegant rooms enhanced and graced by good lighting. Illumination in the domed room comes from shielded lamps that make ceiling surfaces the brightest elements in the field of view. The ornate ceiling acts as a luminaire reflecting and diffusing light throughout the space.

In the rectangular room a central luminaire provides a bright decorative focal point *and* illuminates the ceiling. Both rooms are ideal settings for effective lighting because of the brightness, shade, and shadow patterns. Light adds to their interesting surfaces and rich architectural details.

Lighting design is easy when illuminated surfaces are interesting. These sketches show rooms with elaborate surfaces where any illumination will create a variety of attractive luminance contrasts. The rectangular room with its decorative luminaire and the domed room with its indirect fixtures are both examples of good lighting design.

Less exciting rooms demand more from lighting designers who must add brightness patterns, decorative fixtures, and task lighting to create visual interest.

FIGURE 4.24

sets, candles, prisms, lamps, reflectors, sunrise, daylight, and stained glass—all are potential luminaires, and all are potentially beautiful.

The preceding pages emphasized "architectural" lighting. Fixtures with concealed lamps illuminated large surfaces, and the visual results were as attractive and interesting as the illuminated architecture. Decorative luminaires use exposed lamps, reflectors, diffusers, shapes, and color in the field of view to illuminate and *beautify* (see Figure 4.26). Such fixtures add focal points and brightness patterns; they can grace elegant rooms or make ordinary rooms more attractive. Most successful lighting designs include both shielded and decorative luminaires.

Selecting the best fixture for a specific room is a talent built on experience. Artistic designers study lighting installations like professional golfers study courses. They continually create and save memory images of attractive lighting scenes and the fixtures that help create such scenes. Brightness contrast, pattern, color, and motion are design tools; but memory images of lighting effects are a designer's reference library.

The source of a memory image affects its quality; the best images are created by observation of an actual lighting installation. Lesser images may be taken from a lighting showroom, a manufacturer's catalog, and this achromatic text.

Build your memory library of lighting images by continual observation as you shop, dine, travel, and recreate.

add color

FIGURE 4.25

"Decorative" is a poor descriptor for the visual beauty an elegant luminaire can create. Imagine the colors, patterns, and contrasts in a sunset and compare them to the experience of viewing a fine stained glass lamp (see Figure 4.25). The scale varies but the visual sensations are nearly identical. Windows, sun-

luminaires by Spring City Electrical

some look better with lamps off ~ all look good with dim lamps.

FIGURE 4.26

A

B

C

D

E

F

FIGURE 4.27

*The black and white illustrations here are only a beginning for lighting study. Serious students will enjoy *Detailing Light* by Jean Gorman, ©1995, Whitney Library of Design, New York; and *Perception and Lighting as Formgivers for Architecture* by William Lam, ©1977, McGraw-Hill, New York.

REVIEW QUESTIONS AND TEMPLATES

1. Name two possible design intentions that can aid luminaire selection.
2. A lighting designer who wants to emphasize a crystal vase of flowers will consider a(n) _____ fixture.
3. A lighting designer who wants to enhance an ornate ceiling will consider a(n)_____ fixture.
4. Template sketches are repeated in Figures 4.27A through 4.27F to encourage illustration.* Experiment with pencils, pens, or markers to add accents, shade, shadow, and color.

ANSWERS

1. illuminate surfaces and objects *or* create decorative focal points (and illumination)
2. adjustable recessed can with a narrow beam spot lamp
3. cove

CHAPTER

5

Sunlight and Daylight

Architecture is the masterly, correct and magnificent play of forms of light.

Le Corbusier

———◦◉◦———

Sunlighting designs trust the same tools used for lamplighting. People respond to:

- brightness contrast,
- form and pattern,
- color, and
- motion

regardless of the light source.

Sunlight and lamplight designs seek identical goals and use identical techniques. The sun replaces lamps. Windows or apertures serve as luminaires. Sunlighting designs use light to create decorative focal points or to illuminate objects and surfaces.

Architects consider views, site features, and sun angles before locating windows that decorate and illuminate interior spaces. Talented architects create exciting interior patterns and contrasts by exploiting sunlight intensity and its changing angle of incidence. Lesser architects measure and estimate sunlight to model potential lamplight cost savings. Accomplished architects and designers detail sunlighting apertures to minimize summer heat gain and maximize winter heat gain.

———◦◉◦———

5.0 SUNLIGHT OR DAYLIGHT?

Sunlight design is emphasized on the following pages. Daylight designs are appropriate in climates where the usual sky condition is overcast. Sunlight offers a moving, directional source, five to ten times more intense than daylight (see Figure 5.1). Designs that exploit sunlight are effective in overcast climates, but designs based on daylight will overheat in warm sunny climates.

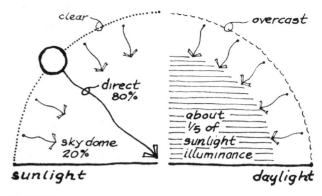

FIGURE 5.1

SUNLIGHT DESIGNS

The eye cannot distinguish sunlight from lamplight, but designers using sunlight for indoor illumination exploit the sun's changing intensity and angle of incidence. Because most light is invisible until reflected the two principles of luminaire selection are appropriate for sunlighting designs. **Use sunlight to (1) create decorative focal points, *or* (2) illuminate and emphasize objects or surfaces** (see Figure 5.2).

This choice is an important starting point for each sunlighting aperture because it shapes occupant perceptions, and suggests details for windows or clerestories. Designing and detailing sunlight apertures is more complex than selecting light fixtures because more variables are involved. Size, shape, proportions, location, light control, glazing, mullion pattern, view, and orientation are only the beginning of an extensive list of design decisions.

Focal point apertures include stained glass windows or windows that capture beautiful views. Apertures used to illuminate surfaces or objects include skylights, clerestories, and light shelves (see Figure 5.3). Brightness contrast is the primary tool of lighting design. Bright views, bright windows, and bright surfaces command visual attention.

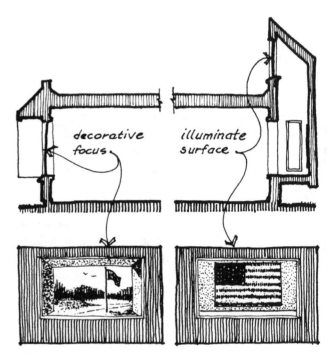

FIGURE 5.2

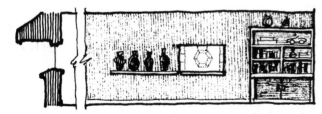

FIGURE 5.3

5.1 FOCAL POINT SUNLIGHTING

A design intent to use sunlight as a focal point *or* to illuminate surfaces, helps locate, shape, and size windows. Intent is not an absolute because all sunlight will illuminate surfaces and bright surfaces command attention, but choosing a primary purpose for each sunlighting aperture is the first step in a creative design effort.

Beveled, etched, or stained glass windows are classic examples of focal point sunlighting (see Figure 5.4).

Window pattern and color are beyond the scope of this text, but window size and orientation are not. In homes, *small* openings are appropriate, and orientation should be suited to the occupants' schedule. A decorative bedroom window will probably face east for morning brightness, but a living room window may face west if entertaining hours fall near sunset.

In churches, architects select larger stained glass areas to suit sanctuary size. Window location will be chosen carefully so that colors and brightness contrast complement (but don't overwhelm) services. Stained glass facing southeast will ensure maximum brightness contrast during morning services, and it may even improve a dull Sunday sermon!

View windows are interior focal points (see Figure 5.5). They command visual attention like stained glass when an outdoor scene is bright and stimulating. Well-designed view windows frame scenes and can grace landscape with mullion pattern (see Figure 5.6). Talented architects consider exterior appearance, landscape, and interior light when they shape, locate, size, and detail view windows.

Because inviting views are found at all compass orientations, exterior shading that excludes direct summer sun is an important design consideration.

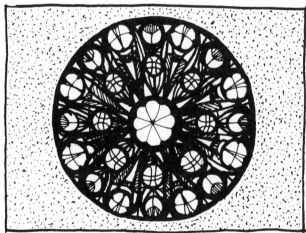

FIGURE 5.4

FIGURE 5.6

FIGURE 5.5

recessed apertures frame views *and* illuminate surfaces.

day↑ night↓

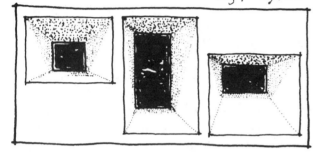

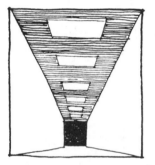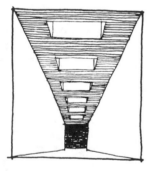

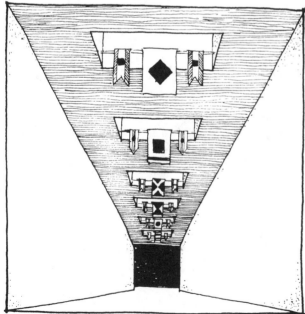

FIGURE 5.7

5.2 SUNLIGHTING SURFACES

When an exterior view is unpleasant or when privacy is desired, sunlighting designs configure openings to illuminate interior surfaces. A most important design consideration for successful surface lighting designs is that *the surface to be illuminated should be interesting.*

The Pantheon in Rome is a classic surface-lighting design. On clear days sunlight passing through the dome aperture paints the coffered dome and rotunda walls with a moving bright ellipse. On cloudy days diffuse daylight softens interior details.

Skylights, clerestories, and light wells do *not* offer interesting views, and light entering these apertures is invisible until it illuminates a surface. A skylight illuminating a room is as boring as a fluorescent troffer doing the same job. A row of skylights and a row of fluorescent troffers are equally depressing, but a row of clerestories with flags suspended below each can be visually interesting (see Figure 5.7).

Visual interest is essential for successful sunlighting of interior surfaces. Intense sunlight (or daylight) allows designers to use illuminated surfaces as focal planes. An aperture designed to wash a wall with sunlight can be enhanced by changing the wall texture or color. A tapestry, a plant, or a piece of pottery displayed on the bright wall will make the room more interesting and inviting.

Surface sunlighting effects can be imitated using lamplight. Architects detail lamps in skylight and clerestory apertures to minimize a "black hole" appearance at night (see Figure 5.8).

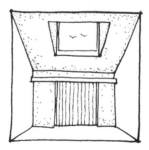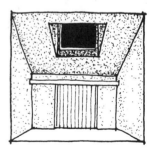

FIGURE 5.8

5.3 ORIENTATION

Advantages and disadvantages of selected sunlight orientations between 26 and 50 degrees north latitude follow.

North. Most uniform light intensity during daylight hours, but north-facing windows lose heat all winter. In cold climates, north-facing windows are a poor choice.

East. Great sunrise views, but overheating is likely on summer mornings. Heat gain can be limited with well-placed deciduous trees or vertical exterior shading devices. Interior blinds will also reduce summer heat gain; but with interior blinds closed for most summer mornings, light and view are lost.

South. More light and heat in winter, less light and heat in summer—*good!*

South is the best orientation for heat control. Overhangs can make south-facing windows even more effective by excluding most summer heat without limiting winter heat gain. South-facing windows can provide "free heat" during winter months, and south-facing windows with double glass and insulated night curtains can save heating dollars.

West. Great for watching sunsets, but will cause afternoon overheating in summer. Excess summer heat can be controlled with well-placed deciduous trees or vertical exterior shading devices. Interior blinds will also reduce summer heat gain; but with interior blinds closed for most summer afternoons, light and view are lost.

Clerestories. Clerestories and skylights don't offer interesting views so heat control is a primary design consideration. Clerestory windows facing south ensure easy control of summer heat and maximize winter heat and light. South-facing clerestories with night insulation can cut winter heating costs.

Skylights. Horizontal or sloping roof openings are poor sunlighting apertures because they magnify summer heat gain and maximize winter heat loss. Thoughtful architects use clerestories instead of skylights.

CONTROL HEAT

Because direct sun is a blessing in winter and a curse in summer, effective sunlighting designs *invite heat in winter and exclude it in summer.* Such heat control is easy with south-facing windows in the northern hemisphere. On a clear winter day south-facing windows receive three times the solar heat as east or west windows, and on a sunny summer afternoon south-facing glass will gain only one-third as much heat as west-facing glass.

Windows and clerestories combined with overhangs, reflectors, louvers, diffusers, and special glazing are the stuff of heat control. Their design is not difficult, requiring only an intent to control heat as sunlight is used for surface illumination *or* to create bright focal points. Direct winter sunlight will make interior surfaces more inviting on a cold day and add "free" heat. Summer sun can be used to create *small* bright interior focal points without overheating. Carefully detailed windows will accommodate summer views as they exclude direct sun.

Buildings designed for effective external sun control use different shading forms and details at each compass orientation (see Figure 5.9). Well-designed sun-control elements catch summer heat outside the building without blocking views. Interior blinds can reduce building heat gains, but they limit views.

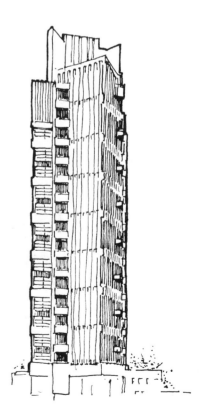

FIGURE 5.9
Frank Lloyd Wright
Price Tower
Bartletsville, OK
1953

5.4 SUNLIGHT CONTROL

The size, shape, orientation, and shading of a sunlight aperture should be based on a design intent to use the opening as a focal point or to illuminate interior objects and surfaces. The sun charts and the section angle overlay (in back of text) will help you plan sunlight control details and interior brightness patterns. Study the examples and then solve the review problems on page 65.

Using only the 30°N sun chart, find the time and location of sunrise on 21 April.

time = 5:30 AM
location = 15° north of east

Find the sun's bearing (compass direction from observer) at 2 PM, 21 September.

bearing = 50° west of south

Using the section angle overlay, pin through the center marks on the overlay and the 30°N sun chart. Set the window faces arrow by rotating the overlay. Read the red section angle directly above the time-date point on the sun chart.

Find the section angle at 3 PM, 21 August for a window facing south.

answer = 75°

Find the section angle at 3 PM, 21 August for a window facing 35° west of south.

answer = 50°

See Figure 5.10.

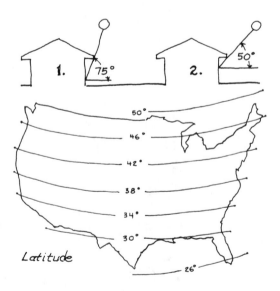

FIGURE 5.10

EXAMPLES

Draw the shadow cast by a pole projecting from a wall. Figure 5.11 shows pole and wall dimensions. All examples use the 30°N sun chart.
Use an adjustable triangle or a protractor.

Example 1 Wall faces south. Draw the pole's shadows at noon, 21 March; and 3 PM, 22 December. Study the following solution and verify all angles used to locate the shadows. Then overlay the solution example with tracing paper and draw shadows for examples 2, 3, 4, and 5 before looking at the answers in Figure 5.12.

Example 1 Solution (Figure 5.11)

- At noon the sun bears due south: 0°.
- Draw a line through 3 PM, 22 December, and read the sun's bearing: 45° west of south.
- Draw lines on the *plan* from the sun's bearing through the end of the pole to the wall.
- Place the section angle overlay on the sun chart with the "window faces" arrow pointing south and read the red section angle values. Noon, 21 March: 60°; and 3 PM, 22 December: 26°.
- Plot the section angles on the *section* and project.

Example 2 Wall faces south-west. (45° west of south). Draw the pole's shadows at noon, 21 March; and 3 PM, 22 December.

Example 3 Wall faces south-west. Draw the pole's shadows on 21 August at 1 PM, 3 PM, and 5 PM.

Example 4 Wall faces south-east. Draw the pole's shadows on 21 June at 8 AM, noon, and 4 PM.

Example 5 Wall faces south-east. Draw the pole's shadows on 22 December at 8 AM, noon, and 4 PM.

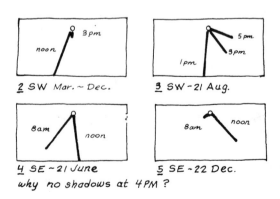

FIGURE 5.12

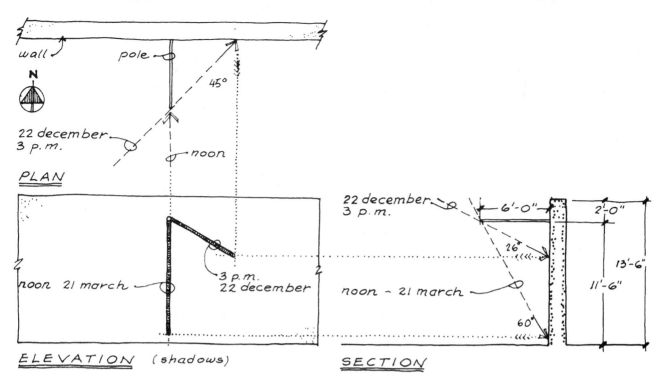

FIGURE 5.11

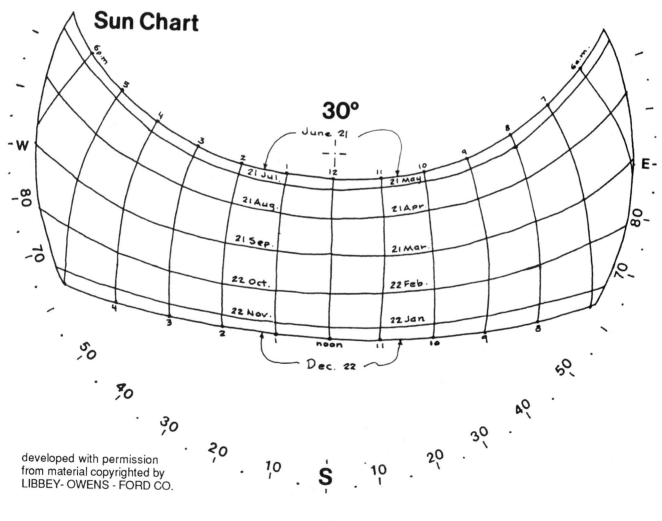

5.5 SUNLIGHTING DESIGNS

Solve the following problems and check the proposed answers. Size the apertures and shading elements using the 30°N sun chart and the section angle overlay.

1. Find the orientation that will maximize annual sunlight on a stained glass window at 10 AM.

2. A new luncheon restaurant wants winter sunlight on a decorative interior fountain. Find the required height of a vertical slot window intended to bring noon sun to the fountain from 1 October through 1 March. The window will be located in a south-facing wall. The fountain is 4 feet tall and 8 feet from the wall.

3. How wide should the window in the preceding example be to ensure sunlight on the fountain from noon until 1 PM?

4. A window faces west (ugh!). Detail an exterior shading device to exclude summer sun after 4 PM. Assume summer extends from 1 May through 30 September.

5. A clerestory faces west (why?). Set the sill height to exclude direct summer sun after 4 PM. Assume summer extends from 1 May through 30 September.

6. A clerestory faces southwest. Set the sill height to exclude direct summer sun after 4 PM. Assume summer extends from 1 May through 30 September.

7. A horizontal trellis is to shade a courtyard located behind a west-facing wall from 4 to 7 PM, between 21 May and 21 September. Find the center-to-center spacing for 2 × 6 wood trellis members that will exclude direct sunlight during this time.

3. At noon the sun bears due south. Compare the sun's bearing at 1 PM on 1 October, 22 December, and 1 March. 1 October shows the greatest bearing change—about 26° west of south. Use a protractor on the plan view to set the window width at 4 feet.

4. The sun is low after 4 PM so horizontal shades will not be effective. Detail vertical shades to exclude summer sun, and allow winter sun. On 30 September at 4 PM the sun bears about 71° west of south. This is the most southerly bearing during the summer months. Detail the vertical shades to exclude all sun bearings exceeding 71° west of south. Use a protractor on a plan view of the window to aim and space vertical shades (see Figure 5.14).

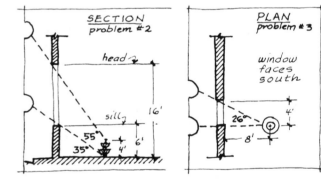

FIGURE 5.13

ANSWERS

1. Study the 10 AM bearings through the year. Sun chart bearings range from 30° east of south to 80° east of south. Select a midrange orientation: *55° east of south.*

2. The red overlay shows a range of noon section angles from 35° in December, to about 55° on 1 October. Use a protractor to set the window sill and head. Set the sill almost 6 feet high, and the head at 16 feet 0 inches high (see Figure 5.13).

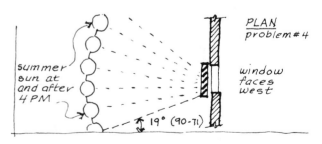

FIGURE 5.14

5. The highest section angle is 35° at 4 PM on 21 June. Use a protractor to set the sill height (see Figure 5.15).

6. The highest section angle is 50° at 4 PM on 21 June. Use a protractor to set the sill height (see Figure 5.16).

7. The highest section angle is 35° at 4 PM on 21 June. Space members 8 inches apart (9.5" centers). Remember a 2 × 6 is actually 1.5" × 5.5". Solar times used on the sun chart must be adjusted for location and daylight savings time.

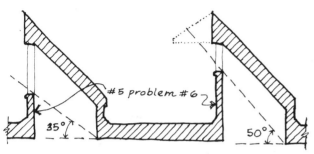

a thoughtful architect would increase head overhang (dotted) #6 to increase winter light.

FIGURE 5.15

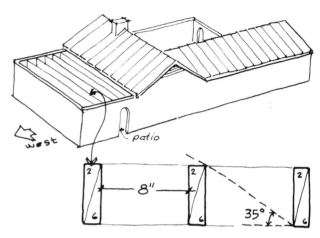

FIGURE 5.16

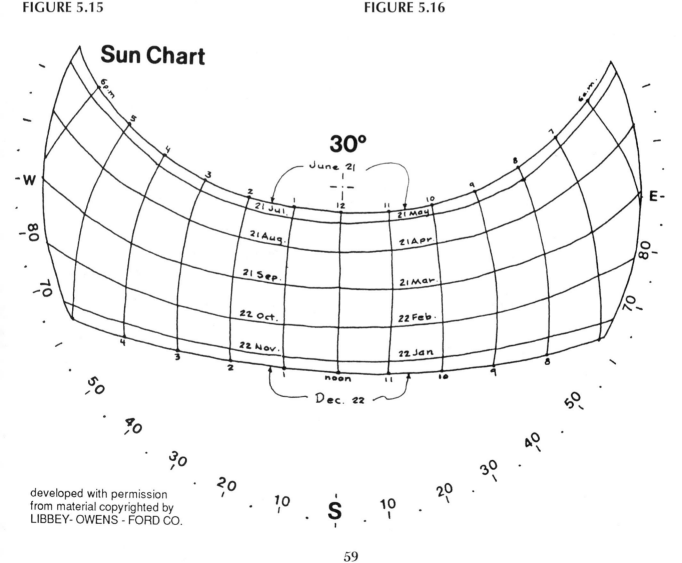

developed with permission from material copyrighted by LIBBEY- OWENS - FORD CO.

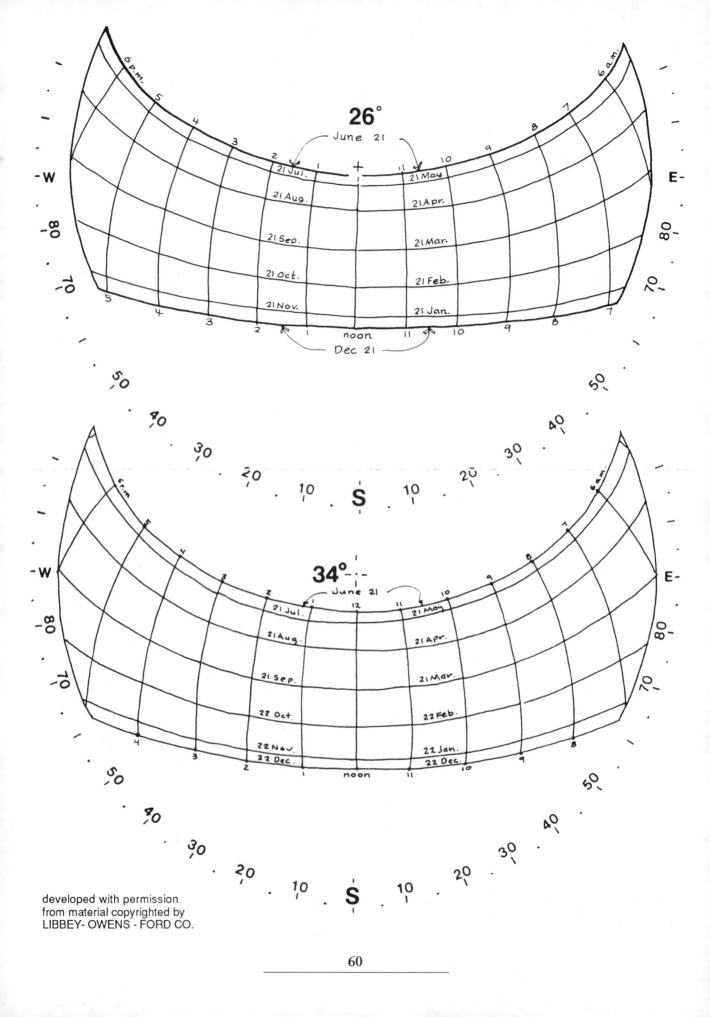

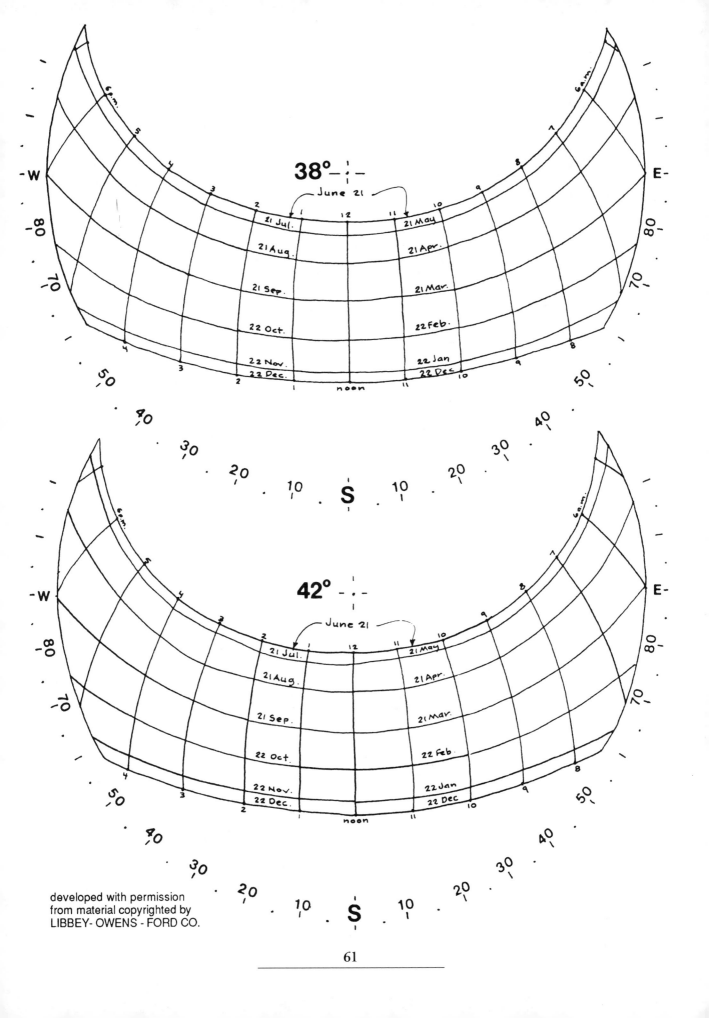

38°

June 21

	6 a.m.	5	4	3	2	1	12	11	10	9	8	7	6 a.m.	
-W					21 Jul.			21 May						E-
80					21 Aug.			21 Apr.						80
70					21 Sep.			21 Mar.						70
					22 Oct.			22 Feb.						
	4		3		22 Nov.			22 Jan		8			
50					22 Dec.			22 Dec				50	
40		30		2	1	noon	11	10	9		40		

20   10   S   10   20   30

42°

June 21

	6 a.m.	5	4	3	2	1	12	11	10	9	8	7	6 a.m.	
-W					21 Jul.			21 May						E-
80					21 Aug.			21 Apr.						80
70					21 Sep.			21 Mar.						70
					22 Oct.			22 Feb.						
	4		3		22 Nov.			22 Jan		8			
50					22 Dec.			22 Dec		9		50	
40		30		2	1	noon	11	10			40		

30   20   10   S   10   20   30

61

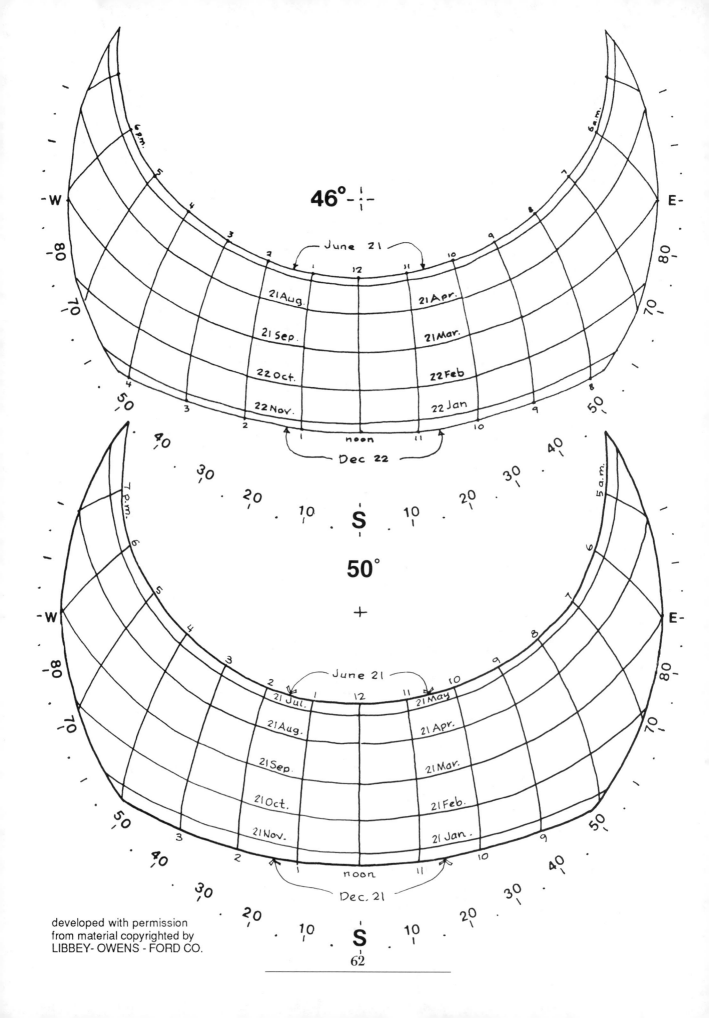

46° -|-

June 21

21Aug.   21Apr.

21Sep.   21Mar.

22Oct.   22Feb

22Nov.   22Jan

noon

Dec 22

W   E

80   80

70   70

50   50

40   40

30   30

20   20

10   10

S

50°

+

June 21

21Jul.   21May

21Aug.   21Apr.

21Sep.   21Mar.

21Oct.   21Feb.

21Nov.   21Jan.

noon

Dec. 21

W   E

80   80

70   70

50   50

40   40

30   30

20   20

10   10

S

62

5.6 DAYLIGHTING

Daylighting considerations shaped industrial America in the early 1900s when sawtooth clerestories illuminated immense factories. Direct sunlight is too intense for most activities where the viewer's eye is adapted to interior lighting levels, so daylighting designs use reflected sunlight or diffuse sky light to replace interior lamplight (see Figure 5.17).

Outdoor clear day illumination can exceed 11,000 footcandles (2,000 from the sky and 9,000 from direct sunlight).

DAYLIGHT FACTOR

A daylight factor (DF) is an estimate of the percent of outdoor horizontal illumination available at an indoor location. A DF of 7 means 7% of the outdoor horizontal illumination is available at the location noted. DFs are calculated by dividing indoor footcandles by outdoor footcandles. Many factors affect daylight penetration into buildings, and the DFs illustrated are maximum values based on ideal conditions (see Figures 5.18 and 5.19).

Some lighting designers enjoy calculating daylight illumination levels in buildings and projecting utility cost savings for replaced lamplight. Many variables are considered in these calculations including:

- **Climate.** Clear or overcast? Number of annual sunshine hours?
- **Illumination.** Sky components? Direct component? Reflected components?
- **Aperture orientation.** Glass transmission? Adjacent buildings or trees? Reflectance of surrounding surfaces?
- **Proportions.** Room sizes and heights? Aperture sizes and locations?
- **Reflectance.** Interior surfaces? Screens? Light shelves?

Readers who enjoy complex estimates can find detailed calculation methods in CIE (Commission Internationale de l'Eclairage) and IES (Illuminating Engineering Society of North America) daylighting publications.

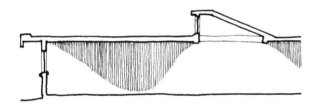

FIGURE 5.17

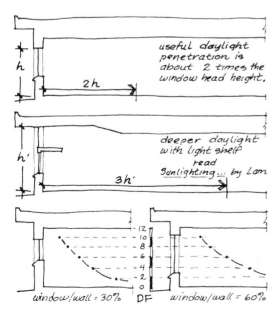

FIGURE 5.18

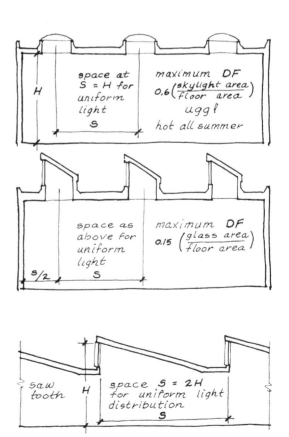

FIGURE 5.19

5.7 GLAZING AND VIEWS

GLASS

Glass transmission of heat and light can be quantified with three factors:

* **U value**—conducted heat transmission
* **SC**—shading coefficient, radiant heat transmission
* **VT**—visible transmission (light)

The "greenhouse" effect is a term used to describe the tendency of glass to act as a heat trap (see Figure 5.20). Clear window glass passes 80 to 90% of incoming short-wave solar radiation, but it's opaque to the long-wave infrared radiation emitted by warm indoor surfaces and objects.

Glass manufacturers offer tinted, reflective, and low E products to limit overheating and provide privacy. Tinted and reflective glass transmit less light and heat than clear glass. Low E glass coatings are thin films that selectively reflect or transmit radiation. Low E glass will transmit light with less accompanying heat than other glasses.

VIEWS AND HEAT CONTROL

Because an elegant view offers much more pleasure than rows of architectural sun-control surfaces, the shape, size, orientation, and location of a view window should be selected to frame a beautiful scene.

Shading devices should *not* limit the pleasure viewers take from the colors, contrasts, brightness patterns, and motions in a fine landscape scene. Where architectural shading devices would limit a wonderful west view, delete them and substitute operable interior blinds (see Figure 5.21).

Remember the initial lighting design choice: use light to create decorative focal points *or* to illuminate objects and surfaces. View windows are decorative focal points, while skylights and clerestories usually illuminate interior surfaces or objects.

Heat and light control are primary design considerations for clerestories that don't offer views. Is a clerestory hung with flags and pennants a luminaire or a decorative focal point?

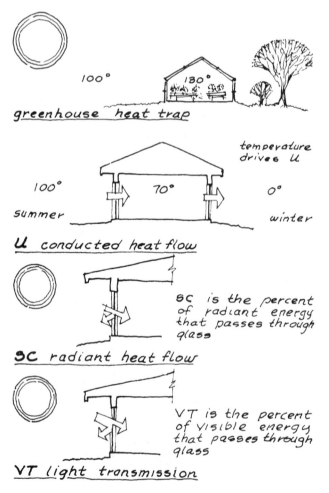

FIGURE 5.20

FIGURE 5.21

REVIEW QUESTIONS

Solve the following problems and verify the proposed answers. Size the apertures and shading elements using the 42°N sun chart and the section angle overlay. If you need help review the examples on page 56–59.

1. Find the orientation that will maximize annual sunlight on a stained glass window at 10 AM.

2. A new luncheon restaurant wants winter sunlight on a decorative interior fountain. Find the required height of a vertical slot window intended to bring noon sun to the fountain from 1 October through 1 March. The window will be located in a south-facing wall. The fountain is 4 feet tall and 8 feet from the wall.

3. How wide should the window in the preceding example be to ensure sunlight on the fountain from noon until 1 PM?

4. A window faces west (ugh!). Detail an exterior shading device to exclude summer sun after 4 PM. Assume summer extends from 1 June through 31 August.

5. A clerestory faces west (why?). Set the sill height to exclude direct summer sun after 4 PM. Assume summer extends from 1 June through 31 August.

6. A clerestory faces southwest. Set the sill height to exclude direct summer sun after 4 PM. Assume summer extends from 1 June through 31 August.

7. A horizontal trellis is to shade a courtyard located behind a west-facing wall from 4 to 7 PM, between 21 May and 21 September. Find the center-to-center spacing for 2 × 6 wood trellis members that will exclude direct sunlight during this time.

8. A north-facing roof slopes 4 in 12. The opening for a 36-inch-square skylight in this roof is 16 inches above the opening in the interior ceiling. Will *direct* summer sun penetrate into the room below this skylight?

ANSWERS

1. Sun's bearing range is 30° to 65° east of south. Face the window 47° east of south.

2. Section angle range is 23° to about 45°. Set the sill 40 inches high and the head 12 feet high.

3. Bearing range is about 20°. Make the window 3 feet wide.

4. Detail vertical shades to exclude all sun bearings exceeding 77° west of south.

5. Set the sill height to exclude section angles less than 35°.

6. Set the sill height to exclude section angles less than 45°.

7. Space 2 × 6 members 8 inches apart to exclude section angles less than 35°.

8. Draw the skylight in section and use a protractor to show the noon section angle in June. Check the 3 PM June section angle.

CHAPTER

6

Design Examples

"Architecture is the careful use of light."

━━◦◉◦━━

The grand white buildings at the World Columbian Exposition (Chicago 1893) were labeled "second eclectic phase" architectural style. Historians speculate about the social factors that led to public understanding and appreciation of their classic forms and details.

The public may have been less taken by neoclassic style than by the opportunity for an evening of social interaction surrounded by dramatic brightness contrast.

". . . As the lights went on, the massed human beings below uttered a great sigh. Then in the seats reserved for them, the Cabinet officers, and the Duke and Duchess of Veragua, and other foreign dignitaries began to cheer. The crowd lustily joined in while tightly corseted women fainted and fell like soldiers in battle. . ."*

In this chapter, black and white sketches illustrate example lighting designs for two rooms. Partial electrical plans are included, and more extensive lighting, switching, and circuiting plans are presented in Chapters 10 and 12. Achromic sketches suggest the brightness contrasts caused by light sources, and the text speculates about perception.

---

*Margaret Cheney. *Tesla, Man Out of Time*, © 1981, Dorset Press.

━━◦◉◦━━

6.0 FAMILY ROOM
PERCEPTIONS

The "mood" of a room will change as lighting changes. Just as outdoor scenes on a sunny day "look and feel" more interesting and stimulating than on an overcast day, an indoor space will change as lighting shifts from diffuse to direct, and as the luminance of interior surfaces changes. The effects of light on perception and mood are real design opportunities. They allow lighting design to *influence* viewers.

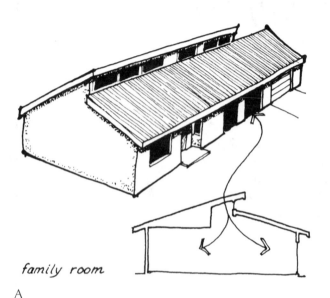

family room

A

Light is invisible until it interacts with reflective surfaces or objects, and words describing this interaction are less effective than visual images. Here sketches show contrasts and patterns, but lack depth, shade, shadow, highlights, motion, and color.

Study a favorite painting on a dark wood wall and then move it to a white wall. Notice the changes in the painting's colors and your perception of the scene. As your color experience grows you'll find that all whites are not equal. "White" is the product of many colors and a given white background will enhance some objects and fade others.

These achromic pages offer only a starting point for lighting design. Maturing designers build a library of mental images of the "good lighting" sensations driven by color, highlights, textures, shade, and shadows missing here. The thoughtful use of light to influence perception, mood, or behavior distinguishes quality lighting design.

The example family room is 13 feet wide and 27 feet long (see Figure 6.1A). A window is centered in the north wall. Sliding glass doors and a clerestory face south. The room accommodates a variety of activities including reading, studying, TV viewing, eating, and entertaining. Entertaining may include dancing, singing, gaming, drinking, or quiet conversation. The number of occupants can vary from 1 to 20 or more. The line perspective view in Figure 6.1B will be used to illustrate family room brightness contrasts on the following pages.

B

FIGURE 6.1

DESIGN

Because perception is driven by contrast, sketches emphasize the brightness contrasts created by locating and controlling light sources. Brightness contrast attracts the eye, but lighting design is much more. It is the thoughtful use of *brightness contrast, form-pattern, motion, and color,* to inform, interest, and influence.

Many design decisions precede fixture selection and location (see Figure 6.2). Good lighting and good design begin with thoughtful selection of visible materials, textures, furnishings, and colors. The light-reflecting, light-absorbing, and light-transmitting characteristics of ceilings, walls, doors, windows, and floors generate viewer perceptions, so talented designers visualize day and night lighting opportunities as they select interior colors, textures, and materials.

In Figure 6.3A, dark walls appear closer than light walls. They seem to reduce the apparent room depth. Light walls make the room seem wider and more spacious.

A dark ceiling in Figure 6.3B reduces apparent room height and size. Ceiling board edges or floor tile joints can make the room seem deeper or wider.

Interior furnishings, shapes, colors, and patterns create visual interest (see Figure 6.3C). Some architects and interior designers use an "all white except the floors" formula for interior surfaces to emphasize colors in art and accessories.

FIGURE 6.2

A

B

C

FIGURE 6.3

F.L.Wright   1912

FIGURE 6.4

Coolney Playhouse clerestories are elegant daylight luminaires (see Figure 6.4). Heads, jambs, and sills frame the playhouse sky, and Wright's stained glass patterns pleasure children at play. Light, pattern, and color delight the mind and excite imagination.

On clear days, windows are a room's largest and most intense light sources. They illuminate interior surfaces *and* they can grace a room by framing and accenting bright scenes. Family room forms, colors, textures, and furnishings are initial lighting-design considerations. Sunlight and daylight deserve equal attention.

The clerestory and sliding doors face south so eaves exclude direct summer sun, but welcome winter sunlight (see Figure 6.5A). South is the only window orientation that allows free winter heat and easy control of summer heat. Capable architects consider solar angles and sunlight penetration when they orient a home on a site. Decisions about the location, size, and orientation of windows should support daylighting, view, and interior design concepts.

On a clear winter day, brilliant sunlight fills the clerestory slot and the south end of the family room. Summer daylight will be less intense than winter sunlight, but the room's summer and winter appearance and mood will be nearly identical due to adaptation.

At night the clerestory becomes a dark slot and window views go black. Privacy is lost to passersby and the windows are dark planes that detract from the comfortable ambience of the room (see Figure 6.5B). Family room blinds are drawn, and lamps recreate the sensation of enclosure and shelter lost to the darkness (see Figure 6.5C).

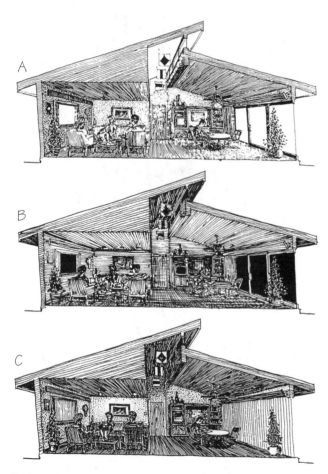

FIGURE 6.5

clerestory

south

north

all

FIGURE 6.6

Because daylight is such a dominant light source, luminaires should be selected *after* visualizing the room in daylight and sunlight. ***Luminaires should be selected to emphasize objects or surfaces or to be decorative focal points.***

Perception and mood are set by light sources, and by the light-reflecting characteristics of interior surfaces, colors, and furnishings. Family room luminaires were selected and located to complement, emphasize, and enhance these surfaces and furnishings.

Cove fixtures were located to illuminate the clerestory and to wash walls and drapes with bands of brightness. Flags add color and visual interest in the clerestory, and bright drapes make the room seem more spacious. Interior settings that complement a variety of family activities can be achieved using one, two, or all three coves (see Figure 6.6).

Three recessed can fixtures with adjustable apertures emphasize painting(s) on the east wall. A fan light kit is the only decorative luminaire illustrated. It was selected to illuminate the work table, and its stained glass shade provides a decorative color accent. (Be careful selecting fan light kits. Visible lamps will be glare sources with ceilings lower than 8 feet.)

Look back at the sketches and notice the variety of scenes light can paint. The coves and cans increase construction costs, but they add value for owners who take pride in the sensations their homes create. Colors, patterns, shades, shadows, textures, and highlights paint viewer perceptions. Add just a single color to any of these sketches and it will command attention at the expense of the surrounding illustrations.

Lighting variety makes the family room interesting, comfortable, and responsive to the variety of likely family activities. Additional decorative fixtures will add focal points and make the room even more attractive.

Panel Schedule

100 Amp. Two-pole Main Circuit Breaker

1. air conditioner	2. water heater
3. d.o.	4. d.o.
5. dryer	6. oven
7. d.o.	8. d.o.
9. rangetop	10. furnace fan
11. d.o.	12. garbage disp.
13. dishwasher	14. lighting & duplex
15. lighting & duplex	16. d.o.
17. d.o.	18. d.o.
19. d.o.	20. d.o.
21. d.o.	22. d.o.
23. elect. heat	24. elect. heat
25. d.o.	26. d.o.
27. landscape ltg	28–30. spares

ELECTRICAL PLAN

The schematic plan in Figure 6.7 locates fixtures, outlets, and switches for electrical rough-in. Some code authorities require schematic plans for *residential* electrical permits, but many cities require complete circuiting. A circuit plan is shown on page 172 and detailed switching and circuiting are illustrated on page 169 in Chapter 12.

Curved lines connect switches to the fixtures they control:

$ indicates a single-pole switch.

$_d$ is a dimmer switch.

$_3$ is a three-pole switch that allows control of a fixture from two locations.

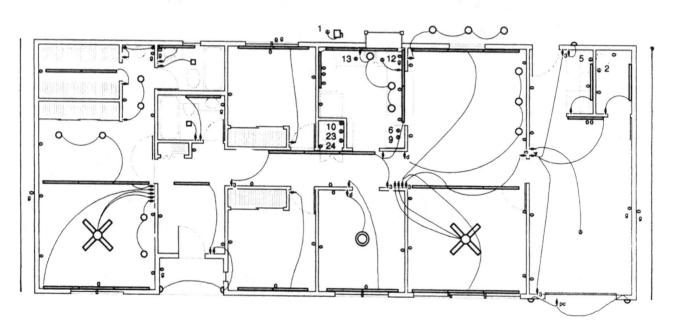

FIGURE 6.7

Where control from more than two locations is required a four-pole switch must be used. Two switches serve the ceiling fan to allow separate control of the fan and the light kit.

Wiring runs through the fluorescent strip fixtures used as cove lights, and the code requires flexible "Greenfield" conduit where the power supply enters these fixtures. Numbers on the plan refer to circuits noted in the panel schedule. A circle with two lines is the symbol for a duplex outlet to be installed 12 inches above the floor unless another height is specified. A circle with an inscribed triangle is the symbol for a special purpose electrical outlet.

6.1 LOBBY

The example office building (Figure 6.9) lobby is used for lighting-design studies. Since it's a first vi-

sual experience for residents and guests, the lobby defines "building image." Planters and display cases flank the entry doors, and two large tapestries suspended below a stained glass ceiling add visual interest in the tall space. A bridge, accessed by elevators

FIGURE 6.8

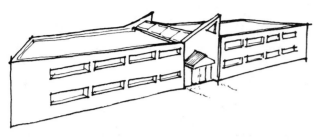

FIGURE 6.9

and a decorative circular stair, carries second-floor resident and guest traffic between the east and west offices. A reception desk, building directory, and small waiting area share the space beneath the bridge (see plan in Figure 6.10).

The perspective sketch in Figures 6.9 and 6.10 is a design template used to invent, visualize, and evaluate brightness patterns and contrasts.

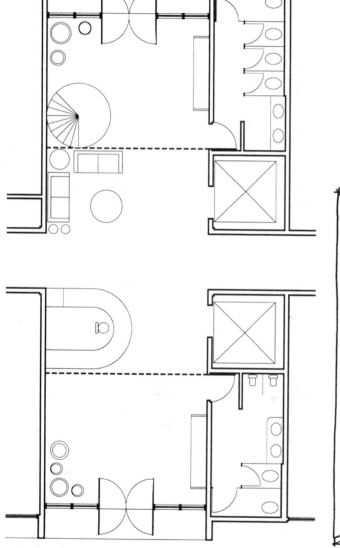

FIGURE 6.10

STAINED GLASS CEILING

Lobby lighting design begins with the decorative stained glass ceiling. Opaque walls surround the ceiling at the bridge level. Ground-floor glazing admits only 5% of ambient illumination, so window brightness will not compete with the ceiling for visual attention.

Because sunlight could make the lobby uncomfortably bright, the lighting designer and the stained glass artist agree to limit maximum lobby illumination to 10% of outdoor levels (see Figure 6.11). Outdoor luminance values can range from zero to 10,000 and electric lighting in the office spaces will produce luminance magnitudes from 1 to 100, so lobby brightness ranges in the 10 to 1,000 range should allow comfortable visual adaptation for visitors or residents. If the stained glass uses deep hues that transmit 20% of ambient light the skylight should pass about 50%, but if the stained glass design uses subtle tints that pass 50% of incident light, the skylight should exclude 80%.

At night, industrial light fixtures mounted in the skylight illuminate the ceiling. These fluorescent fixtures are spaced at 1.5 times their height above the stained glass to eliminate lamp image lines in the ceiling. Ceiling luminance is reduced at night, but the stained glass is equally attractive day or night because of viewer adaptation (see Figure 6.12).

Because daylight varies so much from clear to cloudy and from day to night, a scene controller will dim lobby lamps as outdoor light intensity changes.

Ceiling stained glass colors and patterns may include deep hues or subtle tints. The sketches in Figures

FIGURE 6.11

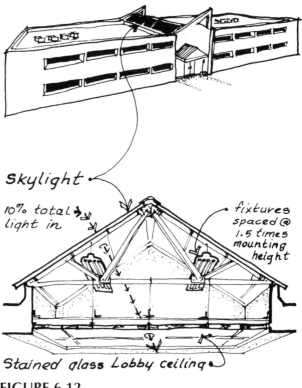

FIGURE 6.12

FIGURE 6.13

FIGURE 6.14

6.13 and 6.14 illustrate both possibilities. With light tints the lobby seems taller, but with dark hues the ceiling provides a dramatic background for the tapestries.

Seven lighting circuits serve lobby light fixtures. Two circuits illuminate the stained glass ceiling, and single circuits light the tapestries, stair, plants, display cases, and porches through dimmer controls that adjust lighting in response to time and daylight changes.

Sketches isolate the ceiling, but perception relates all visible surfaces. Dark brick walls change the lobby's ambience (see Figure 6.15).

An exterior photocell keeps the stained glass backlights off until daylight intensity drops below 200 footcandles. During the evening, ceiling luminance is far below sunny day levels, but the ceiling's stained glass pattern creates a similar visual sensation day or night because of viewer adaptation. After midnight, dimmers cut ceiling backlights to 20% of rated output. When daylight triggers the morning scene, backlights are extinguished.

The spiral stair and the second-floor bridge are attractive lobby structures. Transparent bridge railing panels open the lobby volume and allow visitors to enjoy the complete ceiling pattern. The bridge shades the seating area, reception desk, and ground-

FIGURE 6.15

floor circulation path so recessed fixtures in the bridge floor are used to light these areas.

During daylight hours a ring of spotlights illuminates the tapestries so they are brighter than the stained glass ceiling. Narrow beam lamps are aimed to minimize spill light on the floor below, and the ring dims to 60% of rated output for the evening scene. Ring lamps are off from midnight until morning.

Valence lighting accents the vertical faces of the lobby bridge, and a 400 watt recessed HID lamp lights the spiral stair treads from above. These lamps run at full voltage from morning to evening and dim to 60% of rated output from evening to morning.

The building manager plans changing lobby floral displays each month. Seven recessed ceiling fixtures with narrow beam lamps will illuminate the plants and the wall behind them. The floral circuit is photocell controlled to enhance the plants and flowers during evening hours and on overcast days. These lights are off from midnight until noon.

The sketches in Figures 6.16, 6.17, and 6.18 suggest brightness contrast with differing light source settings and surface reflectances. They are only beginning images of lighting design without color, shade, shadow, highlights, and source luminance. Even so, the lobby seems a dramatically different space in each illustration.

FIGURE 6.17

FIGURE 6.16

FIGURE 6.18

Many design decisions precede fixture selection and location. Good lighting and good design begins with thoughtful selection of the materials, textures, furnishings, and colors that shape viewer perceptions. The Fixture Schedule includes all office building fixtures.

In the plan shown in Figure 6.19, solid lines denote circuits and dotted lines show switching. Switches are not used on circuits A-4 through A-10. Illumination levels are controlled by timer and photocell signals that adjust seven dimmers.

Fixture Schedule

Key	Watts	Fixture
A	110	Fluorescent strip
B*	130	Fluorescent strip
C*	50	Incandescent can
D	500	Incandescent—custom
E*	72	Fluorescent—wall mount
F	200	Fan and light
G	55	Fluorescent strip
H	72	Recessed fluorescent
J*	28	Recessed compact fluorescent
K	70	Built-in display case
L	250	Incandescent pendant
M	50	Incandescent eyeball
N*	240	Industrial fluorescent (*locate between the skylight and the stained glass ceiling*)
O*	600	Incandescent (*a circle of twelve 50 watt MR-16 spots above each tapestry*)
P*	460	HID recessed in ceiling
R*	100	Incandescent can
S*	500	Incandescent—display case
T*	250	Incandescent can
U*	56	Fluorescent recessed
V*	100	Incandescent wall mount
W*	288	Fluorescent directory sign
=	18	Exit lamp with battery pack

Circuit loads for the lobby and offices are tabulated in Chapter 12.
*Fixtures used in the lobby.

Six lighting scenes are programmed:

Morning
Clear winter day
Clear summer day
Cloudy or overcast
Evening
Midnight to sunrise

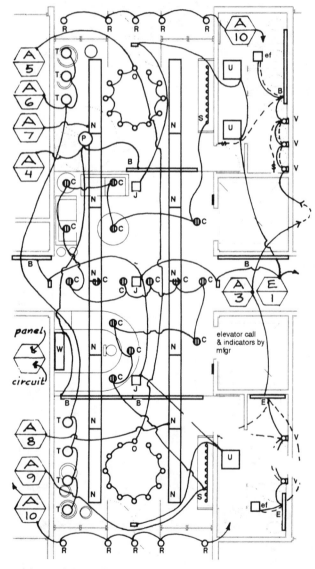

Lobby Lighting Plan

FIGURE 6.19

Scene Circuit Summary

Key	Watts	Fixtures illuminate
A-4	1,138	Stair, bridge, and directory
A-5	1,200	Tapestry (2 @ 600 watts each)
A-6	1,750	Plants (7 @ 250 watts each)
A-7	1,440	Stained glass backlights
A-8	1,440	Stained glass backlights
A-9	1,750	Display cases and under bridge
A-10	1,000	Exterior (10 @ 100 watts)

6.2 DESIGN OPPORTUNITIES

Family room and lobby example sketches are lightness studies lacking shades, shadows, highlights, and color. They are incomplete lighting-design examples, but they serve to illustrate a designer's use of lightness contrasts to inform, interest, and influence people.

When more lighting effects like:

brightness,
color,
shade,
shadows,
highlights, and
motion

are added, creative design opportunities multiply.

Design is only part of architectural practice. Vitruvius' design triad:

firmness
commodity
delight

and recent architectural authors:

form
function
economy

include just a single word for design.

Generous authors view architectural design as a pursuit of grace, beauty, and elegance in buildings, but designs evolve in a framework of constraints. Site, program, budget, codes, construction documents, and program changes shape buildings and compete with design considerations in architectural practice.

Design emphasis is greater with lighting. Enhancing a landscape, a building, or a room with light is a simpler task than creating these spaces. Lighting designers pursue beauty by visualizing spaces where light illuminates objects or surfaces *or* creates decorative focal points. They select or design luminaires to accomplish their visual images.

The following information is an attempt to describe lighting-design opportunities. Use what you find helpful.

Begin by identifying interesting objects, details, or features that can pleasure the eye. For landscape lighting the emphasis might be a tree, a pool, a fountain, or a gate; for building lighting, entries are obvious focal points. In interior spaces, light serves occupant activities *and* adds visual interest by emphasizing surfaces, furnishings, art, and architectural features.

View or visualize the space or object to be illuminated, and identify interesting colors, textures, surfaces, and details. *Use light to illuminate objects or surfaces, or to create decorative focal points.*

Visualize opportunities to enhance spaces, rooms, and interesting features with light by:

- Using brightness contrast to accent interesting objects and details. Visualize the patterns that can be created by light, shade, and shadow until you find one that best complements the object or detail.
- Locating luminaires so that grazing light paints surface textures and architectural moldings with light, shade, and shadow.
- Using luminaires to create brightness patterns that enhance occupant perceptions of space proportions and architectural details.
- Selecting light sources that complement space color schemes, and using colored luminaires or luminaires that decorate colored surfaces.

"Decorative" is a poor descriptor for the visual beauty an elegant luminaire can create. Imagine the colors, patterns, and contrasts in a sunset and compare them to the experience of viewing a fine stained glass lamp.

Selecting decorative luminaires for a specific project is a talent built on experience. Artistic designers study lighting installations like professional golfers study courses. They continually create and save memory images of attractive lighting scenes and the fixtures that help create such scenes. Brightness contrast, pattern, color, and motion are design tools; but memory images of lighting effects are a designer's reference library.

TEMPLATES

Make a few copies of Figures 6.20 and 6.21 and use color to illustrate lighting designs for the family room and lobby. Begin with just a warm earth tone and a single accent color. Compare your work to the preceding black and white sketches and see how much just two colors can add to lighting design.

When you're comfortable with two tones, experiment with complement and split complement color schemes.

FIGURE 6.20

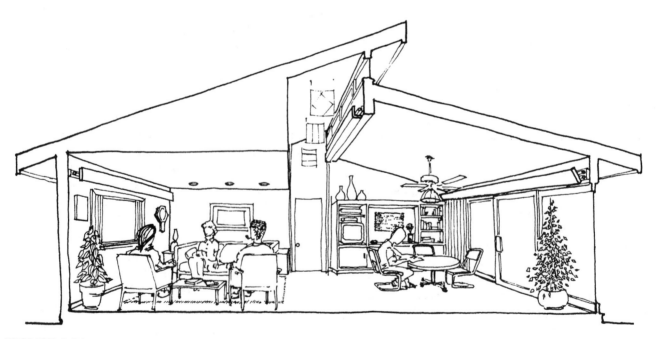

FIGURE 6.21

CHAPTER 7

Lighting Numbers

Calvin—*I'm not going to do my math homework...*
Look at these unsolved problems. Here's a number in mortal combat with another.
One of them's going to get subtracted. But why? How? What will be left of him?...
If I answered these it would kill the suspense. It would resolve the conflict and turn
intriguing possibilities into boring old facts...
Hobbs—*I never really thought about the literary qualities of math.*
Calvin—*I prefer to savor the mystery.*

Bill Watterson, 13 October 1992

⸺⸺◈⸺⸺

This chapter presents photometric numbers and calculations. Accent lighting uses illumination to create bright objects or surfaces that draw attention. Accent footcandles are easy to estimate when candlepower, beam spread, and distance are known.

Few lighting authorities recommend uniform lighting, but it's a lighting scheme used in too many buildings. Unfortunately, "task" lighting recommendations are often spread across large rooms as uniform illumination, instead of directing light to the smaller areas where a task is performed.

The ability to calculate uniform footcandles is a skill expected of lighting professionals, but these calculations are *not* lighting design. Selecting and spacing fixtures to provide uniform footcandles are not design judgments. They're merely skills that disregard adaptation, and the sensations talented lighting designers rely on to shape perception.

⸺⸺◈⸺⸺

7.0 TERMS AND ACCENTS
REVIEW TERMS

Lumen (lm): Unit of *luminous flux*. The lumen is a measure of light quantity based on the eye's sensitivity. By definition 1 watt can yield a maximum of 683 lumens. The following units are all related to the lumen.

Candela (cd) or **candlepower:** Unit of *luminous intensity*. Defined as 1/60 of the intensity of a square centimeter of a blackbody radiator at 2,045 K. One candela = 1 lumen per steradian (sr). A steradian is a solid angle at the center of a sphere which subtends an area on the surface of the sphere equal to the radius squared.

Footcandle (fc) or **lux (lx):** Units of *illuminance*. Density of luminous flux uniformly incident upon a surface. One lumen upon a 1-square-foot area is 1 fc. One lumen upon a square meter is 1 lux. One fc = 10.76 lux.

cd/m^2 or **nit:** Unit of *luminance*. Luminous flux leaving a surface. When 1 lumen is reflected or emitted from a 1-square-meter surface, luminance is **1 cd/m^2** *in the direction being viewed*. When 1 lumen is reflected or emitted from a 1-square-meter *diffusing* surface, luminance is **1/π cd/m^2**.

Consider a sphere with a radius of 1 foot surrounding a 1 *candela* point source of light (see Figure 7.1). By definition, *illuminance* at the sphere surface is 1 footcandle or 1 lumen per square foot or 10.76 lux. The sphere's surface area is 12.57 square feet ($4\pi r^2$), so 1 candela emits 12.57 *lumens*. If the sphere trans-

mits and diffuses 50% of incident lumens its surface *luminance* will be 1.7 cd/m^2.*

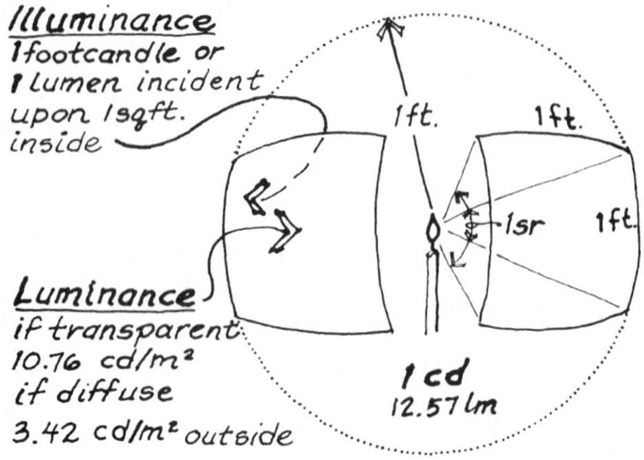

ACCENT LIGHTING

Accent lighting rains lumens on interesting objects or surfaces because brightness contrast commands attention. Designers begin by visualizing highlights, shades, shadows, colors, and textures. They select luminaires that enhance the objects or surfaces. A strong brightness contrast sensation usually occurs when the illuminance at an object or surface is at least 5 times surrounding illuminance. Specifying lamps for a five-fold increase is easy when distance, candlepower, and beam spread are known.

Candlepower sets illuminance at a given distance. Designers seeking brightness contrast use the formula:

$$\text{fc or lx} = \text{candlepower} \div \text{distance}^2$$

to estimate illuminance.

Beam spread and the fixture aperture determine the shape of the illuminance cone, and designers use a protractor or trigonometry to estimate the size of the illuminated area (see Figure 7.2).

Lamp manufacturers provide beam candlepower** and beam spread data for accent lighting applications on the facing pages. Lamp and fixture catalogs also provide data on illuminance and size of the illuminated area for typical applications. Study the following examples and work the sample problems at the end of the chapter so you can estimate illuminance values with confidence.

---

*Sphere radius is 1 foot. Illuminance is 1 fc = 1 lm/ft^2 = 10.76 lm/m^2. Luminance = (50%)(10.76)(1/π) cd/m^2 = 1.7 cd/m^2.

**Manufacturers provide MBCP (maximum beam candlepower) or CBCP (center beam candlepower). Lamps with long filaments produce an elliptical beam instead of a circular beam.

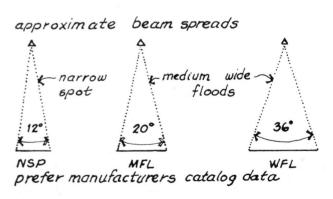

FIGURE 7.1

FIGURE 7.2

Lamp Table	Beam Spread	Beam cp
A. 25W-R14 SP (12v)	32°	1,040
B. 35W-PAR36 MFL (12v)	28°	1,400
C. 75W-PAR 38 SP (120v)	30°	3,800
D. 25W-PAR36 NSP (12v)	18°	4,500
E. 50W-PAR36 NSP (12v)	18°	8,000
F. 25W-PAR36 VNSP (12v)	10°	15,000
G. 50W-PAR36 VNSP (12v)	8°	23,500
H. 25W-PAR36 (5.5v)	5°	30,000

Use the information in the two tables to select lamps for the following examples, **but** use current lamp manufacturer data for real applications.

EXAMPLES

1. Select a lamp that will deliver 200+ fc when aimed at a wall 12 feet away.
   Answer: $fc = cp \div d^2$, $200 = (cp) \div (12)^2$, cp needed is 28,800. Select *lamp H*.

2. How big will the illuminated circle be in example 1? (See Figure 7.3.)
   Answer: Lamp H has a 5° beam spread so the illuminated circle will be about *12 inches in diameter* at a distance of 12 feet. If the lamp axis is not perpendicular to the wall the illuminated area will be an ellipse instead of a circle.

3. You plan to use two lamps to illuminate a small sculpture displayed on a 20-inch-diameter pedestal. You can mount two H lamps 20 feet away, or two F lamps 10 feet away. Which lamps will deliver maximum illuminance?
   Answer: $fc = cp \div d^2$, two *F lamps* will deliver a total of 300 fc.

4. Average illumination on two intersecting walls is 11 fc. You want to illuminate a heart-shaped area in the corner to accent a floral arrangement (see Figure 7.4). Select the lowest wattage lamp that will increase illuminance by at least 55 fc and produce a heart about 30 inches tall. The lamp will be located 4 feet away from the corner and 3 feet above the center of the accent area.
   Answer: Select 35 watt lamp B. It will deliver 56 fc and produce a heart about 30 inches high. The 25 watt lamps with less beam spread don't produce a tall enough heart. Lamp A only adds 42 fc.

Illuminated Area Table

Beam Spread	5°	10°	20°	30°	40°
5' distance	5"	10"	22"	33"	44"
10' distance	10"	20"	44"	66"	88"
20' distance	20"	40"	88"	136"	176"

Inches are diameters of illuminated circles.

Note: Most lamps have elliptical beam cones. Use manufacturers' catalog data instead of these example values.

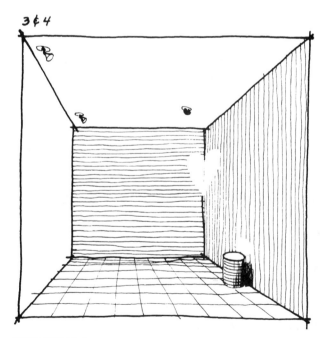

FIGURE 7.3

FIGURE 7.4

7.1 HOW MUCH LIGHT?

Because the eye adapts, most people can comfortably read this page at any luminance between 4 cd/m^2 and 4,000+ cd/m^2. Illuminance is easier to quantify than luminance. The corresponding illuminance range for reading this page would be 2 to 2,000 footcandles.

Some argue that adaptation and the adapted eye's range make most illuminance recommendations frivolous, but arguments have not discouraged lamp manufacturers, engineers, fixture manufacturers, academics, or government agencies from offering recommendations for lighting visual "tasks." Unfortunately, task lighting is frequently spread over large areas as uniform lighting, instead of emphasizing smaller areas where the task in question is performed.

The graph in Figure 7.5 plots the Davis Reading Test, "speed of comprehension" versus illumination. Two age groups were tested using high- and low-contrast documents.

The graph shows no change in performance between 1 and 500 footcandles, except low contrast for the 60-year age group showed no change from 10 to 500 footcandles.[*]

The IES Handbook defines nine types of visual tasks ranging from easy to difficult, and recommends nine appropriate illumination levels. *General* (uniform) lighting, up to 20 footcandles, is recommended *only* for simple tasks. When illumination exceeding

---

[*]For more detail and findings read: S. W. Smith, and M. S. Rea, *Performance of Office-Type Tasks Under Different Types and Levels of Illumination*, The Institute for Research in Vision, Ohio State University, October 1976; and D. K. Ross, *The Limitations of Illumination as a Determinant of Task Performance*, Ross & Baruzzini Inc., St. Louis, March 1978.

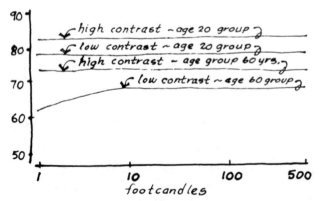

Speed of Comprehension Scores

FIGURE 7.5

20 footcandles is recommended, the IES specifies, "illuminance on task."

Activity		fc
Reading	CRT screen	5–10
	8 and 10 point type	20–50
	Glossy magazines	20–50
	Maps	50–100
Sewing, hand sewing		
Occasional sewing, high contrast		20–50
Light to medium fabrics		50–100
Dark fabrics, low contrast		100–200
Jewelry and watch manufacturing		200–500

Spaces		fc
Auditoriums, assembly		10–20
Barber shops		50–100
Court rooms	Seating	10–20
	Activity areas	50–100
Food service	Dining	5–10
	Cashier	20–50
	Kitchen	50–100
Hospitals	Lobby	10–20
	Corridor, night	2–5
	Corridor, day	10–20
	Nurse desk	50–100
Surgery scrub room		100–200
Surgery operating room		100–200
Surgery operating table (78 sq. in.)		2,500
Machine shops	Rough work	20–50
	Medium work	50–100
	Fine work	100–200
	Extra fine work	500–1,000
Residence	General	5–10
	Kitchen counter	20–50

Outdoors		fc
Construction	Excavation	2
	General construction	10
Ice hockey	Recreational	10
	Amateur	20
	College or professional	50
Service station	Approach	1–2
	Pump area	20

Reprinted with permission from the IESNA Handbook, Illuminating Engineering Society of North America, 1987 Application Volume.

Because different activities may require different illumination levels, and because accent lighting is effective when it is at least five times the general illumination level, designers should be able to calculate the number of footcandles delivered by a specific lighting installation.

7.2 LUMINAIRE PHOTOMETRICS

Calculating the number of fixtures needed to provide general lighting in a room is more complex than selecting accent lighting. Fixture manufacturers provide photometric data for uniform lighting, and designers use this data to calculate the number of fixtures required to yield a given illuminance (see Figure 7.6).

CANDLEPOWER PLOTS

Candlepower plots illustrate fixture light output. The plots show candlepower in a circular field, and two or three plots may be given for fixtures with asymmetrical distribution patterns. An ideal distribution for a uniform lighting application spreads light as far as possible from the fixture, but limits light output in the glare zone above 45°.

S/MH

In uniform lighting applications the spacing to mounting height ratio (S/MH), indicates a fixture's ability to spread light. As S/MH increases, the number (and cost) of fixtures decreases. Fixture manufacturers include S/MH with candlepower plots, and when fixture light distribution is asymmetrical, S/MH values are given both parallel and perpendicular to fixture.

COEFFICIENT OF UTILIZATION

Coefficient of utilization (CU), is an index of fixture efficiency; it is the percent of lamp lumens that reach the work plane *in a given room*. CU values vary with room proportions and reflectances, so preparatory calculations are required before selecting a CU.

LIGHT LOSS FACTOR

The light loss factor (LLF) is an estimate of illuminance depreciation. Operating considerations such as lamp temperature, lamp age, lamp cleanliness, supply voltage, and the ballast factor affect lumen output.

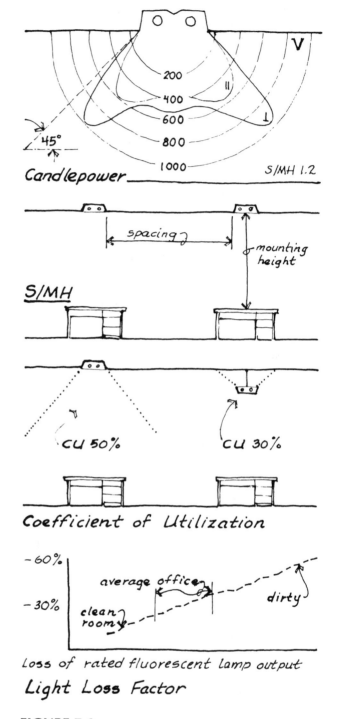

Candlepower

S/MH

Coefficient of Utilization

Light Loss Factor

FIGURE 7.6

Danger! Approximate LLFs are used in this text. Readers seeking greater precision must use a more comprehensive reference to study LOF (lamp operating factor), LLD (lamp lumen depreciation), and LDD (luminaire dirt depreciation).

7.3 FOOTCANDLE CALCULATIONS

This section and the Footcandle Calculation form describe a zonal cavity illumination calculation. Read the instructions here first if you're not familiar with the calculation method; then study the example calculation that follows.

Begin by entering the project name, your initials, and the date; then fill in the room dimensions. Next select the fixture and lamp(s) you intend to use, complete the fixture information box, and attach a copy of the manufacturer's photometric data to the form. Note your lamp lumens and total fixture lumens in the right-hand summary column.

1. Room size, proportions, and reflectances affect footcandles; enter three *cavity height* dimensions in the room view box and the right column summary. The ceiling cavity height is the distance from the ceiling to the fixture. The room cavity extends from the fixture to the work plane. The floor cavity extends from the work plane to the floor. When recessed fixtures are used the ceiling cavity height is zero. The work plane is usually at desk or countertop height, but in a lobby or bowling alley the work plane is the floor.

    White rooms or large rooms welcome more work plane footcandles than black rooms or small rooms. Enter three *reflectances:* ceiling (pc), wall (pw), and floor (pf).

    Ideally reflectances are measured with a light meter for specific room finishes, but they are often estimated.

2. Calculate three cavity ratios—CCR, RCR, and FCR—using the formula:

    $CR = (5hc) (L + W) \div (L \times W)$

    CR = cavity ratio, hc = height of cavity,
    L = room length, and W = room width.

3. Look up pcc (effective ceiling cavity reflectance) in the table using CCR, pc, and pw. This approximate calculation does not calculate effective floor cavity reflectance because its CU impact is small. Manufacturers' CU tables assume an effective floor cavity reflectance of 20%.

4. Look up the coefficient of utilization (CU) on the manufacturer's data sheet using pcc, pw, and RCR. CU is the percent of lamp lumens expected at this room's work plane using the selected fixture.

5. Use the LLF (light loss factor) table to estimate lumen depreciation.

6. Select required footcandles from the IES recommendations given earlier in the chapter.

7. Calculate the number of fixtures required to ensure a given illumination level using the formula:

$$\# \text{ fixtures} = \frac{(\text{footcandles})(\text{room area})}{(\text{FL})(\text{CU\%})(\text{LLF\%})}$$

FL = fixture lumens (total)
CU = coefficient of utilization
LLF = light loss factor

pcc Table (pcc's in field, CCR at left)

pc	80%	70%	50%
pw	70 50 30	70 50 30	50 30
0	80 80 80	70 70 70	50 50
1	71 66 61	63 58 53	42 39
2	64 56 48	56 48 41	37 30
3	58 47 38	51 40 32	32 24
4	52 40 30	46 35 26	29 20
5	48 35 25	43 32 22	26 17

Example CUs (% CUs in field, RCR left)

pcc	80%	70%	50%
pw	70 50 30	70 50 30	50 30
0	74 74 74	72 72 72	69 69
1	70 68 67	69 67 66	65 63
2	66 63 61	65 62 59	60 58
3	62 58 55	61 57 54	65 53
4	58 54 50	58 53 49	51 48
5	55 49 45	54 49 45	47 44

LLF Values

	%*
Good	75–80
Average	60–75
Poor	40–60

*Best—85% electronics assembly clean room.

Average—70% classroom or office.

Worst—40% wood cabinet shop.

Direct fixtures up to 85%, indirect to 70%.

Footcandle Calculation   project

Fixture Information

Manufacturer - model #
_____

option(s) _____
_____

lamp(s) _____
_____

Fixture Lumens ↘
FL |_____

ballast _____

Room View

1, 2, 3

ceiling reflectance ↗ |___ pc

ceiling cavity height |___

average wall reflectance |___ pw

room cavity height |___

floor cavity height |___

floor reflectance |___ pf

Room Plan & Fixture Layout

by _____ date _____

Room _____
dimensions _____ x ___
area _____ sqft.

Selected Fixture
lamp lumens _____
# of lamps _____
Fixture lumens _____
                                FI

1
cavity height & reflectance
ceiling ____' pc _____%
wall   ____' pw _____%
floor   ____' pf _____%

2
Cavity Ratio's
CR = (5 hc) (L+W) ÷ (LxW)
ceiling ~ CCR _____
room   ~ RCR _____
floor   ~ FCR _____

3
effective ceiling cavity
reflectance ~ pcc _____

4
Coefficient of Utilization
_____ CU

5
Light Loss Factor _____
                        LLF

6
Footcandles required ____
                        FC

7
Number of Fixtures =

(FC)(area)÷(FL)(CU)(LLF)

_____

87

EXAMPLE CALCULATION

Fluorescent fixtures will be used to illuminate a classroom measuring $20' \times 30' \times 9'$. How many fixtures should be installed to yield 50 footcandles at desktops 30 inches above the floor?

Use a manufacturer's catalog to select a fixture and fill in the fixture information box of the Footcandle Calculation form. The fixture in this example uses three F40 (34 watt CW) fluorescent lamps rated at 2,900 lumens each.

1. Complete the room view box information by entering cavity heights and reflectances. White ceiling reflectance (pc) = 80%, but the average wall reflectance (pw) = 50% because of blackboards and windows.
2. Calculate cavity ratios using the formula:

$$CR = 5hc (L + W) \div (L \times W)$$

CR = cavity ratio
hc = height of cavity
L = room length
W = room width

The ceiling cavity height is zero so CCR = 0. Room cavity height is 6'-6" so the RCR is 2.7.

$$(5)(6.5)(20 + 30) \div (600) = 2.7$$

3. Look up pcc in the table. With a CCR (ceiling cavity ratio) of zero, pcc = 80%.
4. Enter the CU table using pcc = 80%, pw = 50%, and RCR = 2.7. Interpolate to select CU = 60% (actually 59.5%).
5. Use the LLF table to estimate LLF = 70%.
6. Required horizontal illumination for this example is 50 footcandles.
7. Calculate the number of fixtures required using the formula:

$$\frac{number}{of\ fixtures} = \frac{(footcandles)(room\ area)}{(FL)(CU\%)(LLF\%)}$$

$$8.21 = \frac{(50)\ (600)}{(8,700)(60\%)(70\%)}$$

8. Lay out fixtures. Eight or nine fixtures will work. Use nine for this room plan—best fit for the ceiling grid, seating arrangement, and blackboard location. With nine fixtures the calculated illumination increases to about 55 footcandles.

Lamp Output (initial*)	Lumens
Fluorescent Lamps	
F 40 CW	3,200
F 40 BX (compact)	3,150
F 40 CW (34 watt)	2,900
F 48 CW/HO (60 watt)	4,300
F 48 CW/VHO (110 watt)	6,900
F 96 CW (75 watt)	6,300
F 96 CW/HO (110 watt)	9,200
F 96 CW/VHO (215 watt)	16,000

*Values are approximate. Consult lamp manufacturers for exact lamp lumens.

pcc Values (pcc's in field, CCR at left)

pc	80%	70%	50%
pw	70 50 30	70 50 30	50 30
CCR			
0	80 80 80	70 70 70	50 50
1	71 66 61	63 58 53	42 39
2	64 56 48	56 48 41	37 30
3	58 47 38	51 40 32	32 24
4	52 40 30	46 35 26	29 20
5	48 35 25	43 32 22	26 17

Fixture CU Table for this Example

CU Values (% CU in field, RCR at left)

pcc	80%	70%	50%
pw	70 50 30	70 50 30	50 30
RCR			
0	74 74 74	72 72 72	69 69
1	70 68 67	69 67 66	65 63
2	66 63 61	65 62 59	60 58
3	62 58 55	61 57 54	55 53
4	58 54 50	58 53 49	51 48
5	55 49 45	54 49 45	47 44

*All field CU values are given as percents.

The example fixture is fixture #2 in the following CU tables. Manufacturers' CU tables assume an effective floor cavity reflectance (pfc) of 20%.

LLF Values	%*
Good	75–80
Average	60–75
Poor	40–60

Best—85% electronics assembly clean room.
Average—70% classroom or office.
Worst—40% wood cabinet shop.
Direct fixtures up to 85%, indirect to 70%.

Footcandle Calculation

project *Anson Elem. School*

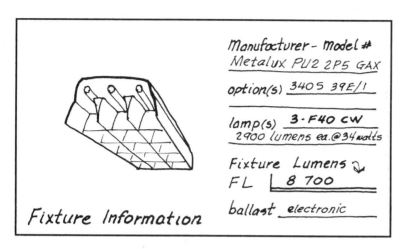

Manufacturer - Model #
Metalux PU2 2P5 GAX

option(s) *340S 39E/1*

lamp(s) **3 - F40 CW**
2900 lumens ea.@34 watts

Fixture Lumens ↘
FL | **8 700**

ballast *electronic*

Fixture Information

by *A.P.* date *2-7-99*

Room *Classroom 112*
dimensions *20' x 30'*
area *600* sqft.

Selected Fixture
lamp lumens *2,900*
# of lamps *3*
Fixture lumens *8,700*   F

1
cavity height & reflectance
ceiling *0'* pc *80* %
wall *6.5'* pw *50* %
floor *2.5'* pf *20* %

2
Cavity Ratio's
CR = (5 hc) (L+W) ÷ (LxW)
ceiling ~ CCR *0*
room ~ RCR *2.7*
floor ~ FCR *1.0*

3
effective ceiling cavity
reflectance ~ pcc *80%*

4
Coefficient of Utilization
60% CU

5
Light Loss Factor *70%*
LLF

6
Footcandles required *50*
FC

7
Number of Fixtures = ↘

(FC)(area)÷(FL)(CU)(LLF)

8.2 use 9 ★

★ *55 footcandles with 9*

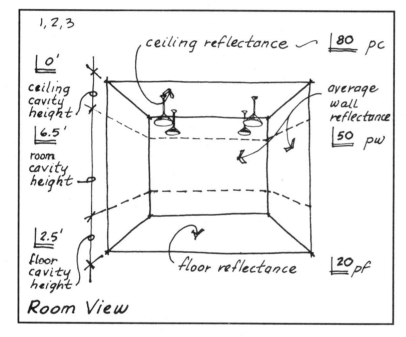

1, 2, 3

ceiling reflectance ~ | **80** pc

0'
ceiling cavity height

6.5'
room cavity height

2.5'
floor cavity height

average wall reflectance
| **50** pw

floor reflectance | **20** pf

Room View

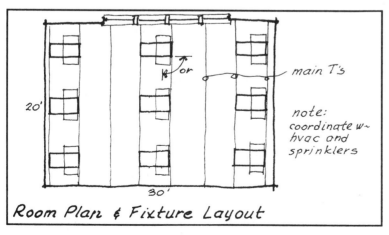

20'

30'

or
main T's

note: coordinate w~ hvac and sprinklers

Room Plan & Fixture Layout

FOOTCANDLE TABLES

Use these tables and the Footcandle Calculation form with manufacturers' CU tables to estimate illumination in a specific room using a particular fixture.

Lamp Output	Lumens*
Incandescent	
50 watt A-19	800
100 watt A-19	1,700
200 watt PS-30	3,700
300 watt PS-30	6,100
Fluorescent	
F 40 CW	3,200
F 40 BX (compact)	3,150
F 40 CW (34 watt)	2,900
F 48 CW/HO (60 watt)	4,300
F 48 CW/VHO (110 watt)	6,900
F 96 CW (75 watt)	6,300
F 96 CW/HO (110 watt)	9,200
F 96 CW/VHO (215 watt)	16,000
MH-HID	
175 watt MH	15,000
250 watt MH	22,000
400 watt MH	40,000
1,000 watt MH	120,000

*Values are approximate. Consult lamp manufacturers' catalogs for exact lumens.

Reflectances

A footcandle meter can provide accurate surface reflectance values. Measure the light reflected by a surface and then rotate the light meter to measure incident light. The reflectance is equal to the reflected value divided by incident value.

The following approximate values are an imperfect starting point for estimates:

Surface	% Reflectance
Mirror	90–95
White (paint)	80–90
Off white (paint)	60–85
White (ceiling tiles)	70–90
Colored paint (Munsell values)*	
Light value colors (7–9)	40–80
Medium value colors (4–6)	10–40
Dark value colors (1–3)	1–10
Concrete	10–60
Birch (clear finish)	20–40
Walnut (oil finish)	5–15
Grass (or similar carpet)	5–15
Slate blackboard	1–10

*Vary with gloss, texture, age, etc.

pcc Values (pcc's in field, CCR at left)

pc	80%	70%	50%
pw	70 50 30	70 50 30	50 30
pcc			
0	80 80 80	70 70 70	50 50
1	71 66 61	63 58 53	42 39
2	64 56 48	56 48 41	37 30
3	58 47 38	51 40 32	32 24
4	52 40 30	46 35 26	29 20
5	48 35 25	43 32 22	26 17

LLF Values

	%*
Good	75–80
Average	60–75
Poor	40–60

*Best—85% electronics assembly clean room.
*Average—70% classroom or office.
*Worst—40% wood cabinet shop.
Direct fixtures up to 85%, indirect to 70%.

Footcandle Recommendations

Activity		fc
Reading	CRT screen	5–10
	8 and 10 point type	20–50
	Glossy magazines	20–50
	Maps	50–100
Jewelry and watch manufacturing		200–500

Spaces		fc
Auditoriums, assembly		10–20
Barber shops		50–100
Court rooms	Seating	10–20
	Activity areas	50–100
Food service	Dining	5–10
	Cashier	20–50
	Kitchen	50–100
Hospitals	Lobby	10–20
	Corridor, night	2–5
	Corridor, day	10–20
	Nurse desk	50–100
Surgery scrub room		100–200
Surgery operating room		100–200
Surgery operating table (78 sq. in.)		2,500
Machine shops	Rough work	20–50
	Medium work	50–100
	Fine work	100–200
	Extra fine work	500–1,000
Residence	General	5–10
	Kitchen counter	20–50

Reprinted with permission from the IESNA Handbook, Illuminating Engineering Society of North America, 1987 Applications Volume.

Footcandle Calculation   project _____

Fixture Information

Manufacturer - model #
_____

option(s) _____

lamp(s) _____

Fixture Lumens ↘
FL |_____

ballast _____

1, 2, 3

ceiling reflectance ⌐ |__ pc

average wall reflectance |__ pw

ceiling cavity height

room cavity height

floor cavity height

floor reflectance |__ pf

Room View

Room Plan & Fixture Layout

---

by _____ date _____

Room _____
dimensions ____ x ___
area _____ sqft.

Selected Fixture
lamp lumens _____
# of lamps _____
Fixture lumens _____
                                    F

1
cavity height & reflectance
ceiling ____' pc _____%
wall ____' pw _____%
floor ____' pf _____%

2
Cavity Ratio's
CR = (5 hc) (L+W) ÷ (LxW)
ceiling ~ CCR _____
room ~ RCR _____
floor ~ FCR _____

3
effective ceiling cavity
reflectance ~ pcc _____

4
Coefficient of Utilization
_____ CU

5
Light Loss Factor _____
                                LLF

6
Footcandles required ____
                                FC

7
Number of Fixtures =

(FC)(area)÷(FL)(CU)(LLF)

_____

7.4 COEFFICIENT OF UTILIZATION

EXAMPLE CUS

Danger! These CU values are generic and approximate! Use manufacturers' CUs for precise calculations.

1.

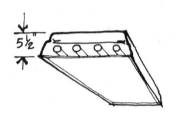

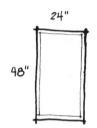

2.

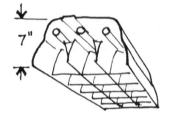

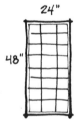

3.

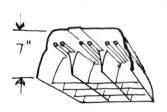

2′ × 4′, 4 F40 FLUORESCENT LAMPS, FLAT PRISMATIC LENS, S/MH 1.5, VCP 55-65

CU Values (% CU in field, RCR left)*

pcc	80%			70%			50%	
pw	70	50	30	70	50	30	50	30
RCR								
0	71	71	71	69	69	69	66	66
1	64	62	60	63	61	59	59	57
2	59	55	51	56	53	50	51	48
3	52	48	43	50	47	43	45	41
4	47	42	37	45	41	37	40	36
5	42	37	32	41	36	31	35	30

* CU values are in percent. pfc = 20%.

2′ × 4′, 3 F40 FLUORESCENT LAMPS, PARABOLIC LENS, S/MH 1.3, VCP 94-99

CU Values (% CU in field, RCR left)*

pcc	80%			70%			50%	
pw	70	50	30	70	50	30	50	30
RCR								
0	74	74	74	72	72	72	69	69
1	70	68	67	69	67	66	65	63
2	66	63	61	65	62	60	60	58
3	62	58	55	61	57	54	55	53
4	58	54	50	58	53	49	51	48
5	55	49	45	54	49	45	47	44

*CU values are in percent. pfc = 20%.

2′ × 2′, 3 F40 FLUORESCENT LAMPS (COMPACT), PARABOLIC LENS, S/MH 1.3, VCP 80-90

CU Values (% CU in field, RCR left)*

pcc	80%			70%			50%	
pw	70	50	30	70	50	30	50	30
RCR								
0	77	77	77	75	75	75	72	72
1	73	71	70	72	70	68	67	66
2	69	66	63	68	65	62	63	61
3	65	61	57	64	60	57	58	55
4	61	56	52	60	55	51	54	50
5	57	51	47	56	55	47	49	46

*CU values are in percent. pfc = 20%.

1' × 4', 1 F40 FLUORESCENT LAMP, PARABOLIC LENS, S/MH 1.3, VCP 94-97.
CU Values (% CU in field, RCR left)*

pcc	80%			70%			50%	
pw	70	50	30	70	50	30	50	30
RCR								
0	73	73	73	72	72	72	68	68
1	69	67	66	68	66	64	63	62
2	65	62	59	64	61	58	59	57
3	61	56	53	60	56	52	54	51
4	57	52	48	56	51	47	50	46
5	53	47	43	52	46	42	45	42

*CU values are in percent. pfc = 20%.

4.

2' × 2' WITH MH-HID LAMP, 175-250 OR 400 WATT, S/MH 1.4, 12' MOUNTING HEIGHT.
CU Values (% CU in field, RCR left)*

pcc	80%			70%			50%	
pw	70	50	30	70	50	30	50	30
RCR								
1	81	77	74	79	75	72	71	69
2	74	69	64	72	69	62	63	60
3	68	61	55	66	62	53	56	52
4	63	54	48	62	55	46	51	46
5	58	49	42	57	50	41	45	40

*All CU values are in percent. pfc = 20%.

5.

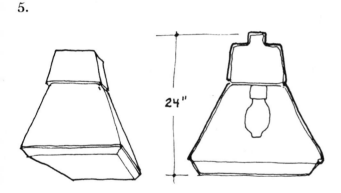

MH-HID 1,000 WATT LAMP, S/MH 1.5, MOUNTING HEIGHT 25'.
CU Values (% CU in field, RCR left)*

pcc	80%			70%			50%	
pw	70	50	30	70	50	30	50	30
RCR								
1	86	84	82	85	82	79	78	77
2	81	79	76	80	77	74	74	72
3	76	74	70	75	73	70	70	68
4	72	70	66	70	68	65	66	64
5	67	65	61	66	64	61	63	60

*All CU values are in percent. pfc = 20%.

6.

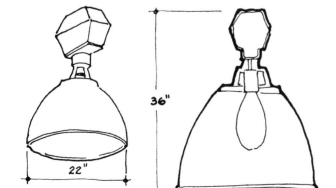

7.

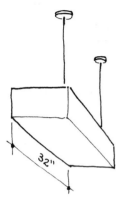

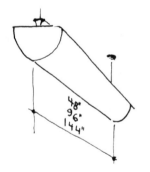

INDIRECT MH-HID 400 WATT LAMP, SUSPEND FIXTURE 3′ BELOW CEILING AND 8′ ABOVE FLOOR

CU Values (CUs in field, RCR left)*

pcc	80%			70%			50%	
pw	70	50	30	70	50	30	50	30
RCR								
1	63	60	57	53	51	49	35	34
2	54	52	48	46	44	41	30	28
3	48	46	41	41	39	35	27	25
4	42	40	35	33	31	26	24	21
5	37	35	30	33	31	26	21	18

*All CU values are in percent. pfc = 20%.

8.

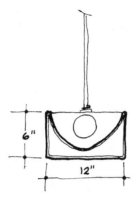

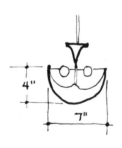

INDIRECT FLUORESCENT, 2 F40 LAMPS, SUSPEND 2′ BELOW CEILING

CU Values (CUs in field, RCR left)*

pcc	80%			70%			50%	
pw	70	50	30	70	50	30	50	30
RCR								
1	56	54	52	51	48	46	35	33
2	50	48	46	47	43	41	47	43
3	45	43	40	42	38	36	41	36
4	40	38	34	37	34	31	36	30
5	35	33	28	32	29	25	20	18

*All CU values are in percent. pfc = 20%.

Danger! These CU values are generic and approximate! Use manufacturers' CU's for precise calculations.

7.5 LIGHTING QUALITY NUMBERS

Glare is defined as an excessive or uncomfortable brightness contrast. Auto headlights glare at night but not in daylight. The reflected image of a lamp or window on this page can make reading difficult. Lighting engineers describe such images as "veiling reflections."

Three numerical indices—VCP, ESI, and CRF—attempt to quantify lighting quality.

VCP

Visual comfort probability is a fixture glare rating for the worst viewing position in a test room (see Figure 7.7). VCP = 100 means that 100% of observers will be visually "comfortable" (untroubled by glare) in a room illuminated by rated fixtures. VCPs above 80 are considered comfortable.

ESI

Equivalent sphere illumination is a term used to describe diffuse shadow-free lighting inside a uniformly illuminated white sphere. Laboratory spheres are used to compare and evaluate lighting installations because an observer looking into such a sphere will *not* see reflected glare or veiling reflections.

The extent to which a given lighting installation duplicates spherical lighting is sometimes quantified in *ESI footcandles*. Individuals who take pleasure in such activity calculate ESI footcandles and compare them with the "raw" horizontal footcandles a light meter measures. A dark room with shielded recessed fixtures might measure 50 "raw" footcandles at the work plane, but calculations could show only 20 spherical ESI footcandles. Raw footcandles and ESI footcandles will be nearly equal in rooms with luminous ceilings, white walls, white furnishings, and white floors.

CRF

Contrast rendition factor is a numerical index that compares the uniformity of a specific lighting installation for various viewer locations. Where ESI footcandles and raw footcandles are nearly equal, the CRF value approaches 1. Lighting installations with CRF values near 1.0 are theoretically glare-free, but they can be visually boring—lacking shade, shadows, and brightness contrast.

FIGURE 7.7

VDTs

Bright fixtures can create annoying veiling reflections on the specular viewing surface of TVs, computer monitors, and other *visual display terminals* (see Figure 7.8). Suffering users overcome such screen reflections by moving to change the reflection geometry. Lighting designers select indirect or well-shielded fixtures to minimize veiling reflections in VDT work spaces (see Figure 7.9).

Typical VDT screen brightness is about 70 cd/m², and many authorities recommend a maximum 5 to 1 ratio for brightness contrasts in VDT workspaces. A 5:1 contrast draws attention, but the adapted eye sees comfortably when field brightnesses range from 10 times to one-tenth the adaptation level. A window can easily be 100 times brighter than a computer screen, but some VDT users prefer the visual interest windows provide in otherwise uniformly dim and bland VDT workspaces.

FIGURE 7.8

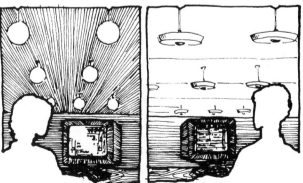

FIGURE 7.9

7.6 ESTIMATES

ESTIMATE WITH WATTS

Limiting the lighting load can reduce electrical costs. New schools and office buildings usually install lighting systems that use less than 2 *watts per square foot*. Review the following example and notice that lighting *watts/sq. ft.* is related to footcandles for a given lamp/fixture combination.

Example

A 20′ × 30′ classroom is illuminated at 55 footcandles by nine 3-lamp fluorescent fixtures. Each lamp is rated at 34 watts including ballast load. Calculate:

- Watts/sq. ft.
- Footcandles per watt/sq. ft.
- Utility $/year to light the classroom

Answers

- 1.5 watts/sq. ft.

$$(9)(3)(34) \div (20)(30) = 1.5$$

- 36 footcandles per watt/sq. ft.

$$55 \div 1.5 = 36$$

- $184 utility $/year. Assumes 2,500 lighting hours per year and an average electrical cost of $0.08 per kWh including demand charges.

$$(9)(3)(34)(2,500)(\$0.08) = \$183.60$$

Do more calculations to compare alternate lamp-fixture combinations. Be sure to include ballast watts in such comparisons. Efficient electronic fluorescent ballasts may operate lamps at rated watts, but magnetic HID ballasts can add up to 15% to lamp watts.

FOOTCANDLES PER WATT/SQ. FT.

Rough estimates of the *maximum* expected footcandles in large rooms using the most efficient fluorescent or MH-HID fixtures can be made using the following table.

Footcandles per Watt (per Square Foot)

Fixture	Space Reflectances	fc watt/ sq. ft.
Direct	High (white walls and ceiling)	50
	Low (dark surfaces and shelves)	40
Indirect	High (white walls and ceiling)	30
	Low (dark surfaces and shelves)	15

Example

Estimate lighting watts/sq. ft. when using direct fluorescent fixtures to provide 90 footcandles in an open office area with white walls and ceilings.

Answer

Allow 1.8 watts/sq. ft.

$$(90 \div 50 = 1.8)$$

FOOTCANDLES OR cd/m^2

Because illuminance is invisible until reflected, Louis Erhardt proposes luminance (cd/m^2) as a better lighting index than footcandles. His lighting recommendations recognize the eye's ability to adapt to a great range of luminance values and see comfortably at luminances a log step above or below the adapted level.

Erhardt's Lighting Design Recommendations for Interior Activities

Activity	cd/m^2
Casual	1
Normal	10
Demanding	100

Louis Erhardt, *Lighting Design and Application,* January 1993.

Footcandles are easier to calculate than cd/m^2 because reflectances vary for each viewing position, but there is an approximate way to relate illuminance and luminance.

$$\text{luminance} = (\text{illuminance})(\text{reflectance}) \div \pi$$

When reflectance is 32%, footcandles and cd/m^2 will be numerically equal. Interior scene reflectances range from 16% to 64%, and 32% is probably typical for many residential interiors. Dark interiors such as a paneled library with bookshelves on all four walls might have an average reflectance near 16%. Light interiors, for example, a white tiled restroom, may approach 64%.

With 100 fc, the dark room = 50 cd/m^2 and the white room = 200 cd/m^2 (see Figure 7.10).

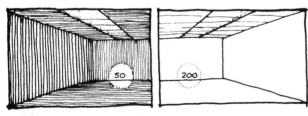

FIGURE 7.10

Convert footcandles to approximate cd/m^2 using the following ratios.

Reflectance	Luminance ÷ Illuminance
16% Low (dark walls and floors)	0.5
32% Average	1
64% High (most interior surfaces white)	2

If illuminance is 10 footcandles, luminance will be 5 cd/m^2 at 16%, 10 cd/m^2 at 32%, and 20 cd/m^2 at 64%.

7.7 LAMP TABLES

INCANDESCENT LAMPS (see Figure 7.11)

The following lamp data is provided for academic spotlighting calculations. The tables are *not* inclusive. Many more lamps are available and new lamps are introduced frequently. Use a current GE, Philips, or Osram Sylvania catalog instead of these tables for designs that will be bid and built.

- *Center beam candlepower* (CBCP) is the intensity in candelas at the center of the beam.
- *Beam spread* is the approximate total angle of the directed beam to where the beam intensity falls to 50% of the maximum value. Two beam spread angles are given for elliptical beams.

12 Volt Halogen Spot- and Floodlights*

Watts	Lamp	Beam Spread°	CBCP
20	MR11	30°	600
	MR16	11°	4,500
	MR16	24°	900
	MR16	36°	450
35	MR11	20°	3,000
	MR11	30°	1,300
	MR16	8°	8,100
	MR16	18°	3,240
	MR16	38°	870
50	MR16	10°	10,800
	MR16	21°	3,330
	MR16	38°	1,395
	MR16	60°	630

120 Volt Halogen Spot and Floodlights*

Watts	Lamp	Beam Spread°	CBCP
50	PAR20	8°	6,000
	PAR20	27°	1,500
50	PAR30	8°	17,000
	PAR30	26°	3,000
50	PAR38	9°	14,000
	PAR38	27°	3,000
100	PAR38	10°	29,000
	PAR38	27°	7,500

*Federal Energy Legislation bars 50, 75, and 100 watt R30 lamps, and 75, 100, and 150 watt R40 and PAR38 lamps. Halogen lamps are approved replacements for the PARs and reduced wattage or halogen lamps replace R30s and R40s.

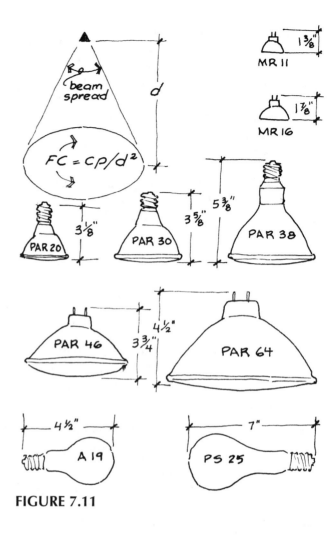

FIGURE 7.11

$$FC = CP/d^2$$

Standard A and PS incandescent lamps can be used with reflectors in floodlighting applications. Reflector design determines beam candlepower. Fixture manufacturers will provide such information.

120 Volt Incandescent Spot- and Floodlights*

Watts	Lamp	Beam Spread	CBCP
200	PAR46	12°x8°	31,000
	PAR46	27°x13°	11,500
300	PAR56	10°x8°	68,000
	PAR56	23°x11°	24,000
	PAR56	37°x18°	11,000
500	PAR64	12°x7°	110,000
	PAR64	23°x11°	37,000
	PAR64	42°x20°	13,000

*Lamp data produced with permission from *GE Lighting's Spectrum 9200 Lamp Catalog,* 21st edition, 1993.

FLUORESCENT LAMPS (see Figure 7.12)

Length, watts, and initial lumens are given for selected fluorescent lamps. The following tables are *not* inclusive. Many more lamps are available and new lamps are introduced frequently. Use these tables for academic calculations, but get a current GE, Philips, or Osram Sylvania catalog for designs that will be bid and built.

Use lamp watts for preliminary circuit load estimates, but remember ballast efficiency can increase watts. Use lumens in zonal cavity lighting calculations.

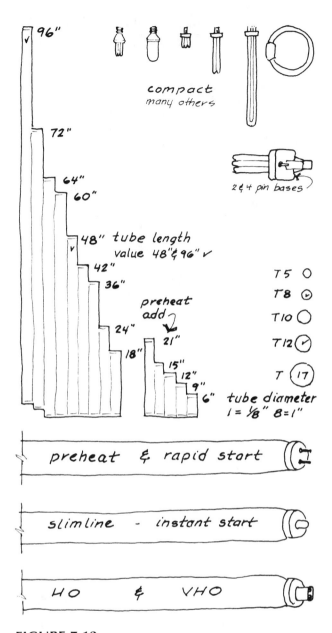

FIGURE 7.12

Compact

Compact Lamp and Ballast, 10,000 Hour Life

Length	Watts	Lamp	Lumens
5.4″	15	FLE15TBX	825
6″	20	FLE20TBX	1,200
6.6″	30	FLE30QBX	1,750

Compact pin Base Lamp, 10,000 Hour Life

Length	Watts	Lamp	Lumens
4.2″	5	F5BX	250
7.5″	3	F13BX	825
10.5″	18	F18BX	1,250
12.8″	27	F27/24BX	1,800
16.5″	39	F39/36BX	2,850
22.5″	50	F50BX	4,000

Tubes

T12 Preheat Lamp, 9,000 Hour Life

Length	Watts	Lamp	Lumens
18″	15	F15T12CW	760
24″	20	F20T12SPX	1,300

T8 Rapid Start Lamp, 20,000 Hour Life

24″	17	F17T8SPX	1375
36″	25	F25T8SPX	2150
48″	32	F32T8SPX	2950

T12 Rapid Start Lamp, 18 to 20,000 Hour Life

36″	25	F30T12SP	2,025
36″	30	F30T12SPX	2,375
48″	32	F40SP	2,650
48″	34	F40SPX	2,900
48″	40	F40SPX	3,350

T12U U-Shape Rapid Start Lamp, 18,000 Hour

22.5″	35	F40LW-U	2,500
22.5″	40	F40SPX-U	3,100

T12 Slimline (Instant Start) Lamp, 12,000 Hour

60″	50	F60T12SP	3,750
72″	55	F72T12SPX	4,800
96″	60	F96T12SPX	6,000
96″	75	F96T12SPX	6,800

T8 Rapid Start Lamp, 15,000 Hour Life

96"	59	F96T8SPX	5,950

T12-HO 800 mA, High Output Lamp, 12kWh

48"	60	F48T12SPX	4,350
72"	85	F72T12SPX	6,800
96"	110	F96T12SPX	9,350

T12-VHO 1,500 mA, Very-High-Output Lamp, 10,000 Hour Life

48"	110	F48T12CW	6,200
72"	165	F72T12CW	9,700
96"	215	F96T12CW	13,500

Reproduced with permission from *GE Lighting's Spectrum 9200 Lamp Catalog,* 21st edition © 1993.

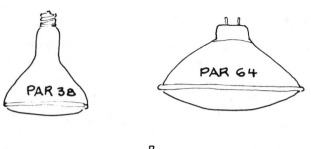

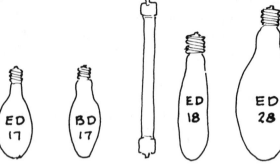

Metal Halide
Spot- and Flood Applications

Watts	Lamp	Beam Spread	CBCP
70°	PAR38	12	50,000
70°	PAR38	40	6,500
100°	PAR38	12	54,000
100°	PAR38	40	10,000
150°	PAR64	3	300,000
150°	PAR64	13	50,000

The lamps below can also be used with reflectors in spot and flood applications.

Watts	Lamp	Life	CRI	Lumens
32	ED17	10k	70	2,500
50	ED17	5k	70	3,500
70	ED17	12k	70	5,500
100	BD17	15k	70	9,000
150	BD17	15k	70	13,000
175	BD17	15k	65	14,000
250	ED28	10k	65	21,500
400	ED37	20k	65	36,000
1,000	BT56	12k	65	110,000
1,500	BT56	14k	65	155,000
2,000	T7	3k	65	200,000

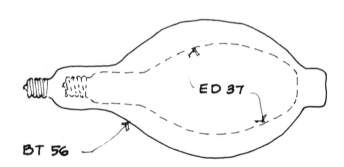

FIGURE 7.13

HID LAMPS (see Figure 7.13)

High-intensity discharge lamps are used for sports lighting, roadway lighting, and interior lighting. When these lamps are used with reflectors in floodlighting applications the reflector design determines beam intensity.

These tables are *not* inclusive. Many more lamps are available and new lamps are introduced frequently. Use them for academic calculations, but get a current GE, Philips, or Osram Sylvania catalog for designs that will be bid and built.

Remember all HID lamps are ballasted. The ballast usually adds 15% to the rated lamp wattage. Also remember many HID lamps must be used in enclosed fixtures.

Sodium

HPS High-Pressure Sodium Clear

Watts	Lamp	Life	CRI	Lumens
250	ED18	24k	22	28,000
400	ED18	24k	22	51,000
1,000	ED18	24k	22	140,000

HPS High Pressure Sodium Coated

Watts	Lamp	Life	CRI	Lumens
70	ED18	10k	65	3,800
150	ED18	15k	65	10,500
250	ED18	15k	65	22,500
400	ED18	15k	6	37,400

SOX Low-Pressure Sodium

Watts	Lamp	Life	CRI	Lumens
55	SOX35	18k	-	7,650
90	SOX90	16k	-	12,750
135	SOX135	16k	-	22,000
180	SOX180	16k	-	33,000

Mercury

Watts	Lamp	Life	CRI	Lumens
175	ED28	24k	15	7,950
250	ED28	24k	15	11,200
400	BT37	24k	15	22,100

Replacement sodium lamps are available, less watts, more lumens.

Lamp data reproduced with permission from *GE Lighting's Spectrum 9200 Lamp Catalog,* 21st edition.

Lamp length is not given in the illustrations because it varies with lamp wattage.

7.8 CU TABLES

Manufacturers provide CU tables for specific fixtures. The following selected generic CU tables are included for readers who find section 7.4 too brief.

Typical Luminaire	Typical Intensity Distribution and Per Cent Lamp Lumens		ρcc →	80			70			50			30			10			0	WDRC	ρcc →
			ρw →	50	30	10	50	30	10	50	30	10	50	30	10	50	30	10	0		ρw →
	Maint. Cat.	SC	RCR ↓	Coefficients of Utilization for 20 Per Cent Effective Floor Cavity Reflectance (ρ_{FC} = 20)																	RCR ↓
1	V	1.5	0	.87	.87	.87	.81	.81	.81	.70	.70	.70	.59	.59	.59	.49	.49	.49	.45		
	 35½% 45%		1	.71	.66	.62	.65	.61	.58	.55	.52	.49	.46	.44	.42	.38	.36	.34	.30	.368	1
			2	.60	.53	.48	.55	.50	.45	.47	.42	.38	.39	.35	.32	.31	.29	.26	.23	.279	2
			3	.52	.44	.38	.48	.41	.36	.40	.35	.31	.33	.29	.26	.27	.24	.21	.18	.227	3
			4	.45	.37	.32	.42	.35	.29	.35	.30	.25	.29	.25	.21	.23	.20	.17	.14	.192	4
			5	.40	.32	.27	.37	.30	.25	.31	.25	.21	.26	.21	.18	.21	.17	.14	.12	.166	5
			6	.35	.28	.23	.33	.26	.21	.28	.22	.18	.23	.19	.15	.19	.15	.12	.10	.146	6
			7	.32	.25	.19	.29	.23	.18	.25	.20	.16	.21	.16	.13	.17	.13	.11	.09	.130	7
			8	.29	.22	.17	.27	.20	.16	.23	.17	.14	.19	.15	.12	.15	.12	.09	.07	.117	8
Pendant diffusing sphere with incandescent lamp			9	.26	.19	.15	.24	.18	.14	.21	.16	.12	.17	.13	.10	.14	.11	.08	.07	.107	9
			10	.24	.17	.13	.22	.16	.12	.19	.14	.11	.16	.12	.09	.13	.10	.08	.06	.098	10
	II	N.A.	0	.83	.83	.83	.72	.72	.72	.50	.50	.50	.30	.30	.30	.12	.12	.12	.03		
			1	.72	.69	.66	.62	.60	.57	.43	.42	.40	.26	.25	.25	.10	.10	.10	.03	.018	1
			2	.63	.58	.54	.54	.50	.47	.38	.35	.33	.23	.22	.20	.09	.09	.08	.02	.015	2
			3	.55	.49	.45	.47	.43	.39	.33	.30	.28	.20	.19	.17	.08	.07	.07	.02	.013	3
	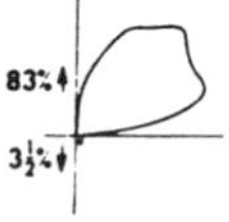 83% 3½%		4	.48	.42	.37	.42	.37	.33	.29	.26	.23	.18	.16	.15	.07	.06	.06	.02	.012	4
2			5	.43	.36	.32	.37	.32	.28	.26	.23	.20	.16	.14	.12	.06	.06	.05	.01	.011	5
			6	.38	.32	.27	.33	.28	.24	.23	.20	.17	.14	.12	.11	.06	.05	.04	.01	.010	6
			7	.34	.28	.23	.30	.24	.21	.21	.17	.15	.13	.11	.09	.05	.04	.04	.01	.009	7
			8	.31	.25	.20	.27	.21	.18	.19	.15	.13	.12	.10	.08	.05	.04	.03	.01	.008	8
Concentric ring unit with incandescent silvered-bowl lamp			9	.28	.22	.18	.24	.19	.16	.17	.14	.11	.10	.09	.07	.04	.03	.03	.01	.008	9
			10	.25	.20	.16	.22	.17	.14	.16	.12	.10	.10	.08	.06	.04	.03	.03	.01	.007	10
	IV	1.3	0	.99	.99	.99	.97	.97	.97	.93	.93	.93	.89	.89	.89	.85	.85	.85	.83		
			1	.87	.84	.81	.85	.82	.79	.82	.79	.77	.79	.76	.74	.76	.74	.72	.71	.323	1
	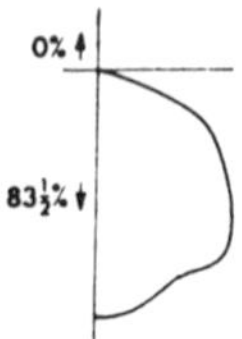 0% 83½%		2	.76	.70	.65	.74	.69	.65	.71	.67	.63	.69	.65	.62	.66	.63	.60	.59	.311	2
			3	.66	.59	.54	.65	.59	.53	.62	.57	.53	.60	.56	.52	.58	.54	.51	.49	.288	3
			4	.58	.51	.45	.57	.50	.45	.55	.49	.44	.53	.48	.44	.51	.47	.43	.41	.264	4
3			5	.52	.44	.39	.51	.44	.38	.49	.43	.38	.47	.42	.37	.46	.41	.37	.35	.241	5
			6	.46	.39	.33	.46	.38	.33	.44	.38	.33	.43	.37	.33	.41	.36	.32	.31	.221	6
			7	.42	.34	.29	.41	.34	.29	.40	.33	.29	.39	.33	.29	.38	.32	.28	.27	.203	7
			8	.38	.31	.26	.37	.31	.26	.36	.30	.26	.35	.30	.25	.34	.29	.25	.24	.187	8
Porcelain-enameled ventilated standard dome with incandescent lamp			9	.35	.28	.23	.34	.28	.23	.33	.27	.23	.32	.27	.23	.32	.26	.23	.21	.173	9
			10	.32	.25	.21	.32	.25	.21	.31	.25	.21	.30	.24	.21	.29	.24	.20	.19	.161	10
13	V	N.A.	0	.87	.87	87	.85	.85	.85	.80	.80	.80	.76	.76	.76	.73	.73	.73	.71		
			1	.75	.72	.69	.73	.70	.68	.70	.67	.65	.66	.64	.63	.63	.62	.60	.59	.312	1
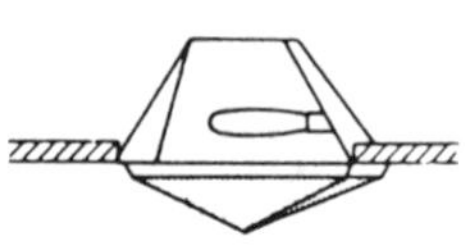	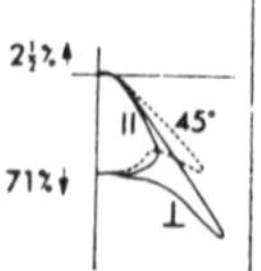 2½% 45° 71%		2	.66	.60	.56	.64	.59	.55	.61	.57	.54	.58	.55	.52	.56	.53	.51	.49	.279	2
			3	.58	.51	.47	.56	.51	.46	.54	.49	.45	.51	.47	.44	.49	.46	.43	.41	.251	3
			4	.51	.44	.39	.50	.44	.39	.48	.42	.38	.46	.41	.37	.44	.40	.37	.35	.226	4
			5	.45	.39	.34	.44	.38	.33	.42	.37	.33	.41	.36	.32	.39	.35	.32	.30	.206	5
			6	.41	.34	.29	.40	.33	.29	.38	.33	.28	.37	.32	.28	.35	.31	.28	.26	.188	6
			7	.37	.30	.26	.36	.30	.25	.35	.29	.25	.33	.28	.25	.32	.28	.24	.23	.173	7
			8	.33	.27	.23	.33	.27	.22	.31	.26	.22	.30	.25	.22	.29	.25	.22	.20	.159	8
Bilateral batwing distribution—clear HID with dropped prismatic lens			9	.30	.24	.20	.30	.24	.20	.29	.23	.20	.28	.23	.19	.27	.22	.19	.18	.148	9
			10	.28	.22	.18	.27	.22	.18	.26	.21	.18	.26	.21	.17	.25	.20	.17	.16	.138	10
14	V	1.3	0	.78	.78	.78	.77	.77	.77	.73	.73	.73	.70	.70	.70	.67	.67	.67	.66		
			1	.71	.69	.67	.69	.67	.65	.67	.65	.63	.64	.63	.61	.62	.61	.60	.58	.188	1
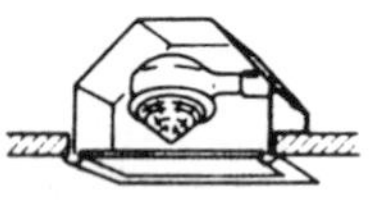	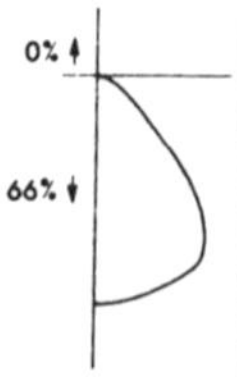 0% 66%		2	.64	.60	.57	.62	.59	.56	.60	.57	.55	.58	.56	.54	.56	.54	.53	.51	.183	2
			3	.57	.53	.49	.56	.52	.49	.54	.51	.48	.53	.50	.47	.51	.49	.46	.45	.173	3
			4	.52	.47	.43	.51	.46	.43	.49	.46	.42	.48	.45	.42	.47	.44	.41	.40	.161	4
			5	.47	.42	.38	.46	.42	.38	.45	.41	.38	.44	.40	.37	.43	.40	.37	.36	.151	5
			6	.43	.38	.34	.42	.38	.34	.41	.37	.34	.40	.36	.34	.39	.36	.33	.32	.141	6
			7	.39	.34	.31	.39	.34	.31	.38	.34	.30	.37	.33	.30	.36	.33	.30	.29	.132	7
			8	.36	.31	.28	.36	.31	.28	.35	.31	.28	.34	.30	.27	.34	.30	.27	.26	.124	8
Clear HID lamp and glass refractor above plastic lens panel			9	.34	.29	.25	.33	.28	.25	.32	.28	.25	.32	.28	.25	.31	.28	.25	.24	.117	9
			10	.31	.26	.23	.31	.26	.23	.30	.26	.23	.30	.26	.23	.29	.25	.23	.22	.110	10
15	V	1.4	0	.85	.85	.85	.83	.83	.83	.80	.80	.80	.76	.76	.76	.73	.73	.73	.72		
			1	.77	.75	.73	.76	.74	.72	.73	.71	.69	.70	.69	.67	.67	.66	.65	.64	.189	1
	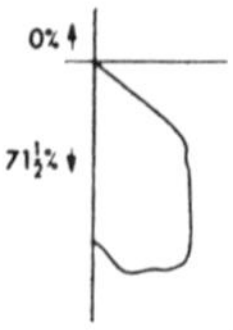 0% 71½%		2	.70	.66	.63	.68	.65	.62	.66	.63	.60	.64	.61	.59	.61	.60	.58	.56	.190	2
			3	.63	.58	.54	.62	.57	.54	.60	.56	.53	.58	.54	.52	.56	.53	.51	.50	.183	3
			4	.56	.51	.47	.56	.51	.47	.54	.50	.46	.52	.49	.46	.51	.48	.45	.44	.174	4
			5	.51	.46	.42	.50	.45	.41	.49	.44	.41	.48	.44	.40	.46	.43	.40	.39	.164	5
			6	.46	.41	.37	.46	.41	.37	.45	.40	.36	.43	.39	.36	.42	.39	.36	.34	.155	6
			7	.42	.37	.33	.42	.37	.33	.41	.36	.33	.40	.36	.32	.39	.35	.32	.31	.146	7
			8	.39	.33	.30	.38	.33	.29	.37	.33	.29	.37	.32	.29	.36	.32	.29	.28	.137	8
Enclosed reflector with an incandescent lamp			9	.36	.30	.27	.35	.30	.27	.35	.30	.27	.34	.30	.26	.33	.29	.26	.25	.129	9
			10	.33	.28	.24	.33	.28	.24	.32	.27	.24	.31	.27	.24	.31	.27	.24	.23	.122	10

IES Lighting Handbook, 1984 Reference Volume. Reproduced with permission.

Coefficients of Utilization for 20 Per Cent Effective Floor Cavity Reflectance ($\rho_{FC} = 20$)

Header (applies to all tables below):

RCR	ρcc=80, ρw=50	30	10	ρcc=70, ρw=50	30	10	ρcc=50, ρw=50	30	10	ρcc=30, ρw=50	30	10	ρcc=10, ρw=50	30	10	ρcc=0, ρw=0	WDRC

19 — "High bay" intermediate distribution ventilated reflector with phosphor coated HID lamp
Maint. Cat. III | SC 1.0 | 6½% ↑ | 75½% ↓

RCR	50	30	10	50	30	10	50	30	10	50	30	10	50	30	10	0	WDRC
0	.96	.96	.96	.93	.93	.93	.88	.88	.88	.83	.83	.83	.78	.78	.78	.76	
 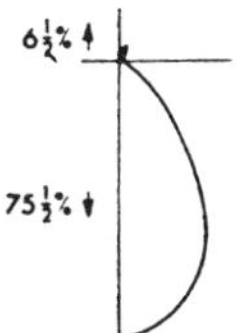 1	.88	.86	.83	.86	.83	.81	.81	.79	.78	.77	.75	.74	.73	.72	.71	.69	.167
2	.80	.76	.73	.78	.74	.71	.74	.71	.69	.71	.68	.66	.68	.66	.64	.62	.168
3	.73	.68	.64	.71	.67	.63	.68	.64	.61	.65	.62	.60	.63	.60	.58	.56	.162
4	.67	.61	.57	.65	.60	.57	.63	.59	.55	.60	.57	.54	.58	.55	.52	.51	.155
5	.61	.56	.52	.60	.55	.51	.58	.53	.50	.56	.52	.49	.54	.50	.48	.46	.147
6	.57	.51	.47	.56	.50	.46	.54	.49	.45	.52	.48	.45	.50	.46	.44	.42	.139
7	.52	.47	.43	.51	.46	.42	.50	.45	.42	.48	.44	.41	.47	.43	.40	.39	.132
8	.49	.43	.39	.48	.42	.39	.46	.42	.38	.45	.41	.38	.44	.40	.37	.36	.125
9	.45	.40	.36	.45	.39	.36	.43	.39	.35	.42	.38	.35	.41	.37	.34	.33	.118
10	.42	.37	.33	.42	.37	.33	.41	.36	.33	.39	.35	.32	.38	.35	.32	.31	.112

20 — "High bay" wide distribution ventilated reflector with phosphor coated HID lamp
Maint. Cat. III | SC 1.5 | 12% ↑ | 69% ↓

RCR	50	30	10	50	30	10	50	30	10	50	30	10	50	30	10	0	WDRC
0	.93	.93	.93	.90	.90	.90	.83	.83	.83	.77	.77	.77	.72	.72	.72	.69	
 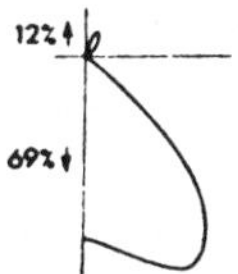 1	.85	.82	.80	.82	.79	.77	.76	.74	.73	.71	.70	.69	.66	.65	.65	.62	.168
2	.76	.72	.69	.74	.70	.67	.69	.66	.64	.65	.63	.61	.61	.59	.58	.56	.168
3	.69	.64	.60	.67	.62	.59	.63	.59	.56	.59	.56	.54	.56	.54	.51	.49	.163
4	.62	.57	.52	.61	.55	.51	.57	.53	.50	.54	.51	.48	.51	.48	.46	.44	.156
5	.57	.51	.46	.55	.50	.46	.52	.48	.44	.49	.46	.43	.47	.44	.41	.39	.148
6	.52	.45	.41	.50	.45	.40	.48	.43	.39	.45	.41	.38	.43	.40	.37	.35	.141
7	.47	.41	.37	.46	.40	.36	.44	.39	.35	.42	.37	.34	.40	.36	.33	.32	.133
8	.43	.37	.33	.42	.36	.33	.40	.35	.32	.38	.34	.31	.37	.33	.30	.29	.126
9	.40	.34	.30	.39	.33	.29	.37	.32	.29	.35	.31	.28	.34	.30	.27	.26	.120
10	.37	.31	.27	.36	.30	.27	.34	.29	.26	.33	.28	.25	.31	.28	.25	.23	.114

21 — "Low bay" rectangular pattern, lensed bottom reflector unit with clear HID lamp
Maint. Cat. V | SC 1.8 | 0° ↑ | 68½% ↓

RCR	50	30	10	50	30	10	50	30	10	50	30	10	50	30	10	0	WDRC
0	.82	.82	.82	.80	.80	.80	.76	.76	.76	.73	.73	.73	.70	.70	.70	.68	
 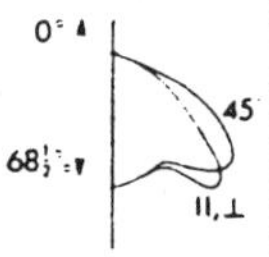 1	.73	.70	.68	.71	.69	.67	.68	.66	.64	.65	.64	.62	.63	.62	.61	.59	.231
2	.64	.60	.56	.63	.59	.55	.60	.57	.54	.58	.55	.53	.56	.54	.52	.50	.227
3	.56	.51	.47	.55	.51	.47	.53	.49	.46	.52	.48	.45	.50	.47	.44	.43	.213
4	.50	.44	.40	.49	.44	.40	.48	.43	.39	.46	.42	.39	.44	.41	.38	.37	.199
5	.45	.39	.34	.44	.38	.34	.42	.38	.34	.41	.37	.33	.40	.36	.33	.32	.184
6	.40	.34	.30	.39	.34	.30	.38	.33	.29	.37	.33	.29	.36	.32	.29	.28	.171
7	.36	.30	.26	.36	.30	.26	.35	.29	.26	.34	.29	.26	.33	.29	.25	.24	.159
8	.33	.27	.23	.32	.27	.23	.31	.26	.23	.31	.26	.23	.30	.26	.23	.21	.148
9	.30	.24	.20	.29	.24	.20	.29	.24	.20	.28	.23	.20	.27	.23	.20	.19	.138
10	.27	.22	.18	.27	.22	.18	.26	.22	.18	.26	.21	.18	.25	.21	.18	.17	.129

22 — "Low bay" lensed bottom reflector unit with clear HID lamp
Maint. Cat. V | SC 1.9 | 3% ↑ | 68% ↓

RCR	50	30	10	50	30	10	50	30	10	50	30	10	50	30	10	0	WDRC
0	.83	.83	.83	.81	.81	.81	.77	.77	.77	.73	.73	.73	.70	.70	.70	.68	
 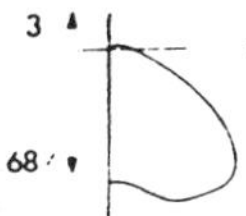 1	.72	.69	.66	.70	.67	.65	.67	.64	.62	.63	.62	.60	.60	.59	.57	.56	.302
2	.62	.57	.53	.61	.56	.52	.58	.54	.50	.55	.52	.49	.52	.50	.47	.46	.279
3	.54	.48	.43	.53	.47	.43	.50	.45	.41	.48	.44	.40	.46	.42	.39	.38	.253
4	.47	.41	.36	.46	.40	.35	.44	.39	.35	.42	.37	.34	.40	.36	.33	.31	.229
5	.42	.35	.30	.41	.34	.30	.39	.33	.29	.37	.32	.29	.36	.31	.28	.26	.208
6	.37	.30	.26	.36	.30	.25	.35	.29	.25	.33	.28	.25	.32	.27	.24	.23	.189
7	.33	.27	.22	.33	.26	.22	.31	.26	.22	.30	.25	.21	.29	.24	.21	.19	.173
8	.30	.24	.19	.29	.23	.19	.28	.23	.19	.27	.22	.19	.26	.22	.18	.17	.159
9	.27	.21	.17	.27	.21	.17	.26	.20	.17	.25	.20	.17	.24	.19	.16	.15	.147
10	.25	.19	.15	.24	.19	.15	.24	.18	.15	.23	.18	.15	.22	.18	.15	.13	.137

23 — Wide spread, recessed, small open bottom reflector with low wattage diffuse HID lamp
Maint. Cat. IV | SC 1.7 | 0% ↑ | 56% ↓

RCR	50	30	10	50	30	10	50	30	10	50	30	10	50	30	10	0	WDRC
0	.67	.67	.67	.65	.65	.65	.62	.62	.62	.60	.60	.60	.57	.57	.57	.56	
 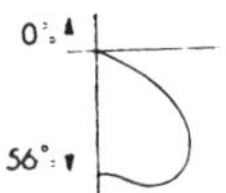 1	.60	.58	.56	.58	.57	.55	.56	.55	.53	.54	.53	.52	.52	.51	.50	.49	.177
2	.53	.49	.46	.52	.48	.46	.50	.47	.45	.48	.46	.44	.46	.44	.43	.42	.179
3	.46	.42	.39	.46	.42	.38	.44	.41	.38	.42	.40	.37	.41	.39	.37	.35	.172
4	.41	.36	.33	.40	.36	.33	.39	.35	.32	.38	.34	.32	.37	.34	.31	.30	.161
5	.37	.32	.28	.36	.31	.28	.35	.31	.28	.34	.30	.27	.33	.30	.27	.26	.150
6	.33	.28	.24	.32	.28	.24	.31	.27	.24	.30	.27	.24	.30	.26	.24	.23	.139
7	.30	.25	.21	.29	.25	.21	.28	.24	.21	.28	.24	.21	.27	.23	.21	.20	.129
8	.27	.22	.19	.26	.22	.19	.26	.22	.19	.25	.21	.19	.24	.21	.19	.17	.120
9	.25	.20	.17	.24	.20	.17	.24	.20	.17	.23	.19	.17	.22	.19	.17	.16	.112
10	.22	.18	.15	.22	.18	.15	.22	.18	.15	.21	.18	.15	.21	.17	.15	.14	.105

24 — Open top, indirect, reflector type unit with HID lamp (mult. by 0.9 for lens top)
Maint. Cat. VI | SC N.A. | 78% ↑ | 0% ↓

RCR	50	30	10	50	30	10	50	30	10	50	30	10	50	30	10	0	WDRC
0	.74	.74	.74	.63	.63	.63	.43	.43	.43	.25	.25	.25	.08	.08	.08	.00	
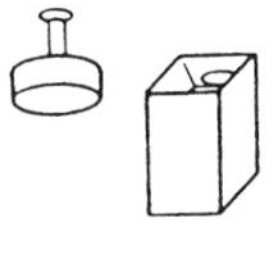 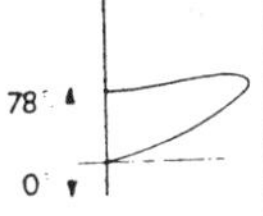 1	.64	.62	.59	.55	.53	.51	.38	.36	.35	.22	.21	.20	.07	.07	.07	.00	.000
2	.56	.52	.48	.48	.45	.42	.33	.31	.29	.19	.18	.17	.06	.06	.06	.00	.000
3	.49	.44	.40	.42	.38	.35	.29	.26	.24	.17	.15	.14	.05	.05	.05	.00	.000
4	.43	.38	.34	.37	.33	.29	.26	.23	.20	.15	.13	.12	.05	.04	.04	.00	.000
5	.38	.33	.28	.33	.28	.25	.23	.20	.17	.13	.12	.10	.04	.04	.03	.00	.000
6	.34	.28	.24	.29	.25	.21	.20	.17	.15	.12	.10	.09	.04	.03	.03	.00	.000
7	.31	.25	.21	.26	.22	.18	.18	.15	.13	.11	.09	.08	.03	.03	.03	.00	.000
8	.28	.22	.18	.24	.19	.16	.16	.13	.11	.10	.08	.07	.03	.03	.02	.00	.000
9	.25	.20	.16	.21	.17	.14	.15	.12	.10	.09	.07	.06	.03	.02	.02	.00	.000
10	.23	.17	.14	.20	.15	.12	.14	.11	.09	.08	.06	.05	.03	.02	.02	.00	.000

IES Lighting Handbook, 1984 Reference Volume. Reproduced with permission.

Typical Luminaire	Typical Intensity Distribution and Per Cent Lamp Lumens		ρcc →	80			70			50			30			10			0	WDRC	ρcc →
	Maint. Cat.	SC	ρw → / RCR ↓	50	30	10	50	30	10	50	30	10	50	30	10	50	30	10	0		ρw → / RCR ↓

25 — Porcelain-enameled reflector with 35°CW shielding. II, SC 1.3. 22½% up, 65% down.

ρcc →	80			70			50			30			10			0	WDRC	RCR
RCR	50	30	10	50	30	10	50	30	10	50	30	10	50	30	10	0		
0	.99	.99	.99	.94	.94	.94	.85	.85	.85	.77	.77	.77	.69	.69	.69	.65		0
1	.87	.84	.81	.83	.80	.77	.75	.73	.71	.68	.66	.65	.62	.60	.59	.56	.236	1
2	.77	.71	.67	.73	.68	.64	.67	.63	.60	.60	.58	.55	.55	.53	.51	.48	.220	2
3	.68	.62	.56	.65	.59	.54	.59	.55	.51	.54	.50	.48	.49	.46	.44	.41	.203	3
4	.61	.54	.48	.58	.52	.47	.53	.48	.44	.48	.44	.41	.44	.41	.38	.35	.186	4
5	.54	.47	.42	.52	.46	.41	.48	.42	.38	.44	.39	.36	.40	.36	.33	.31	.170	5
6	.49	.42	.37	.47	.40	.36	.43	.38	.34	.40	.35	.32	.36	.33	.30	.27	.157	6
7	.45	.37	.32	.43	.36	.32	.39	.34	.30	.36	.32	.28	.33	.29	.26	.24	.145	7
8	.41	.34	.29	.39	.33	.28	.36	.31	.27	.33	.29	.25	.31	.27	.24	.22	.135	8
9	.37	.31	.26	.36	.30	.25	.33	.28	.24	.31	.26	.23	.28	.24	.22	.20	.126	9
10	.34	.28	.24	.33	.27	.23	.31	.25	.22	.28	.24	.21	.26	.22	.20	.18	.118	10

26 — Diffuse aluminum reflector with 35°CW shielding. II, SC 1.5/1.3. 17% up, 66% down.

ρcc →	80			70			50			30			10			0	WDRC	RCR
RCR	50	30	10	50	30	10	50	30	10	50	30	10	50	30	10	0		
0	.95	.95	.95	.91	.91	.91	.83	.83	.83	.76	.76	.76	.69	.69	.69	.66		0
1	.85	.82	.79	.81	.79	.76	.75	.73	.71	.69	.67	.66	.63	.62	.61	.58	.197	1
2	.75	.71	.67	.72	.68	.65	.67	.63	.61	.62	.59	.57	.57	.55	.53	.51	.194	2
3	.67	.61	.57	.65	.59	.55	.60	.56	.52	.55	.52	.49	.51	.49	.46	.44	.184	3
4	.60	.54	.49	.58	.52	.48	.54	.49	.45	.50	.46	.43	.46	.43	.41	.39	.173	4
5	.54	.47	.43	.52	.46	.42	.49	.43	.40	.45	.41	.38	.42	.39	.36	.34	.162	5
6	.49	.42	.37	.47	.41	.37	.44	.39	.35	.41	.37	.33	.38	.35	.32	.30	.151	6
7	.44	.38	.33	.43	.37	.32	.40	.35	.31	.38	.33	.30	.35	.31	.28	.27	.141	7
8	.40	.34	.29	.39	.33	.29	.37	.31	.28	.34	.30	.27	.32	.28	.26	.24	.132	8
9	.37	.31	.26	.36	.30	.26	.34	.29	.25	.32	.27	.24	.30	.26	.23	.21	.124	9
10	.34	.28	.24	.33	.27	.23	.31	.26	.23	.29	.25	.22	.28	.24	.21	.19	.117	10

27 — Porcelain-enameled reflector with 30°CW × 30°LW shielding. II, SC 1.0. 23½% up, 57% down.

ρcc →	80			70			50			30			10			0	WDRC	RCR
RCR	50	30	10	50	30	10	50	30	10	50	30	10	50	30	10	0		
0	.91	.91	.91	.86	.86	.86	.77	.77	.77	.68	.68	.68	.61	.61	.61	.57		0
1	.80	.77	.75	.76	.74	.71	.69	.67	.65	.62	.60	.59	.55	.54	.53	.50	.182	1
2	.71	.67	.63	.68	.64	.60	.61	.58	.55	.55	.53	.51	.50	.48	.46	.43	.174	2
3	.63	.58	.53	.60	.55	.51	.55	.51	.47	.50	.46	.44	.45	.42	.40	.38	.163	3
4	.57	.51	.46	.54	.49	.44	.49	.45	.41	.45	.41	.38	.41	.38	.35	.33	.151	4
5	.51	.45	.40	.49	.43	.39	.45	.40	.36	.41	.37	.34	.37	.34	.31	.29	.140	5
6	.46	.40	.35	.44	.38	.34	.41	.36	.32	.37	.33	.30	.34	.30	.28	.26	.130	6
7	.42	.36	.31	.40	.35	.30	.37	.32	.29	.34	.30	.27	.31	.28	.25	.23	.121	7
8	.38	.32	.28	.37	.31	.27	.34	.29	.26	.31	.27	.24	.29	.25	.23	.21	.113	8
9	.35	.29	.25	.34	.28	.25	.31	.27	.23	.29	.25	.22	.27	.23	.21	.19	.106	9
10	.33	.27	.23	.31	.26	.22	.29	.24	.21	.27	.23	.20	.25	.21	.19	.17	.099	10

28 — Diffuse aluminum reflector with 35°CW × 35°LW shielding. II, SC 1.5/1.1. 17% up, 56½% down.

ρcc →	80			70			50			30			10			0	WDRC	RCR
RCR	50	30	10	50	30	10	50	30	10	50	30	10	50	30	10	0		
0	.83	.83	.83	.79	.79	.79	.72	.72	.72	.65	.65	.65	.59	.59	.59	.56		0
1	.74	.72	.70	.71	.69	.67	.65	.63	.62	.59	.58	.57	.54	.53	.52	.50	.160	1
2	.66	.62	.59	.64	.60	.57	.58	.56	.53	.54	.51	.49	.49	.47	.46	.44	.158	2
3	.59	.54	.50	.57	.53	.49	.53	.49	.46	.48	.46	.43	.45	.42	.40	.38	.150	3
4	.53	.48	.44	.51	.46	.42	.47	.43	.40	.44	.41	.38	.40	.38	.36	.34	.141	4
5	.48	.42	.38	.46	.41	.37	.43	.39	.35	.40	.36	.33	.37	.34	.32	.30	.132	5
6	.44	.38	.34	.42	.37	.33	.39	.35	.31	.36	.33	.30	.34	.31	.28	.27	.124	6
7	.40	.34	.30	.38	.33	.29	.36	.31	.28	.33	.30	.27	.31	.28	.25	.24	.116	7
8	.36	.31	.27	.35	.30	.26	.32	.28	.25	.31	.27	.24	.29	.25	.23	.22	.109	8
9	.33	.28	.24	.32	.27	.24	.30	.26	.23	.28	.24	.22	.26	.23	.21	.19	.102	9
10	.31	.25	.22	.30	.25	.22	.28	.24	.21	.26	.22	.20	.25	.21	.19	.18	.096	10

29 — Metal or dense diffusing sides with 45°CW × 45°LW shielding. II, SC 1.1. 39% up, 32% down.

ρcc →	80			70			50			30			10			0	WDRC	RCR
RCR	50	30	10	50	30	10	50	30	10	50	30	10	50	30	10	0		
0	.75	.75	.75	.69	.69	.69	.57	.57	.57	.46	.46	.46	.37	.37	.37	.32		0
1	.66	.64	.62	.61	.59	.57	.51	.50	.48	.42	.41	.40	.33	.33	.32	.28	.094	1
2	.59	.55	.52	.54	.51	.48	.46	.43	.41	.38	.36	.34	.30	.29	.28	.25	.091	2
3	.52	.48	.44	.48	.44	.41	.41	.38	.35	.34	.32	.30	.27	.26	.25	.22	.085	3
4	.47	.42	.38	.43	.39	.35	.37	.33	.31	.31	.28	.26	.25	.23	.22	.19	.079	4
5	.42	.37	.33	.39	.34	.31	.33	.30	.27	.28	.25	.23	.23	.21	.20	.17	.073	5
6	.38	.33	.29	.35	.31	.27	.30	.27	.24	.25	.23	.21	.21	.19	.18	.16	.068	6
7	.35	.29	.26	.32	.28	.24	.28	.24	.21	.23	.21	.19	.19	.17	.16	.14	.063	7
8	.32	.26	.23	.29	.25	.22	.25	.22	.19	.22	.19	.17	.18	.16	.15	.13	.059	8
9	.29	.24	.21	.27	.23	.20	.23	.20	.17	.20	.17	.15	.17	.15	.13	.12	.056	9
10	.27	.22	.19	.25	.21	.18	.22	.18	.16	.19	.16	.14	.16	.14	.12	.11	.052	10

30 — Same as unit #29 except with top reflectors. IV, SC 1.0. 6% up, 46% down.

ρcc →	80			70			50			30			10			0	WDRC	RCR
RCR	50	30	10	50	30	10	50	30	10	50	30	10	50	30	10	0		
0	.61	.61	.61	.58	.58	.58	.55	.55	.55	.51	.51	.51	.48	.48	.48	.46		0
1	.54	.52	.50	.52	.50	.49	.49	.47	.46	.46	.45	.43	.43	.42	.41	.40	.159	1
2	.48	.45	.42	.46	.44	.41	.44	.41	.39	.41	.39	.38	.39	.37	.36	.34	.145	2
3	.43	.39	.36	.42	.38	.35	.39	.36	.34	.37	.35	.33	.35	.33	.31	.30	.132	3
4	.39	.35	.32	.38	.34	.31	.36	.32	.30	.34	.31	.29	.32	.30	.28	.27	.121	4
5	.35	.31	.28	.34	.30	.27	.32	.29	.27	.31	.28	.26	.29	.27	.25	.24	.111	5
6	.32	.28	.25	.31	.27	.25	.30	.26	.24	.28	.25	.23	.27	.25	.23	.22	.102	6
7	.29	.25	.22	.28	.24	.22	.27	.24	.22	.26	.23	.21	.25	.23	.21	.20	.095	7
8	.27	.23	.20	.27	.23	.20	.25	.22	.20	.24	.21	.19	.23	.21	.19	.18	.088	8
9	.25	.21	.19	.25	.21	.18	.24	.20	.18	.23	.20	.18	.22	.19	.17	.16	.083	9
10	.23	.20	.17	.23	.19	.17	.22	.19	.17	.21	.18	.16	.20	.18	.16	.15	.077	10

Coefficients of Utilization for 20 Per Cent Effective Floor Cavity Reflectance (ρFC = 20)

Typical Luminaire	Typical Intensity Distribution and Per Cent Lamp Lumens			ρCC → 80			70			50			30			10			0	WDRC	ρCC → ρW → RCR ↓
	Maint. Cat.	SC	RCR ↓	ρW→ 50	30	10	50	30	10	50	30	10	50	30	10	50	30	10	0		

Coefficients of Utilization for 20 Per Cent Effective Floor Cavity Reflectance (ρFC = 20)

31 — 150 mm × 150 mm (6 × 6") cell parabolic wedge louver—multiply by 1.1 for 250 × 250 mm (10 × 10") cells
Maint. Cat. IV, SC 1.5/1.2, 0%↑, 58%↓

RCR	80-50	30	10	70-50	30	10	50-50	30	10	30-50	30	10	10-50	30	10	0	WDRC	RCR
0	.69	.69	.69	.67	.67	.67	.64	.64	.64	.62	.62	.62	.59	.59	.59	.58		0
1	.62	.61	.59	.61	.59	.58	.59	.57	.56	.57	.55	.54	.55	.54	.53	.52	.159	1
2	.56	.53	.50	.55	.52	.50	.53	.50	.47	.51	.49	.47	.49	.48	.46	.45	.160	2
3	.50	.46	.43	.49	.46	.43	.48	.44	.42	.46	.43	.41	.45	.42	.41	.39	.155	3
4	.45	.41	.37	.44	.40	.37	.43	.39	.36	.42	.38	.36	.40	.38	.36	.34	.147	4
5	.40	.36	.32	.40	.36	.32	.39	.35	.32	.38	.34	.32	.37	.34	.31	.30	.139	5
6	.37	.32	.29	.36	.32	.28	.35	.31	.28	.34	.31	.28	.33	.30	.28	.27	.131	6
7	.33	.29	.25	.33	.28	.25	.32	.28	.25	.31	.28	.25	.30	.27	.25	.24	.123	7
8	.30	.26	.23	.30	.26	.22	.29	.25	.22	.28	.25	.22	.28	.25	.22	.21	.115	8
9	.28	.23	.20	.27	.23	.20	.27	.23	.20	.26	.23	.20	.26	.22	.20	.19	.109	9
10	.26	.21	.18	.25	.21	.18	.25	.21	.18	.25	.24	.18	.24	.20	.18	.17	.102	10

32 — 2-lamp, surface mounted, bare lamp unit—photometry with 460 mm (18") wide panel above luminaire—lamps on 150 mm (6") centers
Maint. Cat. I, SC 1.3, 9½%↑, 78%↓

RCR	80-50	30	10	70-50	30	10	50-50	30	10	30-50	30	10	10-50	30	10	0	WDRC	RCR
0	1.02	1.02	1.02	.99	.99	.99	.92	.92	.92	.86	.86	.86	.81	.81	.81	.78		0
1	.85	.80	.76	.82	.78	.74	.76	.73	.70	.71	.68	.66	.67	.64	.62	.60	.467	1
2	.72	.65	.59	.70	.63	.58	.65	.60	.55	.61	.56	.52	.57	.53	.50	.47	.387	2
3	.63	.55	.48	.60	.53	.47	.56	.50	.45	.53	.47	.43	.49	.45	.41	.38	.331	3
4	.55	.46	.40	.53	.45	.39	.50	.43	.37	.46	.41	.36	.43	.38	.34	.32	.289	4
5	.49	.40	.34	.47	.39	.33	.44	.37	.32	.41	.35	.31	.39	.34	.29	.27	.255	5
6	.43	.35	.29	.42	.34	.29	.40	.33	.28	.37	.31	.27	.35	.30	.26	.23	.228	6
7	.39	.31	.25	.38	.30	.25	.36	.29	.24	.34	.28	.23	.32	.26	.22	.20	.206	7
8	.36	.28	.22	.35	.27	.22	.33	.26	.21	.31	.25	.21	.29	.24	.20	.18	.188	8
9	.33	.25	.20	.32	.25	.20	.30	.24	.19	.28	.23	.18	.27	.22	.18	.16	.173	9
10	.30	.23	.18	.29	.22	.18	.28	.21	.17	.26	.21	.17	.25	.20	.16	.14	.159	10

33 — Luminous bottom suspended unit with extra-high output lamp
Maint. Cat. VI, SC N.A., 66%↑, 12%↓

RCR	80-50	30	10	70-50	30	10	50-50	30	10	30-50	30	10	10-50	30	10	0	WDRC	RCR
0	.77	.77	.77	.68	.68	.68	.50	.50	.50	.34	.34	.34	.19	.19	.19	.12		0
1	.67	.64	.61	.59	.56	.54	.43	.42	.41	.29	.29	.28	.17	.16	.16	.10	.048	1
2	.58	.54	.50	.51	.48	.44	.38	.36	.34	.26	.24	.23	.14	.14	.13	.08	.045	2
3	.51	.46	.42	.45	.41	.37	.33	.30	.28	.23	.21	.19	.13	.12	.11	.07	.041	3
4	.45	.39	.35	.40	.35	.31	.30	.26	.24	.20	.18	.17	.11	.10	.10	.06	.037	4
5	.40	.34	.30	.35	.30	.26	.26	.23	.20	.18	.16	.14	.10	.09	.08	.05	.034	5
6	.36	.30	.25	.31	.26	.23	.24	.20	.17	.16	.14	.12	.09	.08	.07	.04	.031	6
7	.32	.26	.22	.28	.23	.20	.21	.18	.15	.15	.12	.11	.08	.07	.06	.04	.028	7
8	.29	.23	.19	.26	.21	.17	.19	.16	.13	.13	.11	.09	.08	.06	.06	.03	.026	8
9	.26	.21	.17	.23	.18	.15	.17	.14	.12	.12	.10	.08	.07	.06	.05	.03	.024	9
10	.24	.19	.15	.21	.17	.13	.16	.13	.10	.11	.09	.07	.06	.05	.04	.03	.022	10

34 — Prismatic bottom and sides, open top, 4-lamp suspended unit—see note 7
Maint. Cat. VI, SC 1.4/1.2, 33%↑, 50%↓

RCR	80-50	30	10	70-50	30	10	50-50	30	10	30-50	30	10	10-50	30	10	0	WDRC	RCR
0	.91	.91	.91	.85	.85	.85	.74	.74	.74	.64	.64	.64	.54	.54	.54	.50		0
1	.80	.77	.74	.75	.72	.70	.65	.63	.61	.57	.55	.54	.49	.47	.47	.43	.179	1
2	.70	.65	.61	.66	.62	.58	.58	.54	.52	.50	.48	.46	.43	.42	.40	.37	.166	2
3	.62	.56	.51	.59	.53	.49	.51	.47	.44	.45	.42	.39	.39	.37	.35	.32	.153	3
4	.55	.49	.44	.52	.46	.42	.46	.41	.38	.40	.37	.34	.35	.32	.30	.27	.140	4
5	.50	.43	.38	.47	.41	.36	.41	.37	.33	.36	.33	.30	.32	.29	.26	.24	.129	5
6	.45	.38	.33	.42	.36	.32	.37	.33	.29	.33	.29	.26	.29	.26	.23	.21	.119	6
7	.40	.34	.29	.38	.32	.28	.34	.29	.26	.30	.26	.23	.26	.23	.21	.19	.111	7
8	.37	.30	.26	.35	.29	.25	.31	.26	.23	.28	.24	.21	.24	.21	.19	.17	.103	8
9	.34	.27	.23	.32	.26	.22	.29	.24	.21	.25	.22	.19	.22	.19	.17	.15	.096	9
10	.31	.25	.21	.29	.24	.20	.26	.22	.19	.23	.20	.17	.21	.18	.15	.14	.090	10

35 — 2-lamp prismatic wraparound—see note 7
Maint. Cat. V, SC 1.5/1.2, 11½%↑, 58½%↓

RCR	80-50	30	10	70-50	30	10	50-50	30	10	30-50	30	10	10-50	30	10	0	WDRC	RCR
0	.81	.81	.81	.78	.78	.78	.72	.72	.72	.66	.66	.66	.61	.61	.61	.59		0
1	.71	.68	.66	.68	.66	.63	.63	.61	.59	.58	.57	.56	.54	.53	.52	.50	.223	1
2	.63	.58	.55	.60	.56	.53	.56	.53	.50	.52	.50	.47	.48	.46	.45	.43	.201	2
3	.56	.50	.46	.54	.49	.45	.50	.46	.43	.47	.43	.41	.43	.41	.39	.37	.183	3
4	.50	.44	.40	.48	.43	.39	.45	.40	.37	.42	.38	.35	.39	.36	.34	.32	.167	4
5	.45	.39	.34	.43	.38	.34	.40	.36	.32	.38	.34	.31	.35	.32	.30	.28	.153	5
6	.40	.34	.30	.39	.34	.30	.37	.32	.28	.34	.30	.27	.32	.29	.26	.25	.142	6
7	.37	.31	.27	.35	.30	.26	.33	.29	.25	.31	.27	.24	.30	.26	.23	.22	.131	7
8	.33	.28	.24	.32	.27	.23	.30	.26	.23	.29	.25	.22	.27	.24	.21	.20	.122	8
9	.31	.25	.21	.30	.25	.21	.28	.24	.20	.26	.23	.20	.25	.22	.19	.18	.114	9
10	.28	.23	.19	.27	.22	.19	.26	.21	.18	.24	.21	.18	.23	.20	.17	.16	.107	10

36 — 2-lamp prismatic wraparound—see note 7
Maint. Cat. V, SC 1.2, 24%↑, 50%↓

RCR	80-50	30	10	70-50	30	10	50-50	30	10	30-50	30	10	10-50	30	10	0	WDRC	RCR
0	.82	.82	.82	.77	.77	.77	.69	.69	.69	.61	.61	.61	.53	.53	.53	.50		0
1	.71	.67	.65	.67	.64	.61	.59	.57	.55	.52	.51	.49	.46	.45	.44	.40	.234	1
2	.62	.57	.53	.59	.54	.51	.52	.49	.46	.46	.44	.41	.41	.39	.37	.34	.194	2
3	.55	.49	.45	.52	.47	.43	.46	.42	.39	.41	.38	.36	.37	.34	.32	.30	.168	3
4	.49	.43	.39	.47	.41	.37	.42	.37	.34	.37	.34	.31	.33	.30	.28	.26	.150	4
5	.44	.38	.34	.42	.36	.32	.38	.33	.30	.34	.30	.27	.30	.27	.25	.23	.135	5
6	.40	.34	.29	.38	.32	.28	.34	.30	.26	.31	.27	.24	.28	.25	.22	.21	.123	6
7	.36	.30	.26	.35	.29	.25	.31	.27	.23	.28	.25	.22	.25	.22	.20	.18	.112	7
8	.33	.27	.23	.32	.26	.23	.29	.24	.21	.26	.22	.20	.23	.20	.18	.16	.104	8
9	.30	.25	.21	.29	.24	.20	.26	.22	.19	.24	.20	.18	.22	.19	.16	.15	.097	9
10	.28	.23	.19	.27	.22	.18	.25	.20	.17	.22	.19	.16	.20	.17	.15	.14	.090	10

Typical Luminaire	Typical Intensity Distribution and Per Cent Lamp Lumens	Maint. Cat.	SC	RCR	ρcc → 80, pw 50	30	10	70, pw 50	30	10	50, pw 50	30	10	30, pw 50	30	10	10, pw 50	30	10	0	WDRC	RCR
37 — 2-lamp diffuse wraparound—see note 7	8% up, 37½% down	V	1.3	0	.52	.52	.52	.50	.50	.50	.46	.46	.46	.43	.43	.43	.39	.39	.39	.38		0
				1	.44	.42	.40	.42	.40	.39	.39	.37	.36	.36	.35	.33	.33	.32	.31	.30	.201	1
				2	.38	.35	.32	.37	.33	.31	.34	.31	.29	.31	.29	.27	.28	.27	.25	.24	.171	2
				3	.33	.29	.26	.32	.28	.25	.29	.26	.24	.27	.25	.22	.25	.23	.21	.20	.149	3
				4	.29	.25	.22	.28	.24	.21	.26	.23	.20	.24	.21	.19	.22	.20	.18	.17	.132	4
				5	.26	.22	.19	.25	.21	.18	.23	.20	.17	.21	.18	.16	.20	.17	.15	.14	.117	5
				6	.23	.19	.16	.22	.18	.16	.21	.17	.15	.19	.16	.14	.18	.15	.13	.12	.106	6
				7	.21	.17	.14	.20	.16	.14	.19	.15	.13	.17	.15	.12	.16	.14	.12	.11	.096	7
				8	.19	.15	.12	.18	.15	.12	.17	.14	.12	.16	.13	.11	.15	.12	.11	.10	.088	8
				9	.17	.14	.11	.17	.13	.11	.16	.13	.10	.15	.12	.10	.14	.11	.09	.09	.081	9
				10	.16	.12	.10	.15	.12	.10	.14	.11	.09	.14	.11	.09	.13	.10	.09	.08	.075	10
38 — 4-lamp, 610 mm (2') wide troffer with 45° plastic louver—see note 7	0% up, 50% down	IV	1.0	0	.60	.60	.60	.58	.58	.58	.56	.56	.56	.53	.53	.53	.51	.51	.51	.50		0
				1	.53	.51	.49	.52	.50	.49	.50	.48	.47	.48	.47	.46	.46	.45	.44	.43	.168	1
				2	.47	.44	.42	.46	.43	.41	.44	.42	.40	.43	.41	.39	.41	.40	.38	.37	.159	2
				3	.42	.38	.36	.41	.38	.35	.40	.37	.35	.39	.36	.34	.37	.35	.34	.32	.146	3
				4	.38	.34	.31	.37	.34	.31	.36	.33	.30	.35	.32	.30	.34	.32	.30	.29	.135	4
				5	.34	.30	.27	.34	.30	.27	.33	.29	.27	.32	.29	.27	.31	.28	.26	.25	.124	5
				6	.31	.27	.24	.31	.27	.24	.30	.27	.24	.29	.26	.24	.28	.26	.24	.23	.114	6
				7	.29	.25	.22	.28	.24	.22	.28	.24	.22	.27	.24	.21	.26	.23	.21	.20	.106	7
				8	.26	.22	.20	.26	.22	.20	.25	.22	.20	.25	.22	.20	.24	.21	.19	.19	.099	8
				9	.24	.21	.18	.24	.21	.18	.24	.20	.18	.23	.20	.18	.23	.20	.18	.17	.092	9
				10	.23	.19	.17	.22	.19	.17	.22	.19	.16	.22	.19	.16	.21	.18	.16	.16	.086	10
39 — 4-lamp, 610 mm (2') wide troffer with 45° white metal louver—see note 7	0% up, 46% down	IV	0.9	0	.55	.55	.55	.54	.54	.54	.51	.51	.51	.49	.49	.49	.47	.47	.47	.46		0
				1	.49	.48	.46	.48	.47	.46	.46	.45	.44	.45	.44	.43	.43	.42	.42	.41	.137	1
				2	.44	.42	.40	.43	.41	.39	.42	.40	.38	.40	.38	.37	.39	.38	.37	.36	.131	2
				3	.40	.37	.34	.39	.36	.34	.38	.36	.33	.37	.35	.33	.36	.34	.32	.32	.122	3
				4	.36	.33	.30	.36	.33	.30	.35	.32	.30	.34	.31	.29	.33	.31	.29	.28	.113	4
				5	.33	.30	.27	.33	.29	.27	.32	.29	.27	.31	.28	.26	.30	.28	.26	.25	.104	5
				6	.30	.27	.24	.30	.27	.24	.29	.26	.24	.28	.25	.24	.28	.25	.23	.23	.097	6
				7	.28	.25	.22	.28	.24	.22	.27	.24	.22	.26	.24	.22	.26	.23	.22	.21	.090	7
				8	.26	.23	.20	.26	.22	.20	.25	.22	.20	.25	.22	.20	.24	.22	.20	.19	.085	8
				9	.24	.21	.19	.24	.21	.19	.23	.20	.18	.23	.20	.18	.23	.20	.18	.18	.079	9
				10	.23	.19	.17	.22	.19	.17	.22	.19	.17	.22	.19	.17	.21	.19	.17	.16	.075	10
40 — Fluorescent unit dropped diffuser, 4-lamp 610 mm (2') wide—see note 7	1% up, 60½% down	V	1.2	0	.73	.73	.73	.71	.71	.71	.68	.68	.68	.65	.65	.65	.62	.62	.62	.60		0
				1	.63	.60	.58	.62	.59	.57	.59	.57	.55	.56	.55	.53	.54	.53	.51	.50	.259	1
				2	.55	.51	.47	.54	.50	.46	.51	.48	.45	.49	.46	.44	.47	.45	.43	.42	.236	2
				3	.48	.43	.39	.47	.42	.39	.45	.41	.38	.43	.40	.37	.42	.39	.36	.35	.212	3
				4	.43	.37	.33	.42	.37	.33	.40	.36	.32	.39	.35	.32	.37	.34	.31	.30	.191	4
				5	.38	.33	.29	.37	.32	.28	.36	.31	.28	.35	.31	.28	.33	.30	.27	.26	.173	5
				6	.34	.29	.25	.34	.29	.25	.33	.28	.24	.31	.27	.24	.30	.27	.24	.23	.158	6
				7	.31	.26	.22	.31	.26	.22	.30	.25	.22	.30	.25	.21	.28	.24	.21	.20	.144	7
				8	.28	.23	.20	.28	.23	.20	.27	.23	.19	.26	.22	.19	.25	.22	.19	.18	.133	8
				9	.26	.21	.18	.26	.21	.18	.25	.21	.17	.24	.20	.17	.24	.20	.17	.16	.123	9
				10	.24	.19	.16	.24	.19	.16	.23	.19	.16	.22	.19	.16	.22	.18	.16	.15	.115	10
41 — Fluorescent unit with flat bottom diffuser, 4-lamp 610 mm (2') wide—see note 7	0% up, 57½% down	V	1.2	0	.69	.69	.69	.67	.67	.67	.64	.64	.64	.61	.61	.61	.59	.59	.59	.58		0
				1	.60	.58	.56	.59	.57	.55	.56	.55	.53	.54	.53	.51	.52	.51	.50	.49	.227	1
				2	.52	.49	.45	.51	.48	.45	.49	.46	.44	.47	.45	.43	.46	.44	.42	.40	.214	2
				3	.46	.41	.38	.45	.41	.37	.43	.40	.37	.42	.39	.36	.40	.38	.35	.34	.196	3
				4	.41	.36	.32	.40	.35	.32	.39	.34	.31	.37	.34	.31	.36	.33	.30	.29	.178	4
				5	.36	.31	.28	.36	.31	.27	.35	.30	.27	.33	.30	.27	.32	.29	.26	.25	.162	5
				6	.33	.28	.24	.32	.27	.24	.31	.27	.24	.30	.26	.23	.29	.26	.23	.22	.148	6
				7	.30	.25	.21	.29	.25	.21	.28	.24	.21	.28	.24	.21	.27	.23	.21	.20	.136	7
				8	.27	.22	.19	.27	.22	.19	.26	.22	.19	.25	.21	.19	.25	.21	.19	.17	.126	8
				9	.25	.20	.17	.25	.20	.17	.24	.20	.17	.24	.20	.17	.23	.19	.17	.16	.116	9
				10	.23	.18	.15	.23	.18	.15	.22	.18	.15	.22	.18	.15	.21	.18	.15	.14	.108	10
42 — Fluorescent unit with flat prismatic lens, 4-lamp 610 mm (2') wide—see note 7	0% up, 63% down, 60°	V	1.4/1.2	0	.75	.75	.75	.73	.73	.73	.70	.70	.70	.67	.67	.67	.64	.64	.64	.63		0
				1	.67	.64	.62	.65	.63	.61	.63	.61	.59	.60	.59	.58	.58	.57	.56	.55	.208	1
				2	.59	.56	.52	.58	.55	.52	.56	.53	.51	.54	.52	.49	.52	.50	.48	.47	.199	2
				3	.53	.48	.45	.52	.48	.44	.50	.46	.43	.48	.45	.43	.47	.44	.42	.41	.186	3
				4	.47	.42	.38	.46	.42	.38	.45	.41	.38	.44	.40	.37	.42	.39	.37	.35	.172	4
				5	.43	.37	.34	.42	.37	.33	.41	.36	.33	.39	.36	.33	.38	.35	.32	.31	.160	5
				6	.39	.33	.30	.38	.33	.29	.37	.32	.29	.36	.32	.29	.35	.31	.29	.27	.148	6
				7	.35	.30	.26	.35	.30	.26	.34	.29	.26	.33	.29	.26	.32	.28	.26	.24	.138	7
				8	.32	.27	.24	.32	.27	.23	.31	.26	.23	.30	.26	.23	.29	.26	.23	.22	.128	8
				9	.30	.25	.21	.29	.24	.21	.28	.24	.21	.28	.24	.21	.27	.24	.21	.20	.120	9
				10	.27	.22	.19	.27	.22	.19	.26	.22	.19	.26	.22	.19	.25	.22	.19	.18	.113	10

Coefficients of Utilization for 20 Per Cent Effective Floor Cavity Reflectance (ρFC = 20)

Coefficients of Utilization for 20 Per Cent Effective Floor Cavity Reflectance ($\rho_{FC} = 20$)

Typical Luminaire	Maint. Cat.	SC	RCR	80/50	80/30	80/10	70/50	70/30	70/10	50/50	50/30	50/10	30/50	30/30	30/10	10/50	10/30	10/10	0	WDRC
43 — 4-lamp, 610 mm (2') wide unit with sharp cutoff (high angle—low luminance) flat prismatic lens—see note 7	V	1.4/1.3	0	.78	.78	.78	.76	.76	.76	.73	.73	.73	.70	.70	.70	.67	.67	.67	.66	
			1	.71	.68	.66	.69	.67	.65	.66	.65	.63	.64	.63	.61	.62	.61	.60	.58	.181
			2	.63	.60	.57	.62	.59	.56	.60	.57	.55	.58	.56	.54	.56	.54	.52	.51	.180
			3	.57	.52	.49	.56	.52	.48	.54	.51	.48	.52	.49	.47	.51	.48	.46	.45	.173
			4	.51	.46	.43	.50	.46	.42	.49	.45	.42	.47	.44	.41	.46	.43	.41	.39	.164
			5	.46	.41	.37	.46	.41	.37	.44	.40	.37	.43	.39	.36	.42	.39	.36	.35	.154
			6	.42	.37	.33	.41	.37	.33	.40	.36	.33	.39	.35	.32	.38	.35	.32	.31	.145
			7	.38	.33	.29	.38	.33	.29	.37	.32	.29	.36	.32	.29	.35	.32	.29	.28	.136
			8	.35	.30	.26	.35	.30	.26	.34	.29	.26	.33	.29	.26	.32	.29	.26	.25	.127
			9	.32	.27	.24	.32	.27	.24	.31	.27	.24	.31	.27	.24	.30	.26	.24	.22	.120
			10	.30	.25	.22	.30	.25	.22	.29	.25	.22	.28	.24	.22	.28	.24	.21	.20	.113
44 — Bilateral batwing distribution—louvered fluorescent unit	IV	N.A.	0	.71	.71	.71	.70	.70	.70	.66	.66	.66	.64	.64	.64	.61	.61	.61	.60	
			1	.64	.62	.60	.63	.61	.60	.60	.59	.58	.58	.57	.56	.56	.55	.54	.53	.167
			2	.57	.54	.51	.56	.53	.51	.54	.52	.50	.52	.50	.48	.51	.49	.47	.46	.170
			3	.51	.47	.44	.50	.46	.43	.49	.45	.43	.47	.44	.42	.46	.43	.41	.40	.165
			4	.46	.41	.38	.45	.41	.37	.44	.40	.37	.42	.39	.36	.41	.38	.36	.35	.157
			5	.41	.36	.33	.40	.36	.32	.39	.35	.32	.38	.35	.32	.37	.34	.31	.30	.148
			6	.37	.32	.28	.36	.32	.28	.35	.31	.28	.34	.31	.28	.34	.30	.28	.27	.139
			7	.33	.29	.25	.33	.28	.25	.32	.28	.25	.31	.27	.25	.30	.27	.24	.23	.130
			8	.30	.26	.22	.30	.25	.22	.29	.25	.22	.28	.25	.22	.28	.24	.22	.21	.122
			9	.28	.23	.20	.27	.23	.20	.27	.23	.20	.26	.22	.20	.25	.22	.19	.18	.115
			10	.25	.21	.18	.25	.21	.18	.25	.20	.18	.24	.20	.18	.23	.20	.18	.17	.108
45 — Bilateral batwing distribution—4-lamp, 610 mm (2') wide fluorescent unit with flat prismatic lens and overlay—see note 7	V	N.A.	0	.57	.57	.57	.56	.56	.56	.53	.53	.53	.51	.51	.51	.49	.49	.49	.48	
			1	.50	.48	.46	.49	.47	.45	.47	.45	.44	.45	.43	.42	.43	.42	.41	.40	.204
			2	.43	.40	.37	.42	.39	.36	.40	.38	.35	.39	.37	.35	.37	.36	.34	.33	.192
			3	.37	.33	.30	.37	.33	.30	.35	.32	.29	.34	.31	.29	.33	.30	.28	.27	.175
			4	.33	.28	.25	.32	.28	.25	.31	.27	.24	.30	.27	.24	.29	.26	.24	.23	.159
			5	.29	.24	.21	.28	.24	.21	.27	.24	.21	.26	.23	.20	.25	.23	.20	.19	.145
			6	.26	.21	.18	.25	.21	.18	.24	.21	.18	.24	.20	.18	.23	.20	.17	.16	.132
			7	.23	.19	.16	.23	.18	.15	.22	.18	.15	.21	.18	.15	.21	.17	.15	.14	.122
			8	.21	.17	.14	.21	.16	.14	.20	.16	.13	.19	.16	.13	.19	.16	.13	.12	.112
			9	.19	.15	.12	.19	.15	.12	.18	.14	.12	.18	.14	.12	.17	.14	.12	.11	.104
			10	.17	.13	.11	.17	.13	.11	.17	.13	.11	.16	.13	.11	.16	.13	.11	.10	.096
46 — Bilateral batwing distribution—one-lamp, surface mounted fluorescent with prismatic wraparound lens	V	N.A.	0	.87	.87	.87	.84	.84	.84	.77	.77	.77	.72	.72	.72	.66	.66	.66	.64	
			1	.75	.72	.69	.72	.69	.66	.67	.64	.62	.62	.60	.58	.57	.56	.54	.52	.296
			2	.65	.60	.56	.63	.58	.54	.58	.54	.51	.54	.51	.48	.50	.47	.45	.43	.261
			3	.57	.51	.46	.55	.49	.45	.51	.46	.42	.47	.43	.40	.44	.41	.38	.36	.232
			4	.50	.44	.39	.48	.42	.38	.45	.40	.36	.42	.38	.34	.39	.35	.32	.30	.209
			5	.45	.38	.33	.43	.37	.32	.40	.35	.31	.37	.33	.29	.35	.31	.28	.26	.189
			6	.40	.33	.28	.39	.32	.28	.36	.31	.26	.34	.29	.25	.31	.27	.24	.22	.172
			7	.36	.29	.25	.35	.29	.24	.32	.27	.23	.30	.26	.22	.28	.24	.21	.19	.158
			8	.33	.26	.22	.31	.25	.21	.29	.24	.20	.28	.23	.20	.26	.22	.19	.17	.146
			9	.30	.23	.19	.29	.23	.19	.27	.22	.18	.25	.21	.17	.24	.20	.17	.15	.135
			10	.27	.21	.17	.26	.21	.17	.25	.20	.16	.23	.19	.16	.22	.18	.15	.13	.126
47 — Radial batwing distribution—4-lamp, 610 mm (2') wide fluorescent unit with flat prismatic lens—see note 7	V	1.7	0	.71	.71	.71	.69	.69	.69	.66	.66	.66	.63	.63	.63	.61	.61	.61	.60	
			1	.62	.59	.57	.60	.58	.56	.58	.56	.54	.55	.54	.52	.53	.52	.51	.50	.251
			2	.53	.49	.46	.52	.48	.45	.50	.47	.44	.48	.45	.43	.46	.44	.42	.41	.237
			3	.46	.41	.37	.45	.41	.37	.44	.40	.36	.42	.39	.36	.40	.38	.35	.34	.216
			4	.41	.35	.31	.40	.35	.31	.38	.34	.30	.37	.33	.30	.36	.32	.30	.28	.196
			5	.36	.30	.26	.35	.30	.26	.34	.29	.26	.33	.29	.26	.32	.28	.25	.24	.178
			6	.32	.27	.23	.32	.26	.23	.31	.26	.22	.29	.25	.22	.29	.25	.22	.21	.162
			7	.29	.24	.20	.28	.23	.20	.28	.23	.19	.27	.22	.19	.26	.22	.19	.18	.149
			8	.26	.21	.17	.26	.21	.17	.25	.20	.17	.24	.20	.17	.24	.20	.17	.16	.137
			9	.24	.19	.15	.24	.19	.15	.23	.18	.15	.22	.18	.15	.22	.18	.15	.14	.127
			10	.22	.17	.14	.22	.17	.14	.21	.17	.14	.20	.16	.14	.20	.16	.14	.12	.118
49 — 2-lamp fluorescent strip unit with 235° reflector fluorescent lamps	I	1.4/1.2	0	1.13	1.13	1.13	1.09	1.09	1.09	1.01	1.01	1.01	.94	.94	.94	.88	.88	.88	.85	
			1	.95	.90	.86	.92	.87	.83	.85	.82	.78	.79	.76	.74	.74	.72	.69	.66	.464
			2	.82	.74	.68	.79	.72	.66	.73	.68	.63	.68	.64	.60	.63	.60	.56	.53	.394
			3	.71	.62	.55	.69	.61	.54	.64	.57	.52	.59	.54	.49	.55	.51	.47	.44	.342
			4	.62	.53	.46	.60	.52	.45	.56	.49	.43	.52	.46	.41	.49	.44	.40	.37	.300
			5	.55	.46	.39	.54	.45	.39	.50	.43	.37	.47	.40	.36	.44	.38	.34	.32	.267
			6	.50	.41	.34	.48	.40	.33	.45	.38	.32	.42	.36	.31	.39	.34	.30	.27	.240
			7	.45	.36	.30	.44	.35	.29	.41	.34	.28	.38	.32	.27	.36	.30	.26	.24	.218
			8	.41	.32	.26	.40	.32	.26	.37	.30	.25	.35	.29	.24	.33	.27	.23	.21	.199
			9	.37	.29	.24	.36	.28	.23	.34	.27	.22	.32	.26	.22	.30	.25	.21	.19	.183
			10	.34	.26	.21	.33	.26	.21	.32	.25	.20	.30	.24	.20	.28	.23	.19	.17	.170

IES Lighting Handbook, 1984 Reference Volume. Reproduced with permission.

107

REVIEW QUESTIONS

ESTIMATE FOOTCANDLES AND DOLLARS

Lighting professionals estimate illuminance levels and costs for proposed designs. Answer the following questions to refine your estimating skills. Questions 1 through 8 are based on the example footcandle calculation summarized below, but refer back to pages 88 and 89 before answering.

Example Classroom Summary Page 80–81

Dimensions: 20′ W, 30′ L, 9′ H, area = 600 sq. ft.
Fixture: #2, 24″ × 48″, 3 lamp fluorescent
Lamps: F40 CW (34 watt), 2,900 lumens each
Reflectance: pc = 80%, pw = 50%, pf = 20%
Cavity ratios: CCR = 0, RCR = 2.7, FCR = 1.0
Coefficient of utilization: CU = 60%
Light loss factor: LLF = 70%
No. of fixtures required = 8.2 for 50 footcandles
No. of fixtures provided = 9 for 55 footcandles

1. Classroom lighting operates 2,500 hours each year and electricity costs $0.08 per kWh. Find the *annual* cost of lighting the classroom.
2. Classroom lamps are cleaned once a year with a labor cost of $1 per fixture. Fixture re-lamping is scheduled every 6 years (75% of lamp life) at a cost of $6 per fixture for labor and lamps. Find the *annual* cost of cleaning and re-lamping.
3. Estimate the annual *cost per square foot* for classroom lighting.
4. If classroom ceiling reflectance is changed to 50% (instead of 80%) less light will reach the work plane. Find the CU change and the footcandle change.
5. If classroom dimensions are changed to 10′ × 60′ (ugh!), both RCR and CU will change. Estimate the footcandle reduction.
6. Classroom illumination must be increased to 80 fc. Make two proposals for lighting changes, without doing a new calculation.
7. Increase the example classroom ceiling height to 10′ so that indirect fixtures can be mounted

20″ below the ceiling. Replace the example fixtures with nine #8 fluorescent fixtures. Calculate footcandles if each new fixture uses 2 F48 CW/HO (60 watt) lamps.
8. Nine #8 indirect fluorescent fixtures offer diffuse lighting but they're a poor choice for uniform lighting in the example classroom. Why?
9. Make a preliminary comparison of 400 watt MH-HID, and 120 watt fluorescent fixtures being considered for a new 10,000 sq. ft. grocery store. The 400 watt MH lamp produces 36,000 initial lumens. Two 60 watt T8 lamps in the 96″ fluorescent fixture produce 12,000 initial lumens.

   If both fixtures have a CU of 64% and a LLF of 70% in the grocery store, estimate the number of fixtures required to provide 50 footcandles.
10. If electricity costs $0.08 per kWh and grocery store lighting operates for 8,670 hours each year, estimate annual lighting costs for ninety-three 120 watt fluorescent fixtures.

ANSWERS

1. **$184 per year.**
   Each of nine fixtures has three 34 watt lamps.

   (34 watts)(9 fixtures)(3 lamps) = 918 watts

   (0.918 kW)(2,500 hr.)($0.08) = $183.60

   Electrical costs vary and the average cost per kWh must include demand charges.

2. **$18 per year.**

   Clean ($1 per fixture)(6 yr.)(9 fixtures) = $54
   re-lamp ($6 per fixture)(9 fixtures) = $54
   annual cost, $108 ÷ 6 yr. = $18 per year

   Actual costs will be higher because some ballasts and lamps will fail during 6 years of operation.

3. **$0.34 per square foot per year.**
   $184 + $18 ÷ 600 sq. ft. = $0.34

4. **CU and fc drop about 5%.**
   Example CU was 60%, new CU = 57%.
   Example fc was 55, new fc = 52.

5. fc drop 10% from 55 to 50.

Example RCR was 2.7, new RCR = 3.8.
Example CU was 60%, new CU = 55%.
Example fc was 55, new fc = 50.

6. Two ways to get 80 fc.

- Replace 34 watt, 2,900 lumen lamps with 60 watt, 4,300 lumen lamps (and ballasts) to yield 80 fc.
- Nine #2 fixtures produce 55 fc so a new layout using 14 #2 fixtures will yield 80 fc. Which requires the most watts?

7. 37 footcandles (with fixture #8). Review the footcandle calculation on pages 88–89 and use the following blank Footcandle Calculation form to check this answer. If you don't get 37 footcandles recheck each entry on your calculation form as follows. New ceiling cavity height is 1.67¢. New room cavity height is 5.83¢.

F 48 CW/HO (60 watt) lamps yield 4,300 lumens, and with two lamps FL = 8,600.

The new CCR (ceiling cavity ratio) is 0.7, because the ceiling cavity height is 1.67'.

$$(5)(1.67)(20+30) \div 600 = 0.69, \text{ rounded to } 0.7$$

The new RCR (room cavity ratio) is 2.4, because the new room cavity height is 5.83'.

$$(5)(5.83)(20+30) \div 600 = 2.42, \text{ rounded to } 2.4$$

The new pcc (effective ceiling cavity reflectance) is 70% (CCR = 1.67, interpolate).
The new CU = 41% (fixture #8, RCR 2.4, pcc = 70%, pw = 50%, interpolate).
LLF = 70% no change, assumes frequent lamp cleaning in these open fixtures.
Calculate footcandles with 9 fixtures = 37.

$$9 = (\text{fc})(600 \text{ sq. ft.}) \div (8,600)(41\%)(70\%)$$

8. Nine indirect fixtures a poor choice.

- More watts, less footcandles.
- Less uniform, fixture #8 works better in continuous rows because light distribution at fixture ends is poor.
- Less efficient light distribution because #8 has a recommended 24" drop, not 20".

9. 31 MH or 93 fluorescent fixtures. Compare 400 watt MH-HID fixtures and 120 watt fluorescent fixtures at 50 footcandles in a 10,000 sq. ft. grocery store.
MH lamp = 36,000 initial lumens.
Fluorescent lamps = 12,000 initial lumens.
Both fixtures have a CU of 64% and a LLF of 70%.
Solution:
Both fixtures will deliver 45% of initial lamp lumens as usable footcandles.

$$(64\% \text{ CU})(70\% \text{ LLF}) = 45\%$$

50 lumens per square foot = 50 footcandles, so this 10,000 sq. ft. store requires 500,000 lumens.

$$(10,000 \text{ sq. ft})(50 \text{ lumens/sq. ft.}) = 500,000$$

31 MH-HID fixtures are required.

$$500,000 \text{ lm} \div (36,000 \text{ lm})(45\%) = 30.86$$

$$\text{total watts} = 14,260 \text{ (460 incl. ballast)}(31)$$

93 fluorescent fixtures are required.

$$500,000 \text{ lm} \div (12,000 \text{ lm})(45\%) = 92.59$$

$$\text{total watts} = 11,160 \text{ (120)(93)}$$

Danger! This comparison is incomplete; initial costs, lamp life, mean footcandles, operating costs, maintenance costs, and many other considerations are omitted.

10. $7,741 per year.

$$(93)(120)(8,760 \text{ hr})(\$0.08) \div 1,000 \text{ W/kW}$$

Perception begins with light. Color, contrast, form, and pattern are names that describe reflected light, and design.

Lighting numbers can be interesting but they are not metrics for design or perception.

Footcandle Calculation   project

Fixture Information

Manufacturer - model #
_____

option(s) _____

lamp(s) _____
_____

Fixture Lumens
FL |_____

ballast _____

Room View

1, 2, 3

ceiling reflectance ⌐ |__ pc

ceiling cavity height

room cavity height

floor cavity height

average wall reflectance |__ pw

floor reflectance |__ pf

Room Plan & Fixture Layout

---

by _____ date _____

Room _____
dimensions _____ x ____
area _____ sqft.

Selected Fixture
lamp lumens _____
# of lamps _____
Fixture lumens _____
                        FL

1
cavity height & reflectance
ceiling ____' pc _____%
wall ____' pw _____%
floor ____' pf _____%

2
Cavity Ratio's
$CR = (5 hc)(L+W) \div (L \times W)$
ceiling ~ CCR _____
room ~ RCR _____
floor ~ FCR _____

3
effective ceiling cavity
reflectance ~ pcc _____

4
Coefficient of Utilization
_____ CU

5
Light Loss Factor _____
                         LLF

6
Footcandles required ____
                         FC

7
Number of Fixtures =

$(FC)(area) \div (FL)(CU)(LLF)$

_____

ELECTRICAL

ELECTRICAL TERMS

To work with the people who electrify your projects you should speak their language. Skim this list of terms before you begin Part 2 and review it after each chapter to build a language foundation that supports effective communication.

Ampere   Unit of electrical current (flow of electrons). A 1 volt force, acting in a circuit with a resistance of 1 ohm, produces a current of 1 ampere.

AC   Alternating current. Electrons flow forward, then backward to complete a cycle. In 60 cycle AC, electron flow direction reverses 120 times each second.

Alternator   A device that transforms mechanical energy into AC electrical energy.

Bus   A rectangular metal conductor used to carry large currents.

Capacitor   An assembly of layered conductors and insulators. After passing through a capacitor, AC amperes will lead volts.

Circuit   A closed loop that accommodates electron flow.

Circuit breaker   A switch that opens when current exceeds the breaker trip rating.

Coil   A conducting spiral. Coils or windings are found in motors, transformers, and magnetic ballasts.

Conductors   Materials like copper and aluminum that accommodate electron flow.

Conduit   A tube used to protect conductors.

Current   Number of electrons passing a point in one second, measured in amperes. One amp = 6.28×10^{18} electrons/second.

DC   Direct current. Electrons flow in one direction.

Delta   A three-phase service geometry.

Demand   Volt-amperes or kVA.

EMT   Electrical metallic tubing.

Feeders   Conductors that serve large electrical loads.

Generator   A device that transforms mechanical energy into DC electrical energy.

GFI   Ground fault interrupter. A circuit breaker that opens if circuit current varies.

Ground   Electrical connection to earth.

Hz   Frequency. AC cycles per second.

Inductive reactance   A characteristic of conducting coils or windings. After passing through a coil, AC amperes will lag volts.

Insulators   Materials like rubber and glass that resist electron flow.

kVA   Volt-amperes ÷ 1,000.

kW   Kilowatt (1,000 watts). Unit of electrical power.

kWh   Kilowatt hour. Unit of electrical work or energy.

Megawatt   1,000,000 watts.

NEC   National Electric Code of the National Fire Protection Agency (NFPA).

NEMA   National Electrical Manufacturers Association.

Ohm   Unit of electrical resistance. Tendency to resist current flow.

Ohm's law   Relation between ohms, amps, and volts. E = IR. Volts = (amps) (ohms).

Panel   An enclosure where electric power is allocated among individual circuits.

Parallel circuit   A circuit where equal voltage is applied to each electrical load.

Power   Watt or kW.

Resistance   Tendency to resist current flow.

Series circuit   A circuit where equal current flows through all electrical loads.

Service   The conductors and equipment that bring electrical power to a building.

Strip heat   Heat caused by current flow in nichrome wire.

Switchgear   Large electrical load centers that allocate power.

Transformer   A device used to exchange AC volts and amperes.

VA   Volt-ampere. Product of amps and volts.

Volt   Unit of electrical pressure or force. A force of 1 volt, acting in a circuit with a resistance of 1 ohm, causes a current of 1 ampere.

Voltage drop   Voltage lost to resistance, a problem when circuits serve distant loads.

Watt   Unit of electrical power. The rate at which work is done or energy is expended. One watt = 1/746 horsepower.

Winding   A series of conducting loops. Windings or coils are found in motors, transformers, and magnetic ballasts.

Wye   A balanced three-phase service geometry.

CHAPTER

8

Electrical Basics

Electricity seems destined to play a most important part in the arts and industries. The question of its economical application to some purposes is still unsettled, but experiment has already proved that it will propel a street car better than a gas jet and give more light than a horse.

Ambrose Bierce, 1906

Electrical distribution lines and equipment are essential building subsystems. Design and construction professionals study these electrical components so they can make competent judgments about:

- ◆ Lighting and power requirements
- ◆ Space required for switchgear and transformers
- ◆ Optimum location for major components
- ◆ Space required for horizontal and vertical distribution
- ◆ Construction and operating costs
- ◆ Occupant safety

Build your understanding of this short chapter by completing the ending sample problems and reviewing the preceding list of terms.

8.0 ELECTRICITY AND MAGNETISM

ELECTRICITY

Electricity is the flow of electrons in a given direction. Previous courses described matter as atoms consisting of a nucleus surrounded by orbiting electrons. Electrons orbit in a series of "shells" at increasing distances from the nucleus. Outermost shell electrons flow in electrical circuits.

Atoms of many metals hold their outermost shell electrons "loosely." These metals are called *conductors* because a small energy input will cause their electrons to flow from one atom to another. Silver, copper, gold, and aluminum are all good electrical conductors. Other materials such as rubber, glass, wood, air, and most plastics resist electron flow and are called *insulators*.

Circuits

An electrical circuit is a loop designed to accommodate electron flow. The loop consists of a conductor which extends from an electron source, to an electrical device, and back to the electron source. Electrons will not flow without a complete circuit that begins and ends at the source of electrical energy. *Parallel* circuits are used in most building applications while *series* circuits are used extensively in electronics (see Figure 8.1).

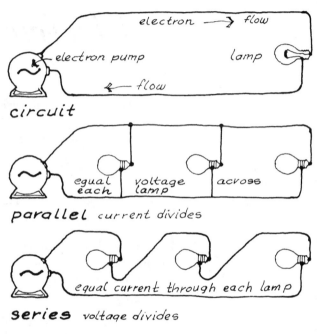

FIGURE 8.1

MAGNETISM

Magnetism and electricity are related phenomena. A magnetic field is an area of electrical influence and a flow of electrons can create a magnetic field.

Magnets are surrounded by force fields called *magnetic flux*. The strength or intensity of a magnetic field is called *flux density*. When a conductor moves through a magnetic field an electrical force is generated. If the conductor is looped to form a circuit, electrons will flow around the loop (see Figure 8.2).

A moving electric field creates a magnetic field, and a moving magnetic field creates an electric field. Because of the relationship between electricity and magnetism, a magnetic field forms around conductors carrying electrical energy. The *left-hand rule* describes this magnetic field based on the direction of electron flow. If a conductor is grasped by the left hand with the thumb pointing in the direction of electron flow, the fingers describe the magnetic field's flux from north to south (see Figure 8.3).

Electromagnets can be made by forming conductors in a coil shape. When electric current flows each coil loop adds to the magnetic field producing the same effect as a natural magnet. An iron bar centered in the coil will increase magnetic flux (see Figure 8.4).

circuit + motion in field = current

FIGURE 8.2

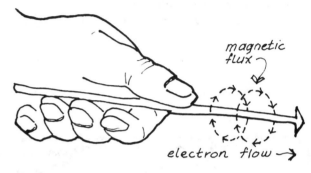

FIGURE 8.3

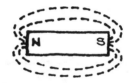 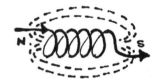

FIGURE 8.4

8.1 ELECTRICAL UNITS

The electromotive force or pressure that causes electron flow is measured in **volts** and the quantity of electrons flowing is measured in **amperes.** Even good conductors like copper wire offer some resistance to electron flow. Electrical resistance is measured in **ohms.** One ampere is defined as the quantity of electrons that will flow through a resistance of 1 ohm when pushed with a pressure of 1 volt. Electrical power is measured in **watts.** An electrical current of 1 ampere pushed by a force of 1 volt is defined as 1 watt.

The analogy of water flow in a pipe may help you visualize electrical terms (see Figure 8.5). The force or pressure pushing water through a pipe is measured in pounds per square inch and is analogous to electrical volts. The quantity of water flowing in a pipe is measured in gallons per minute and is analogous to amperes. Rough pipe offers more resistance to water flow than smooth pipe. In a water supply system this resistance is called *pipe friction* and it is measured as pressure drop when water flows. Similarly, the voltage in an electrical circuit drops when electrons flow. The resistance of electrical conductors causes this voltage drop.

Power required to pump water can be quantified in horsepower. Electrical power is measured in watts—actually thousands of watts or kilowatts.

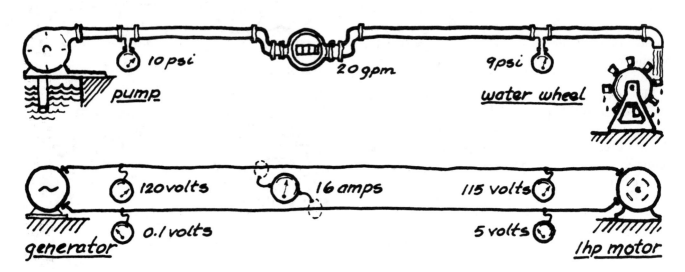

FIGURE 8.5

8.2 CALCULATIONS AND EXAMPLES

RELATIONSHIPS

Electrical calculations use **E** (electromotive force) for voltage, **I** (intensity) for current in amperes, and **R** for resistance in ohms. Three formulas relate these electrical terms.

$$E = IR \qquad \text{volts} = (\text{amps})(\text{ohms})$$

defines the relative magnitude of electrical pressure in volts, current in amperes, and resistance in ohms. This formula is called Ohm's law (for Georg Simon Ohm, 1787–1854) and is useful for calculating voltage drop in long electrical circuits.

Electrical power is measured in **watts** (honoring James Watt, 1736–1819). Increasing flow or pressure in a water system requires an increase in pump power, and increasing current or voltage in an electrical circuit requires an increase in electrical power.

The power formulas:

$$EI = W \qquad (\text{volts})(\text{amps}) = \text{watts}$$

or

$$I^2R = W \qquad (\text{amps})^2(\text{ohms}) = \text{watts}$$

relate volts, amperes, ohms, and power (see Figure 8.6).

CALCULATION EXAMPLES

Most building electrical calculations solve for *current* or *voltage drop*. Current sets conductor size, and excess voltage drop may require an increase in conductor size. The following examples are typical of the electrical math that will be applied later in the text to size building electrical circuits and services.

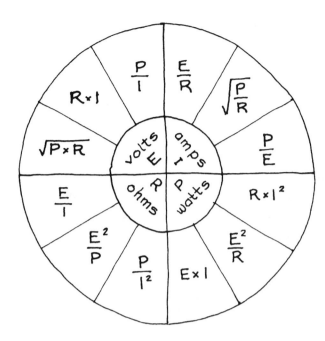

12 variations of 3 formulas

FIGURE 8.6

Example 1

A light bulb is rated at 100 watts. Find the current flow if the bulb operates at 120 volts.

$$EI = W$$
$$(120)(I) = 100 \qquad I = 0.83 \text{ ampere}$$

Example 2

Find the resistance of the light bulb.

$$E = IR$$
$$(120) = (0.83)(R) \qquad R = 144 \text{ ohms}$$

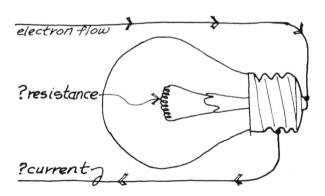

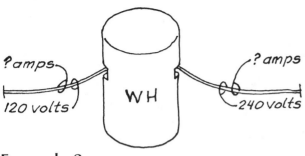

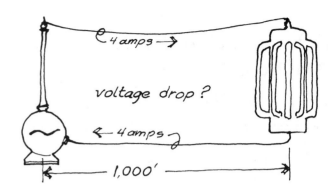

Example 3

A water heater is rated at 4,500 watts. Find the current required at 120 volts, and at 240 volts.

EI = W
(120)(I) = 4,500   I = 37.5 amps
EI = W
(240)(I) = 4,500   I = 18.8 amps

Increased voltage means reduced current and smaller conductors.

voltage drop if a circuit run totals 2,000 feet from the source to the load and back to the source.

total ohms for 2,000 feet = 6

E = IR
E = (4)(6)   E = 24 volts drop

Low voltage can cause motor overloads and light dimming. Voltage drop is a design concern when electrical devices are located more than 100 feet distant from the electrical service entry.

Example 4

The total connected electrical load for all the lights and kilns in a small pottery studio is 125 kW. Find the current required for the studio's electrical service at 240 volts.

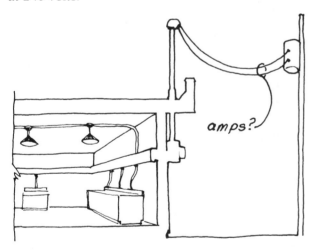

(1 kW = 1,000 watts)
EI = W
(240)(I) = 125,000   I = 521 amps

Example 6

A conductor has a resistance of 20 ohms per 1,000 feet of length. The conductor serves a lamp 200 feet from the power source. If the lamp has a resistance of 72 ohms and source voltage is 120, find voltage drop across the light bulb.

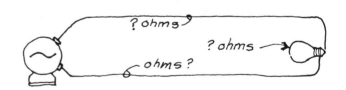

First find total circuit ohms:
The 200-foot circuit loop includes 4 ohms for supply run, 4 more ohms for return run, and 72 ohms for the lamp.

4 + 72 + 4   R = 80 ohms

Example 5

A current of 4 amperes is flowing in a conductor that has a resistance of 3 ohms per 1,000 feet. Find the

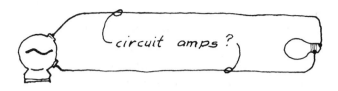

Next find circuit current.

E = IR

120 = (I)(80)   I = 1.5 amps

Current is constant throughout the circuit; voltage drops in proportion to resistance.

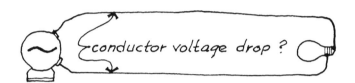

Next find the voltage drop through the circuit conductors.

E = IR

E = (1.5)(4+4)   E = 12 volts drop

These 12 volts were spent overcoming conductor resistance.

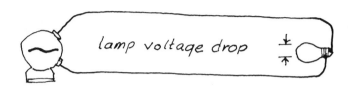

Finally find the actual voltage drop across the lamp.

E = IR

E = (1.5)(72)   E = 108 volts

Light output will be reduced because conductor resistance cuts lamp voltage.

REVIEW QUESTIONS

1. A 115 volt fluorescent lamp is rated at 0.43 amps (430 milliamperes). Find the watts that will be consumed by the lamp and its ballast (*115 volts is specified instead of 120 volts to allow for circuit voltage drop*).

2. Consider 100 watt and 300 watt lamps. Which has the most resistance (ohms)? (*Try to pick the correct answer without referring to the formulas in Figure 8.7.*)

3. Find total current (amperes) for a home with a 230 volt electrical service, if the estimated maximum electrical load from all lights and appliances is 21,000 watts.

4. Find the amperes drawn by a 12 kW range at 230 volts.

5. An outdoor lamp is rated 250 watts at 130 volts. Find the actual voltage across the lamp if it is connected to a 115 volt circuit serving the lamp 500 feet distant from the electrical service. Circuit conductor resistance is 3 ohms per 1,000 feet.

6. Calculate the actual operating watts for the lamp in question 5. How will actual watts affect light output and lamp life?

7. One value is a constant for the lamp in question 5. Which one?

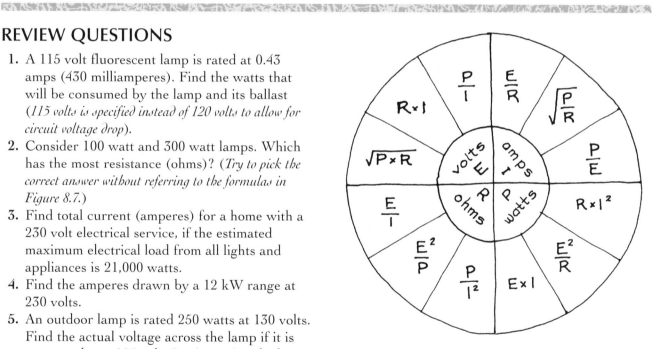

FIGURE 8.7

ANSWERS

1. 49 watts (*actually a bit less because of ballast characteristics, details follow*)
2. 100 watt
3. 91 amps (*nearest standard size is 100 amps*)
4. 52 amps (*1 kW = 1,000 watts*)
5. 110.1 volts
6. 178 watts, less light, longer life. *Conductor voltage drop is 4.9 so actual lamp watts is (110.1) (1.62) = 179 circuit amps @ 115 V = 1.62.*
7. Is the value amps, ohms, volts, or watts?

CHAPTER 9

Generation and Distribution

Work is of two kinds: first altering the position of matter at or near the earth's surface relatively to other such matter; second telling other people to do so. The first kind is unpleasant and ill paid; the second is pleasant and highly paid.

Bertrand Russell, 1935

⸻ ⬦ ⸻

This chapter describes the production and distribution of electrical energy. It introduces terms and concepts that influence the costs of electrical systems and the cost of electricity. These costs are substantial components of building construction and operating budgets.

Read and reread until you're comfortable explaining:

- Why demand and consumption set energy prices for commercial buildings
- Why transformers reduce AC distribution costs
- Why most electrical installations are grounded

Review the terms introduced earlier in the text to support your new vocabulary and work the ending review problems.

⸻ ⬦ ⸻

9.0 DEMAND AND CONSUMPTION

POWER, WORK, AND ENERGY

Power is the rate at which work is done. It may be measured in kilowatts (kW) or horsepower (hp). A kilowatt is a rate of 1,000 joules per second and a horsepower is a rate of 746 joules per second or 550 footpounds per second.

Work is defined as power multiplied by time, or force multiplied by distance. Work is measured in units of power and time; two common measurement units are the kilowatt-hour (kWh) and the horsepower-hour (hph).

Energy can be defined as the ability to do work. "Energy" and "work" are often used interchangeably. However, the word *energy* is also used to describe the heat content of fuels.

DEMAND AND CONSUMPTION

Electric utilities charge commercial customers for both power demand and energy consumption (see Figure 9.1). Power *demand* charges are based on the largest kW load connected during any 15-minute time period. Demand costs can be most of the utility bill for churches or theaters that require large quantities of power for short periods of time. Control systems that limit demand by sequencing electrical loads can reduce demand costs for commercial buildings.

Homes are not metered for demand. Utilities bill energy *consumption* in kWh, using different rate schedules for residential and commercial customers. Utility rate schedules vary remarkably; *don't* attempt to estimate electrical energy costs without an accurate rate schedule.

ELECTRICAL CURRENT, DC OR AC

Electron flow can be caused by batteries or generators. Batteries convert chemical energy to electrical energy and cause external electron flow in one direction—from the negative battery terminal to the positive battery terminal. This flow is called *direct current* (DC). Batteries are used in buildings for emergency

lighting and in some cases for emergency power, computer power, and phones.

Generators use conductors, magnetic flux, and motion to convert mechanical energy into electrical energy. Generators may be designed to deliver DC like a battery, or *alternating current* (AC) where electron flow reverses direction at regular intervals (see Figure 9.2).*

Electric utilities produce AC power because AC can be distributed at high voltage, minimizing line losses, and then easily transformed to safer low voltages suitable for building use.

---

*The correct name for a device that produces AC current is "alternator," but "generator" is widely misused to describe a mechanical device that causes electron flow.

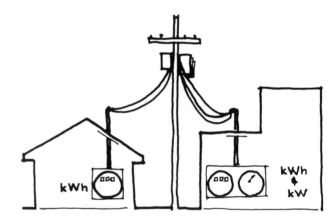

FIGURE 9.1

FIGURE 9.2

9.1 GENERATING EFFICIENCY

ELECTRICAL GENERATION

Utilities use falling water or burning fuel to turn generators. About 10% of U.S. energy is obtained from hydroelectric sources; fossil fuels or nuclear fission reactors account for the remaining 90%. Heat from fuel or nuclear sources is used to turn turbines that drive generators.

The bar graph in Figure 9.3 estimates 2,000 U.S. electrical energy sources. The fuel energy used to produce electricity is nearly equal to the fuel energy used for transportation.

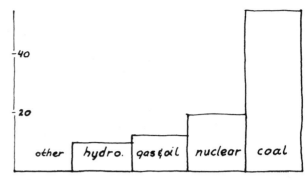

FIGURE 9.3

GENERATING EFFICIENCY

The second law of thermodynamics limits the theoretical efficiency of steam turbine-driven generators to about 60%, and actual industry experience is near 35%.* A typical electric utility converts 10 units of fuel energy into 3.5 units of electrical energy and 6.5 units of waste heat (see Figure 9.4). Nuclear plants are less efficient than fossil fuel plants because they operate with reduced steam temperature.

Although the average thermal efficiency of an electrical generating plant is not nearly as good as an industrial or residential furnace, it is much better than the typical new car.

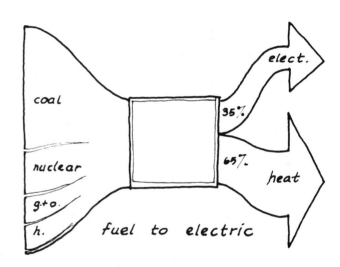

FIGURE 9.4

COGENERATION

Cogeneration and *total energy* are terms used to describe private power producers that conserve fuel by improved utilization of excess heat or generating capacity. Cogeneration describes a power producer that sells surplus heat or electricity to a utility. Total energy usually refers to an on site generating plant that uses waste heat for building heating, water heating, and refrigeration (see Figure 9.5).

---

* Dual cycle generating plants can approach 50% efficiency. They drive one generator with a gas turbine, and a second with steam produced by turbine exhaust.

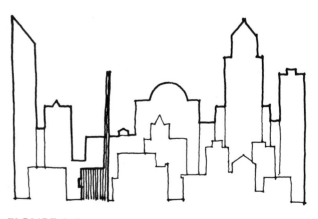

FIGURE 9.5

9.2 ALTERNATING CURRENT AC GENERATORS (*ALTERNATORS*)

Generators convert mechanical energy to electrical energy by rotating a magnetic field in a circle of conductors (see Figure 9.6). Voltage is generated when magnetic flux moves through a conductor, and if the conductor is connected to a circuit, current will flow.

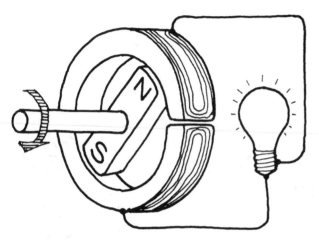

FIGURE 9.6

Utilities in North America use steam-, gas-, or water-driven turbines to generate electric power. Generator drives rotate 60 times each second causing electron flow to change direction or "alternate" 120 times each second. The resulting electrical power is called 60 cycle or 60 hertz alternating current (60 Hz AC).*

When reviewing Figure 9.7 assume a generator uses rotating conductors ** in a stationary magnetic field to cause electron flow. As conductors rotate, their motion relative to the magnetic field is constantly changing. As the conductors cut through more magnetic flux, more voltage is generated and more current flows. The direction of current flow will reverse when the direction of conductor motion in the magnetic field reverses during each revolution.

---

*50 Hz AC is used in Europe and 400 Hz AC is used for some aviation applications.

**As shown in Figure 9-6, the magnetic field rotates and conductors are stationary.

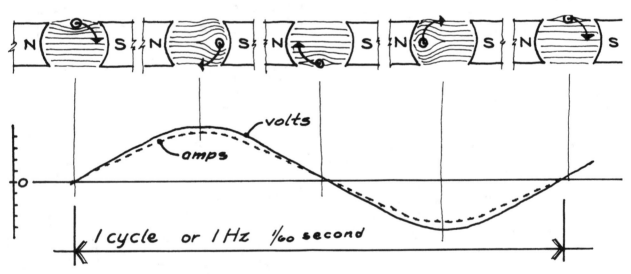

FIGURE 9.7

9.3 SINGLE-PHASE AND THREE-PHASE POWER

High-voltage transmission lines use three conductors (or multiples of three). Utilities generate three-phase power. Their generators cause simultaneous current flow between three separate conductors. At one instant, electrons may be flowing from the power plant in one conductor while they flow back toward the plant in the other two. An instant later the direction and quantity of electron flow will change. Three-phase current and voltage peaks are offset 120 degrees between the three phases, and utilities connect their distribution systems so that nearly equal electrical loads are connected between all three phases. Equalizing connected loads means the energy produced by generators will be used in a complete or *balanced* way.

Residential neighborhoods usually have single-phase power which reduces the number of utility distribution lines needed to serve homes (see Figure 9.8). Utilities designate individual phases A, B, and C. If one neighborhood is served by A and B, the next will be connected across B and C, and the next to C and A so that the total load is balanced for each phase.

Commercial and industrial electrical customers use three-phase power to carry motor loads (see Figure 9.9). Motors are generators operating in reverse. Three-phase motors are more efficient than single-phase motors. Motors larger than 5 horsepower are usually three-phase and where three-phase power is available, motors larger than 1/2 horsepower should be three-phase (see Figure 9.10).

Power in a three-phase electrical system is carried by three conductors. The basic power equation must be modified to account for current flow between these conductors where current peaks are staggered by 120 degrees. With three-phase power:

$$EI\sqrt{3} = W \qquad (volts)(amps)(\sqrt{3}) = watts$$

replaces the single-phase equation $EI = W$. *$\sqrt{3}$ or 1.73 is the cosine of 120° and accounts for the power vectors between three-phase conductors.*

Example Calculations

1. A single-phase, 120 volt electric device requires 20 kW. Find full load current.

$$EI = W$$
$$(120)(I) = 20,000 \qquad I = 167 \text{ amps}$$

167 amps flow in *both* the hot and the neutral conductors.

2. A single-phase, 240 volt electric device requires 20 kW. Find full load current.

$$EI = \backslash W$$
$$(240)(I) = 20,000 \qquad I = 83.3 \text{ amps}$$

83.3 amps will flow in each of *two* hot conductors. This is *not* two-phase.

3. A three-phase, 240 volt electric device requires 20 kW. Find full load current.

$$EI\sqrt{3} = W$$
$$(240)(I)(1.73) = 20,000 \qquad I = 48.2 \text{ amps}$$

48.2 amps flow in each of three hot wires. Three conductors carrying 48 amps use less copper than two conductors carrying 83 amps.

4. A three-phase, 480 volt electric device requires 20 kW. Find full load current.

$$EI\sqrt{3} = W$$
$$(480)(I)(1.73) = 20,000 \qquad I = 24.1 \text{ amps}$$

24.1 amps flow in each of three hot wires — much less copper.

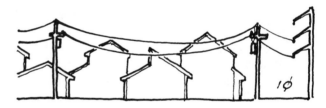

FIGURE 9.8

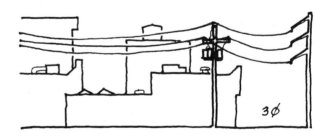

FIGURE 9.9

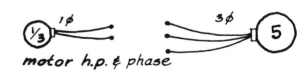

FIGURE 9.10

9.4 TRANSFORMERS
POWER DISTRIBUTION

AC is the power of choice for utilities because it can be transmitted over fairly long distances without excessive distribution losses, and then transformed to lower voltage at the customer's service entry. Very high voltages (up to 500,000 volts) are used on major distribution lines because for a given electrical load more voltage means less current. Reducing current flow reduces transmission losses. The insulators on electrical distribution lines indicate line voltage. Larger insulators are used for higher voltages.

TRANSFORMERS

Transformers permit power distribution at high voltage (minimizing line losses) and deliver a variety of lower voltages for building services. Residential customers may take 240 volts while a commercial building nearby gets 480 volts. A large industrial plant may be served at 13,200 volts. Transformers let utilities serve many customers with differing electrical requirements using a single distribution network.

A transformer is a unique and efficient device without moving parts that trades AC voltage for current. Transformers include an iron core surrounded by two circuit loops called *windings*. One winding is connected to a power supply circuit and the second is connected to building service circuits. *Primary* is the term for the high-voltage or input transformer winding. *Secondary* refers to the low-voltage or output winding.

AC current flow in the transformer primary windings creates a magnetic field which expands and contracts with changing current intensity and direction. This pulsating magnetic field induces current flow in the transformer secondary. Transformers change high-voltage primary power into low-voltage secondary power. Transformer capacity is rated in **kVA** and the reduction of secondary voltage is proportional to the ratio of winding turns from the primary to the secondary side of the transformer.

Example Calculations

1. Find the transformer capacity, and the secondary voltage and current for a residential single-phase (1ø) transformer. Primary power is 13,200 volts at 1.9 amperes, and the ratio of winding turns is 55 to 1 (see Figure 9.11). Transformer capacity in kVA is:

   (volts)(amps) ÷ 1,000
   (13,200)(1.9) = 25,080   or 25 kVA

   Transformer capacity and building service capacity are typically stated in thousands of volt-amperes (kVA) instead of kilowatts (kW) because of power factor considerations.

   Secondary voltage will be 1/55 of the primary voltage because the winding ratio is 55 to 1.

   13,200 ÷ 55 = 240   240 volts

   Secondary current will be 55 times the primary current of 1.9 amperes.

   (55)(1.9) = 104.5   or 100+ amperes

2. Find the three-phase (3ø) transformer capacity required to serve a 60 ampere, 480 volt commercial building load.
   Transformer capacity in kVA is:

   (volts)(amps)($\sqrt{3}$) ÷ 1,000
   (480)(60)($\sqrt{3}$) ÷ 1,000 = 49.8   or 50 kVA

   Utilities frequently use three single-phase transformers instead of a three-phase transformer.
   Large industrial customers can reduce utility costs by building their own electrical distribution network and buying power at 5,000 to 15,000 volts.

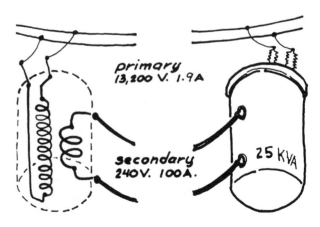

FIGURE 9.11

9.5 POWER FACTOR

POWER FACTOR

Transformers, motors, and ballasts include windings, and all windings have a property called *inductance* which is a tendency to oppose changes in circuit current. *Inductive reactance** is a term describing this tendency to resist changes in current flow. Inductive reactance is a characteristic of windings in AC circuits. Its result is delayed current flow so that current peaks occur after voltage peaks. Lagging current means lower metered kWh and less income for utilities.

Power factor is a number index used to quantify lagging current (see Figure 9.12). A building with no motors or coils will have a power factor of 1.0 (no lag), but buildings with substantial motor loads and/or ballasted lighting loads will have a power factor of less than 1.

The calculation of real power for a building is given by the equations:

$$(amps)(volts)(PF) = Watts$$

for a single-phase service or

$$(amps)(volts)(\sqrt{3})(PF) = Watts$$

for a three-phase service.

Buildings with low power factors use electrical energy less efficiently than similar buildings with power factors near 1, and utilities require capacitors or apply a rate surcharge to low PF buildings. Capacitors improve power factor by causing current peaks to lead voltage peaks.

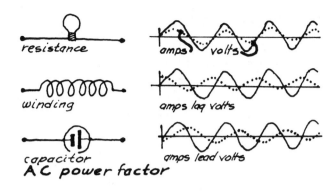

FIGURE 9.12

Example Calculations

1. Calculate the power factor for a building if the connected electrical loads are:

   ◆ 40% resistive loads including water heaters, incandescent lights, and electric heaters with a PF of 1.0
   ◆ 40% fluorescent lighting with a PF of 0.6*
   ◆ 20% electric motors with a PF of 0.8*

   Power factor is the weighted average of all electrical loads.

   $$(0.4)(1) + (0.4)(0.6) + (0.2)(0.8) = PF \quad PF \; 0.8$$

2. If the building in example 1 has a 480 volt three-phase service rated at 600 amperes find the maximum value for *apparent power* (kVA) and *real power* (kW).

   Apparent power is $(A)(V)(\sqrt{3}) \div 1,000$
   $$(600)(480)(\sqrt{3}) \div 1,000 = 498 \; kVA$$
   Real power is $(A)(V)(\sqrt{3})(PF) \div 1,000$
   $$(600)(480)(\sqrt{3})(0.8) \div 1,000 = 399 \; kW$$

---

* Inductive reactance is a characteristic of coils or windings in AC circuits. Capacitive reactance is a characteristic of capacitors in AC circuits.

The general term *inductance* is used to describe the combined effect of resistance, inductive reactance, and capacitive reactance in a circuit.

---

*Manufacturers will provide power factors for their motors or ballasts.

GROUNDING

Grounded means connected to earth. Electrical systems are grounded to dissipate fault currents caused by lightning or equipment failure. A grounded *neutral* conductor is used in most building electrical installations to complete single-pole circuits, and to set a zero potential for safety and reference. The ground connection can be made to underground metal piping or a copper-coated steel rod driven into the earth.

Circuits may be described as loops from a generator to an electrical device and *back to the generator.* Utilities save money by using the earth instead of a conductor to provide a current return path for unbalanced loads (see Figure 9.13).

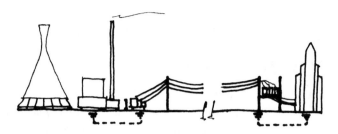

FIGURE 9.13

REVIEW QUESTIONS

1. A home has a single-phase, 240 volt, 150 ampere service. Find the transformer size needed to serve this home.
2. A commercial building has a three-phase, 480 volt, 600 ampere service. Find the required transformer size.
3. A commercial building has a total connected load of 500 kVA. Find the building power factor if the ballasted lighting load of 200 kVA has a power factor of 0.8, and the 150 kVA motor load has a power factor of 0.9. The remaining 150 kVA is resistance load with a power factor of 1.
4. Find the apparent power (kVA) and the real power (kW) for the building in question 3.
5. Find the current required for a 1,000 kVA load at 240 volts, 1ø.
6. Find the current required for a 1,000 kVA load at 240 volts, 3ø.
7. Find the current required for a 1,000 kVA load at 13,200 volts, 3ø.

Add these formulas (see Figure 9.14):

Apparent Power

(amps)(volts) = VA (volt-amperes)

(amps)(volts) ÷ 1,000 = kVA

(amps)(volts)($\sqrt{3}$) ÷ 1,000 = kVA (three-phase)

Real Power

(amps)(volts) = watts (resistive loads)

(amps)(volts)(PF) = watts (inductive loads)

(amps)(volts)($\sqrt{3}$)(PF) = watts (three-phase)

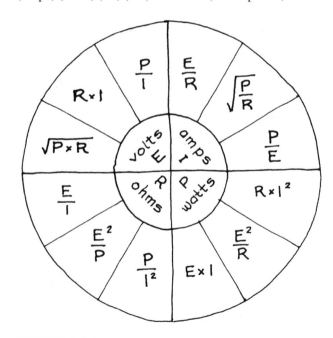

FIGURE 9.14

ANSWERS

1. 36 kVA, 1ø

   Utilities don't size residential transformers for peak demand. They use a diversity factor and allow 5 to 8 kVA per home in residential subdivisions.

2. 500 kVA, 3ø (actually 498.8)

   Utilities size commercial customer transformers to suit building peak demand.

3. 0.89

   $[(200)(0.8) + (150)(0.9) + 150] \div 500 = 0.89$

4. apparent power = 500 kVA

   real power = 445 kW

   $(200)(0.8) + (150)(0.9) + 150 = 445$

5. 4,167 amperes

6. 2,408 amperes

7. 44 amperes

Ending note: Some utilities use high-voltage DC distribution lines because DC line losses are less than AC.

CHAPTER 10

Residential Electrical

*A prophet is not without honor except in his own country, and among his own
people, and in his own house.*

Mark 6:4

—⊷⊶—

This chapter describes residential electrical systems. It begins
with a wall outlet and traces the wires and devices that connect
the outlet to the home's electrical service. Then lighting circuits,
dedicated circuits, and 240 volt circuits are described. Finally,
circuit protection, the electrical panel, and a service calculation
method are explained.

A competent electrician can wire a new home in two long
days, one before and one after wallboard. Allow 6 to 8% of the
total construction budget for electrical work, and plan to spend
more if the owner selects light fixtures. A service calculation
form, and an electrical plan for the example home follow the text.

After reading this chapter you should be able to name,
describe, and select the components of a residential electrical
system. Develop an electrical plan, create a panel schedule, and
then size the service for a house of your choice using the
Residential Service Calculation form. Then review the terms
introduced earlier in the text to support new vocabulary and
complete the ending review problems to verify your abilities.

—⊷⊶—

10.0 DUPLEX OUTLETS
RESIDENTIAL ELECTRICAL

The starting point for this description is a wall outlet that can serve one or two appliances. It is called a *duplex outlet* or a *duplex receptacle*. Follow the electrical components and materials connecting this outlet to the home's electrical service and then add lights, motors, and other electrical devices. A residential service is covered here, but many components and details are also used in commercial buildings.

In North America 120 volt AC power is provided at duplex outlets. Because of voltage drop in home wiring, appliances are usually rated 115 volts (see Figure 10.1). Alternating current (AC) means the direction of electron flow cycles 60 times every second and the power supply is described as 60 cycle AC current or 60 Hz AC.

The three plug blades shown in Figure 10.2 function as follows:

Hot

The hot blade is connected to a *black* conductor carrying 115–120 volt power. Electrons flow from the hot wire through appliances, and voltage drops as electrical energy does work or creates music. The hot conductor insulation is black to identify it as a wire carrying significant voltage.*

Neutral

The neutral blade is connected to a *white* conductor which provides a complete circuit for electron flow. Current is equal in the hot and neutral wires, but voltage in the neutral is minimal—just enough to overcome the resistance of the wire and complete the electrical circuit.

The hot and neutral openings in a duplex outlet differ in size to maintain *polarity* and minimize shock hazard. Hot is the smaller opening (see Figure 10.3). Polarity ensures that only the insulated components of an appliance receive higher voltage. The metal frame of an appliance is connected to the neutral conductor. Before approving an electrical installation, inspectors should check each outlet to verify polarity.

---

*In three-phase commercial installations additional hot conductors will have red or blue insulation.

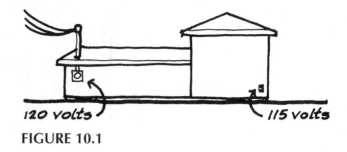

FIGURE 10.1

120 volts   115 volts

neutral   green - ground   neutral   hot   hot

FIGURE 10.2

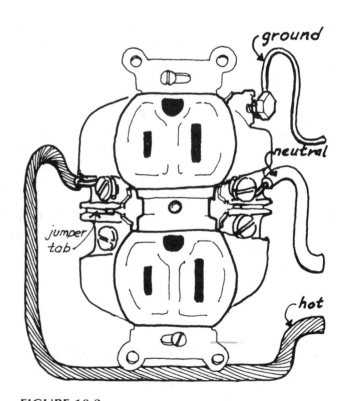

ground   neutral   jumper tab   hot

FIGURE 10.3

Ground

The ground opening in a duplex outlet is connected to a ground conductor. In residential applications the ground conductor is usually an uninsulated wire that provides an extra safe route for fault current. It duplicates the neutral wire throughout the residence, but while the neutral carries electric current to complete a circuit the ground wire carries current *only* in the event of an electrical fault (see Figure 10.3).

Faults may result from worn insulation, loose connections, wet connections, a broken neutral, or inoperative circuit protectors. A very small current flow through the human body can cause death and the ground conductor provides an alternate route for fault current. In commercial applications ground wires may be bare or insulated and color coded green.

VARIATIONS

By breaking off a small jumper, duplex outlets can be wired so separate conductors serve the top and bottom outlet positions. This feature allows two circuits to serve a kitchen appliance outlet, or a wall switch can control a table lamp. Some low-bid home builders provide switched duplex outlets for most rooms and charge extra for built-in wall or ceiling light fixtures.

INSTALLATION

Conductor connections to the terminals of a duplex receptacle are made by stripping insulation and then twisting the conductor around a screw or pushing the conductor into a spring-loaded slot.* Gold tint terminals are reserved for black hot wires, silver tint terminals for white neutral wires, and a green terminal for ground wires (see Figure 10.4).

---

*Wiring to push in spring terminals is forbidden by some local codes.

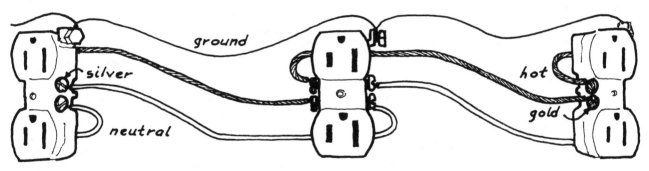

FIGURE 10.4

10.1 CONDUCTORS AND HARDWARE

Copper has less resistance than aluminum, but aluminum conductors are stronger and lighter. Copper conductors are used for *all* duplex and lighting circuits because aluminum wiring tends to fault when thermal expansion and contraction loosen terminal connections.

Aluminum conductors are used for service wiring between the weatherhead and the utility transformer. The National Electrical Code® permits aluminum wiring when terminals are designed to ensure fault-free connections, but many local codes prohibit aluminum wiring in buildings.

CONDUCTOR SIZES

Insulation melting temperature sets the current limit for building wiring. Heat is created when electrical current flows through a conductor. In building wiring, excess heat can cause insulation melting, short circuits, and fire. For a given current, larger conductors will produce less heat.

The smallest conductor permitted in building electrical installations is #14. Its copper core is about a sixteenth of an inch in diameter and will carry 15 amperes safely. It is used for switches and for circuit wiring in many older homes, but slightly larger #12 wire—which will carry 20 amperes—is the preferred wire size for home duplex and lighting circuits. Notice that American Wire Gauge (AWG) conductor area increases as the gauge decreases (see Figure 10.5). A duplex circuit may use #12 wire while a water heater uses #10, and a range may need #6. The largest AWG gauge designation is #4/0. A copper #4/0 conductor can carry a current of more than 200 amperes. Even larger conductors are used in commercial buildings, but their sizes are designated in MCM (thousands of circular mills) instead of AWG.

Copper conductors are made from solid or stranded wire in gauges #14 through #6. Gauge #4 and larger wires are stranded. Aluminum conductors are available in the same gauges. They have less current-carrying capacity than copper but are usually less costly.

RESIDENTIAL WIRING

Only in residential occupancies, and *only* in concealed locations (inside a wall or ceiling) the National Electrical Code® permits the use of type NM wiring (see Figure 10.6). NM stands for the nonmetallic sheath that encloses and protects individual conductors. NM (or Romex) wiring offers low installed cost but it's difficult to add or change circuits after Romex is in place.

ROMEX

Romex is available in three sheath varieties. NM is used for most interior residential applications, NMC in wet or corrosive surroundings, and UF in underground installations. The outer sheath carries printed information about Romex type, number, size of conductors, and maximum allowable voltage. *UF 2#12 WG 600V* designates Romex intended for underground installation. It includes two size #12 wires (one with black insulation and one white) plus a bare #12 ground wire. The insulation is rated for use up to 600 volts.

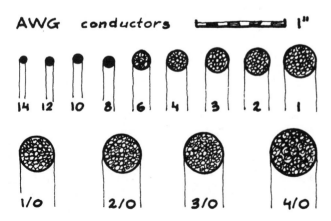

FIGURE 10.5

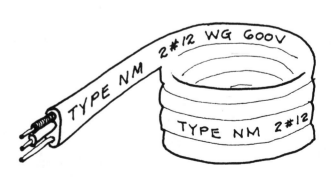

FIGURE 10.6

BOXES

Wiring connections for switches and receptacles are made in protective boxes to prevent contact between conductors and construction materials (see Figure 10.7). Steel and plastic boxes are available. They are secured to wood studs or ceiling joists with nails. When using plastic boxes the ground wire is connected to a green lug on the switch or receptacle frame. When steel boxes are used the ground wire may be connected to a screw terminal inside the box and the green lug on each device.

Boxes are also used to enclose and protect wiring connections. Junction boxes may be round, octagonal, square, or rectangular. Codes require boxes to be accessible when construction is complete. As the number of wires connected in a box increases, larger boxes are required (see Figure 10.8).

Romex conductors serving residential circuits are secured in boxes with internal clamp fittings, and the Romex is also fastened to wood studs or joists supporting the outlet box with a large staple. After several duplex outlets are interconnected, Romex is extended to the power panel where a circuit breaker protects the wiring from excess current.

In wood stud walls, Romex is run through holes drilled in the center of each stud. Good builders are careful to fit insulation around Romex wiring in exterior walls to minimize building heat loss. In attics, Romex is stapled to ceiling joists. Where people or stored items are likely, Romex home runs to the panel must be protected with a plywood cover.

CONDUIT REQUIRED

Romex can only be installed in concealed locations. When an electrical power supply must run outside a wall, floor, or ceiling the Romex is terminated in a box or switch, and conduit is installed to protect the exposed conductors.

Indoors a flexible armored conduit called BX can be used. Outdoors, liquid-tight flexible conduit or rigid metal conduit will be used. The next chapter covers conduit materials and installation.

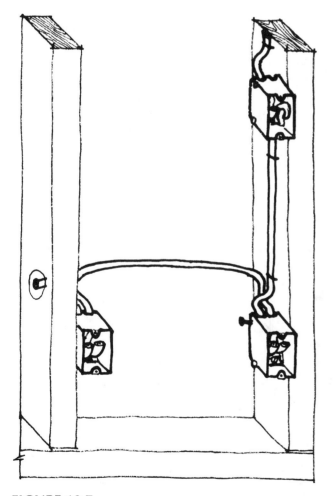

FIGURE 10.7

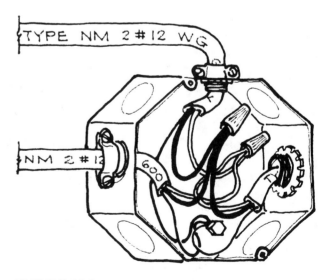

FIGURE 10.8

10.2 DUPLEX CIRCUITS AND THE PANEL

DUPLEX CIRCUITS

Many outlets can be connected on a single circuit by extending circuit wiring from one box to another. Each duplex outlet is counted as 180 watts (even though a single receptacle can supply a 1,500 watt hair dryer). In theory a 20 ampere circuit can serve 13 outlets (see Figure 10.9), but electrical inspectors in most localities limit 20 ampere circuits to eight outlets. Duplex outlets are located so that a six-foot-long cord can reach any point along every wall.

Dedicated Duplex Circuits

The National Electrical Code requires dedicated duplex circuits in residential construction. The kitchen must be served by at least two duplex circuits, and most localities require a third circuit serving only the refrigerator. These three circuits cannot serve a dishwasher, garbage disposal, or exhaust hood so it is easy to dedicate at least six or more circuits in the kitchen alone. The laundry must have a separate circuit for ironing, and custom homes frequently add dedicated circuits for personal computers, security systems, pool pumps, landscape lighting, and shop tools.

PANEL

Each residential circuit draws electrical current in a large metal box called a *panel* (see Figure 10.10). Panel components allocate current among individual circuits and each circuit is protected by a *circuit breaker* that opens when current exceeds the breaker rating. The entire panel is protected by a larger main circuit breaker.

Inside the panel *bus bars* facilitate connection of individual circuit breakers. A bus is a metal bar that carries current. Two hot wires from the utility transformer are connected through the main circuit breaker to two separate bus bars, and individual circuit breakers snap onto these busses. Circuit breakers serving a 120 volt circuit snap on one bus and protect one hot wire (see Figure 10.10); circuit breakers serving a 240 volt circuit snap on both busses and protect two hot wires.

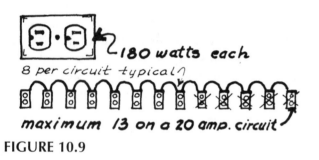

180 watts each

8 per circuit typical

maximum 13 on a 20 amp. circuit

FIGURE 10.9

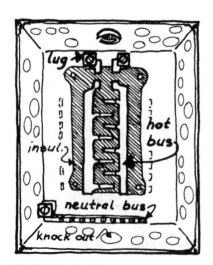
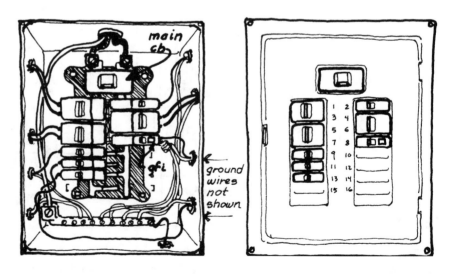

FIGURE 10.10

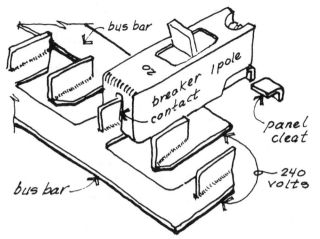

2 pole breaker contacts both bus bars

FIGURE 10.11

open the breaker. Thermal sensors use a bimetal element which opens when excess current causes a temperature rise. Magnetic sensors use an electromagnet to open when excess current increases flux. After a circuit breaker opens, a latch prevents it from closing as it cools or because of magnetic field collapse, breakers must be reset manually to resupply the protected circuit.

Residential circuit breakers are one- or two-pole design. One-pole circuit breakers have one hot wire connected and serve 120 volt circuits. Two-pole circuit breakers protect two hot wires and serve 240 volt circuits.

Neutral conductors are **never** connected to breakers because they must provide an uninterrupted path from electrical loads to the system ground. All circuit neutral wires are connected to a grounded neutral bus. The utility neutral and the system ground are also connected to this neutral bus. The system ground is usually a buried metal water pipe or a copper-coated steel rod driven into the ground near the meter. A bare #6 copper wire connects the system ground to the panel neutral bus.*

Circuit Breaker

A circuit breaker is a switch that opens to disconnect electrical power when it senses excess current (see Figure 10.12). Internal thermal *or* magnetic sensors

GFI

A special circuit breaker may be used in residential panels serving circuits in wet locations. *Ground fault interrupter* circuit breakers sense fault currents by comparing current in circuit hot and neutral wires (see Figure 10.13). If the currents are not equal the GFI opens very quickly to minimize shock hazard.

FIGURE 10.13

---

*Modern residential panels have separate neutral and ground busses. They are bonded in the main panel, but isolated in subpanels.

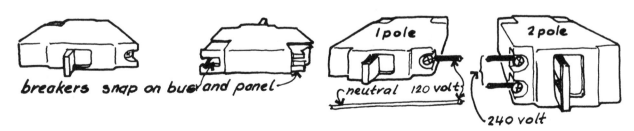

breakers snap on bus and panel

1 pole   neutral   120 volt

2 pole   240 volt

FIGURE 10.12

GFI breakers in the panel protect an entire circuit. GFI protection in an individual outlet will protect downstream outlets. Codes require GFI protection for outlets in bathrooms, garages, and exterior walls; for outlets near kitchen sinks; and for circuits serving swimming pools or hot tubs.

MCB

The panel is protected by a two-pole *main circuit breaker* which will cut off all electrical power in the event of a high current short (see Figure 10.14). Panels should be easily accessible for firefighters and cannot be located in closets, bathrooms, or wet locations.

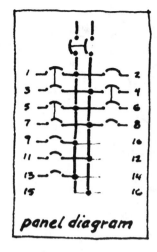

FIGURE 10.14

10.3 OTHER CIRCUITS

LIGHTING CIRCUITS

Commercial buildings separate lighting and duplex circuits, but in residential installations a single circuit can serve *both* duplex outlets and lighting fixtures. Lighting circuits add switches to control individual fixtures, and the NEC allows a maximum of 1,920* watts of lighting load on a 20 ampere 120 volt circuit.

Figures 10.15 and 10.16 show a typical lighting circuit switching connections for controlling lamps. Three-way switches control lights from two locations and should be installed at top and bottom stair landings. Economical dimmer switches are available for incandescent lamps, but dimming fluorescent lamps is usually too expensive for residential work.

Some light fixtures include boxes for making electrical connections and others are mounted on separate square, round, or octagon boxes.

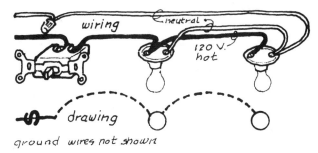

FIGURE 10.15

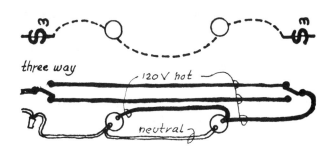

FIGURE 10.16

240 VOLT CIRCUITS

Electric water heaters, ranges, ovens, dryers, air conditioners, heat pumps, large motors, and resistance heat strips are usually served by separate 240 volt circuits. Motors must have flexible connections—cord, BX, or Greenfield indoors and Liquidtight outdoors. Required circuit ampacity is usually listed on the manufacturer's nameplate.

The 240 volt circuits are protected by two-pole circuit breakers that draw power from both panel busses. Two hot wires serve all 240 volt loads, and a neutral or ground wire is usually run on 240 volt circuits for safety should a fault occur.

Current requirements vary for individual appliance circuits. Different outlet configurations are provided to ensure safe connection (see Figure 10.17). Appliances without plugs are *hard wired*—that is, connected directly in a box. For safety a disconnect switch must be installed at strip heat units and central air conditioners or heat pumps when the electrical panel supplying them is not visible to repair personnel (see Figure 10.18).

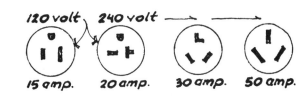

FIGURE 10.17

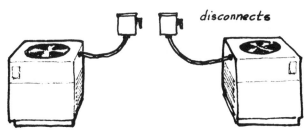

FIGURE 10.18

---

*1,920 watts is 80% of the theoretical circuit capacity.
(120 volts)(20 amps) = 2,400 watts. 80% of 2,400 = 1,920.

SERVICE

A residential *service* includes conductors, conduit, and accessories that connect the home to the utility transformer. The usual residential service is 120/240 volt, single-phase. The utility *service drop* includes two insulated (hot) wires and a bare neutral wire.

Before connecting electrical power to a new home the installation must be inspected and approved for code compliance. Usually the home builder purchases and installs a weatherhead, the meterbox, and all wire and conduit between the weatherhead and the building panel. For overhead services the utility provides conductors from their transformer to the weatherhead and a meter (see Figure 10.19). If an underground service is used the owner usually pays for trenching and underground cable. Removing a home meter disconnects power but exposes live sockets so a cover should be installed for safety whenever a meter is removed.

The service neutral can be smaller than the hot wires because the neutral carries only unbalanced current; 120 volt loads cause neutral current, but 240 volt loads do not. To calculate the maximum neutral current, total the watts *at 120 volts only* for each bus and divide the larger by 120. Service hot wires are sized to carry amperes equal to the main circuit breaker rating.

WEATHERHEAD

The weatherhead keeps rain and snow out of the service conduit. When an overhead service is used check local codes and the National Electrical Code for required clearances above grade, roofs, driveways, and roads (see Figure 10.20).

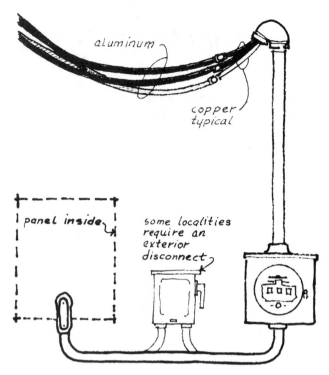

FIGURE 10.19

Service Conductor Amperes*

Amperes	Aluminum	Copper
100	#2*	#4
125	#1/0*	#2
150	#2/0*	#1
175	#3/0*	#1/0
200	#4/0*	#2/0

* Verify ampere capacity with the local code authority. Many local codes prohibit aluminum conductors indoors.

OTHER WIRING

Other home wiring serving TV or phones is run separately from AC power to minimize interference. TV uses a shielded coaxial cable, and phone uses a small four-conductor cable. Both are run unprotected in concealed locations like walls, floors, and ceilings.

Small transformers deliver the low-voltage power used for thermostats, doorbells, and security systems. Low-voltage control wiring can also be used to switch home lighting from many locations. Remote control lighting installations are expensive but they allow you to turn many house lights on from the garage and then turn them all off from your bedroom. Control wiring is usually run in walls, floors, or ceilings, without protection.

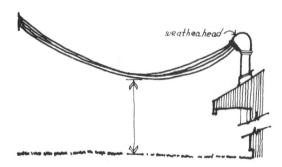

FIGURE 10.20

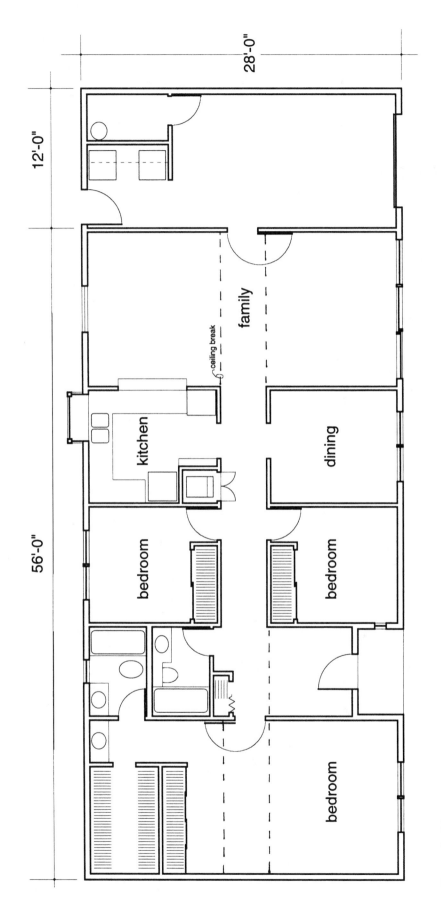

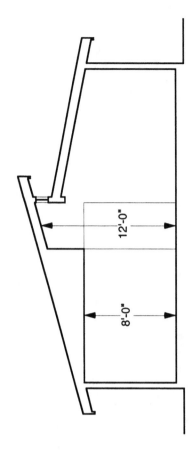

28'-0"

12'-0"

56'-0"

12'-0"

8'-0"

kitchen

family

ceiling break

dining

bedroom

bedroom

bedroom

Example House

The 1,568 square foot home shown here was used earlier in the text to illustrate lighting design. It's used again here to as a template for the electrical plan on the next page. The electrical plan will satisfy many local code authorities, but it's schematic because the lighting and duplex circuit runs are not detailed. If your city requires detailed circuiting examine the commercial electrical plans in Chapter 12.

Study the electrical plan and the panel schedule until you understand all the symbols and circuits and then check the service calculation that follows.

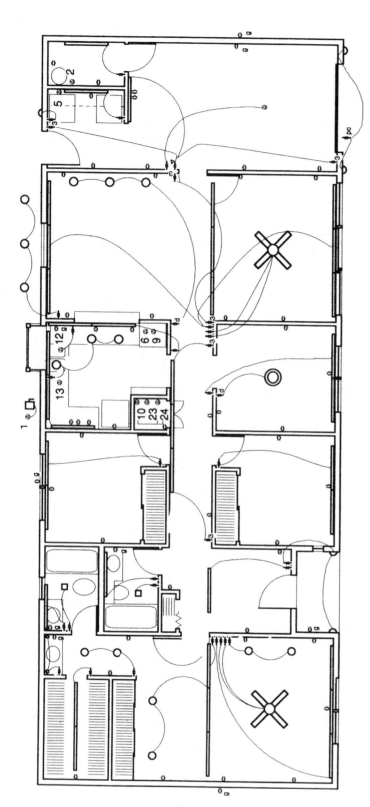

Electrical Plan

The plan shows all duplex outlets, light fixtures, and appliance circuits. Five duplex outlets marked "g" are GFI (ground fault interrupter) protected. The curved lines connecting switches and lights show which switch(s) controls which light(s). Circuits serving 240 volt and and/or hard wired appliances are numbered at their plan location. Each number corresponds to a panel pole, but only one number is used for 2 pole (240 volt) appliances.

Sizing the panel's 125 ampere main circuit breaker is explained on the following residential service calculation form.

Symbols

⊕ duplex outlet, count at 180 watts

⊚ 240 volt equipment OR hard wired equipment, # = circuit

$ switch, 3 = 3 way (2 locations), d = dimmer

Panel

125 Amp, Two-Pole Main Circuit Breaker

1 air conditioner	2 water heater
3 d.o.	4 d.o.
5 dryer	6 oven
7 d.o.	8 d.o.
9 rangetop	10 furnace fan
11 d.o.	12 garbage disp.
13 dishwasher	14 lighting & duplex
15 lighting & duplex	16 d.o.
17 d.o.	18 d.o.
19 d.o.	20 d.o.
21 d.o.	22 refrigerator
23 elect. heat	24 elect.heat
25 d.o.	26 d.o.
27 landscape ltg	28 28-30 spares

Residential Service Calculation

Residential services are not sized for total connected load—an experience-based diversity factor keeps service size below 200 amperes for all but estate size dwellings. Utility services larger than 200 amperes require current transformers and are usually metered as commercial customers. The 1987 NEC optional calculation 220-30 is the basis of this form.

NEC Calculation Requirements

- Lighting, allow 3 watts or VA per square foot 220-3b
- Provide a minimum of two kitchen appliance circuits—allow 1,500 watts or VA each—*these cannot serve exhaust hoods, dishwashers, disposers, or other outlets* 220-16
- Laundry circuit allow a minimum of 1,500 watts or VA 220-4c
- Clothes dryer allow 5,000 watts or VA or nameplate rating (use the larger value) 220-18

Appliance Loads *estimated watt or VA values*

nameplate values are better

attic fan 1/4 hp	700	dishwasher	1,200
disposer 1/2 hp	1,200	dryer	5,000
furnace fan 1/3 hp	900	fan 1/2 hp	1,200
oven	4,500	range	12,000
cook top	6,000	wash. machine	1,200
water heater	4,500	each duplex outlet	180

Air conditioning—allow 1,000 to 1,200 watts per ton

NEC 220-30 Calculation

Select the largest of heating or air-conditioning load weighted as follows:

- AC equipment including heat pumps at **100%** OR
- Central electric space heating including supplemental heat in heat pumps at **65%** OR
- Nameplate rating of electric space heating if less than four separately controlled units at **65%** OR
- Nameplate rating of four or more separately controlled electric space heating units at **40%**

Then ADD 100% of the first 10 kVA of other load and 40% of the remainder of all other load.

Worksheet	Total Watts or VA
Heating OR Cooling (VA)(%)	
Appliance circuits @ 1,500 each	
Laundry circuits @ 1,500 each	
Lighting (floor area)(3)	
Clothes dryer (5,000 or nameplate)	
Cooktop	
Oven(s)	
Range (nameplate)	
Dishwasher	
Exterior lighting	
Freezer	
Garbage disposal	
Landscape lighting	
Pool pump(s)	
Shop	
air compressor	
welder	
saw	
other major tools	
Spa	
Trash compactor	
Water heater	
Other electrical items	
Total watts or VA	

Calculate
first **10,000 VA @ 100%**   10,000
remaining VA **@ 40%**
Service calculation total VA

Minimum required service amperes is the calculated total VA (above) ÷ 240 volts = _____ **AMPERES**
Use next larger standard size—100, 125, 150, 175, or 200A

---

*NEC is a registered trademark of NFPA (National Fire Protection Association).

Residential Service Calculation

Residential services are not sized for total connected load—an experience-based diversity factor keeps service size below 200 amperes for all but estate size dwellings. Utility services larger than 200 amperes require current transformers and are usually metered as commercial customers. The 1987 NEC optional calculation 220-30 is the basis of this form.

NEC Calculation Requirements

• Lighting, allow 3 watts or VA per square foot 220-3b
• Provide a minimum of two kitchen appliance circuits—allow 1,500 watts or VA each—these cannot serve exhaust hoods, dishwashers, disposers, or other outlets 220-16
• Laundry circuit allow a minimum of 1,500 watts or VA 220-4c
• Clothes dryer allow 5,000 watts or VA or nameplate rating (use the larger value) 220-18

Appliance Loads estimated watt or VA values—nameplate values are better

attic fan 1/4 hp	700	dishwasher	1,200
disposer 1/2 hp	1,200	dryer	5,000
furnace fan 1/3 hp	900	fan 1/2 hp	1,200
oven	4,500	range	12,000
cook top	6,000	wash. machine	1,200
water heater	4,500	each duplex outlet	180

Air conditioning—allow 1,000 to 1,200 watts per ton

NEC 220-30 Calculation

Select the largest of heating or air-conditioning load weighted as follows:

• AC equipment including heat pumps at 100% OR
• Central electric space heating including supplemental heat in heat pumps at 65% OR
• Nameplate rating of electric space heating if less than four separately controlled units at 65% OR
• Nameplate rating of four or more separately controlled electric space heating units at 40%

Then ADD 100% of the first 10 kVA of other load and 40% of the remainder of all other load.

Worksheet

Worksheet	Total Watts or VA
Heating OR Cooling (VA)(%) *22,000 × 65%*	14,300
Appliance circuits @ 1,500 each	3,000
Laundry circuits @ 1,500 each	1,500
Lighting (floor area)(3) *(1568 × 3)*	4,704
Clothes dryer (5,000 or nameplate)	5,000
Cooktop	6,000
Oven(s)	4,500
Range (nameplate)	
Dishwasher	1,200
Exterior lighting *6 @ 150*	900
Freezer	300
Garbage disposal	1,200
Landscape lighting	
Pool pump(s) *allow 1,500*	1,500
Shop	
air compressor	
welder	
saw	
other major tools	
Spa	
Trash compactor	
Water heater	4,500
Other electrical items	
Total watts or VA	48,604

example house
1568 square feet
cooling = 3 tons say 3kW
heating = 22 kW
heating is larger

Calculate

	Total watts or VA
first 10,000 VA @ 100%	10,000
remaining VA @ 40% *× 38,604*	15,442
Service calculation total VA	25,442

Minimum required service amperes is the calculated total VA (above) ÷ 240 volts = 100, (125) 150, 175, or 200A   **106**   **AMPERES**

Use next larger standard size—100, (125) 150, 175, or 200A

*NEC is a registered trademark of NFPA (National Fire Protection Association).

Romex Amperes and Gauge

Verify ampacity with local code authority.

Amperes	Aluminum*	Copper
15	#12*	#14
20	#10*	#12
30	#8*	#10
40	#8*	#8
50	#6*	#8
60	#6*	#6

*Most local codes prohibit NM aluminum.

Service Conductor Amperes

Verify ampacity with local code authority.

Amperes	Aluminum*	Copper
100	#2*	#4
125	#1/0*	#2
150	#2/0*	#1
175	#3/0*	#1/0
200	#4/0*	#2/0

*Many local codes prohibit aluminum conductors in buildings.

Type NM cable with THHN insulation @ 30°C ambient—for other conditions see NEC table 310-16.

REVIEW PROBLEMS

1. Which conductor should be connected to the silver terminal on a duplex outlet?
2. A residential duplex circuit is served by three conductors. Name them in order from highest to lowest voltage when the circuit is in use.
3. A residential duplex circuit is served by three conductors. Name them in order from highest to lowest current when the circuit is in use.
4. What type Romex should be used for underground landscape lighting circuits?
5. The maximum number of duplex outlets that can be served by a single 20 ampere, 120 volt circuit is _____.
6. A two-pole circuit breaker is used to protect _____volt circuits.
7. Where is GFI circuit protection required?
8. Why is the hot blade on a plug smaller than the neutral blade?

For 9 through 12, select circuit breakers and copper conductors to serve the circuits:

9. 115 volt lighting circuit with eighteen 100 watt lamps
10. 5,000 watt dryer (230 volts)
11. 11,000 watt heater (230 volts)
12. 1/2 hp fan (9.8 amps @ 115 volts)
13. Use a copy of the Residential Service Calculation form to work this problem:

A large home in Florida has gas heat and four 4 ton air conditioners rated at 5 kW each. Lighting circuits total 12 kW and other dedicated circuits total 40 kW. Find service amperes and aluminum service conductor size @ 240 volts.

ANSWERS

1. the neutral (white) conductor
2. hot, neutral, ground
3. Hot and neutral carry equal current; ground carries none.
4. UF
5. 13 but check local codes. Canada uses 15 amp residential lighting and duplex circuits.
6. 240
7. wet locations
8. polarity
9. 20 amp, one-pole CB and 2 #12 wires
10. 30 amp, two-pole CB and 2 #10 wires
11. 60 amp, two-pole CB and 2 #6 wires (calculates 48 amps BUT add 25% for circuit heat buildup when in operation continuously—3 hours or more)
12. 20 amp, one-pole CB and 2 #12 wires (15 amp looks OK but 20 amp needed to allow for the starting current surge)
13. 150 amps, #2/0 aluminum

Commercial Electrical

"When you believe in things you don't understand, you get into trouble."

Stevie Wonder

$$= \!\!\!\ll\!\!\langle\bullet\rangle\!\!\gg\!\! =$$

Electrical energy claims a large fraction of operating costs, so commercial building owners pursue design and construction options that minimize costs. Electrical hardware in commercial buildings is usually larger and a bit more complex than in homes. Fortunately, there are more similarities than differences.

This chapter builds on the information developed for residential electrical systems, and emphasizes differences between residential and commercial installations. Verify the new terms introduced here by checking each in the list of terms preceding Part II. After reading, you should be able to name and describe the major components of a commercial building's electrical system, and discuss the advantages of increased voltage and three-phase power.

Designing and drawing building electrical systems is covered in Chapter 12.

$$= \!\!\!\ll\!\!\langle\bullet\rangle\!\!\gg\!\! =$$

11.0 CONDUIT AND CONDUCTORS

CONDUIT

Conduit is a pathway for wiring that protects conductors, eases changes, and can serve as a ground (see Figure 11.1).

Duplex and lighting circuits in commercial buildings are nearly the same as their residential equivalents, but conduit is used instead of romex. When conduit provides a continuous metal path to the building ground, it can replace the ground wire.

Steel Conduit

Many varieties of galvanized steel conduit are manufactured. The following five types are extensively used in commercial buildings. Conduit types are listed in order of increasing cost.

Type AC and MC. BX and Greenfield are armored steel conduits that can be installed quickly and economically. They flex to minimize vibration from motors and ballasts. Type AC (BX) includes conductors, and terminations must be made with care so that the steel armor does not cut conductor insulation. Conductors are pulled into Greenfield (type MC) after installation and jacketed Greenfield (Liquidtight) is used in wet locations (see Figure 11.2).

EMT. Electrical metallic tubing is the lightest (least wall thickness) of the rigid steel conduits. Connections can be made with compression fittings or set screws, but compression fittings are preferred when EMT serves as a ground path (see Figure 11.3).

IMC and Rigid. Intermediate metal conduit and rigid are heavier conduits that assemble with threaded connections. Rigid conduit has the greatest wall thickness and offers maximum protection for conductors (see Figure 11.4).

The National Electric Code and local code authorities determine the type of conduit to be used in specific applications. Rigid conduit is commonly used on industrial projects and in areas like loading docks subject to forklift and truck traffic. EMT is used extensively in commercial projects, but flexible conduits are required for motor and fluorescent fixture connections to minimize vibration and noise transmission.

Some commercial lighting installations are prefabricated using Greenfield. This limits site labor to placing fixtures in the ceiling grid, placing switches, and connecting to a power supply.

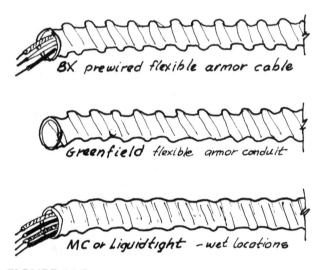

FIGURE 11.2

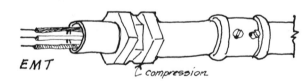

FIGURE 11.3

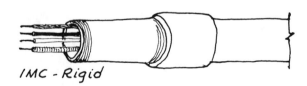

FIGURE 11.4

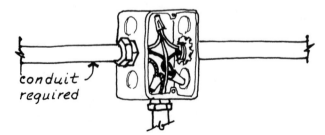

FIGURE 11.1

Aluminum Conduit

Aluminum conduit can be substituted for galvanized steel in many applications, but it should *never* be installed in contact with concrete. Aluminum's lighter weight reduces installation labor allowing competition with steel on a total cost basis.

Plastic Conduit

Plastic conduit (PVC and others) is the conduit of choice for underground installation where corrosion is likely. Plastic conduit is also permitted in some localities for exposed or concealed work. When using plastic a ground conductor or individual equipment ground is required.

Many code authorities prohibit plastic conduit in buildings because of its possible performance in the event of a fire.

Fittings

Couplings, elbows, bends, pull-boxes, and assorted fittings and connectors are used to complete conduit installations. In hazardous locations—where electrical arcing could ignite flammable gasses, vapors, or dust—special *explosion-proof* fittings, switches, and devices are used. Gasketed, weather-tight fittings are used outdoors (see Figure 11.5).

CONDUCTORS

Most commercial buildings are wired with copper conductors. Aluminum conductors are used for some high-current loads where special terminals are designed to ensure fault-free connections, but many local codes prohibit aluminum conductors in buildings.

Conductor Insulation

Thermoplastic or rubber insulation is used for most building wiring. **T** identifies *thermoplastic* and **R** *rubber.* **W** indicates insulation that can be used in *wet* locations, and **H** (*heat*) identifies insulation with an allowable operating temperature of 75°C (see Figure 11.6). A conductor can carry more current when its insulation has a higher temperature rating. For example

#8 RHW is an 8 gauge conductor with rubber insulation, rated for both high heat (75°C) and wet location use.

#6 THHN is a 6 gauge conductor with thermoplastic insulation rated for extra high heat (90°C) applications (N *indicates nylon reinforcing*).

Most building wiring is done with THHN, THWN, or XHHW (polyethylene). These insulations are thinner than equally rated rubber, and a thinner insulating jacket allows more conductors in a given conduit. Fewer wires are used in commercial power and lighting circuits because three-phase circuits can share a single neutral conductor.

Large buildings demand more amperes than residences, and large conductors are specified in MCM (thousand circular mil) instead of AWG (American Wire Gauge).

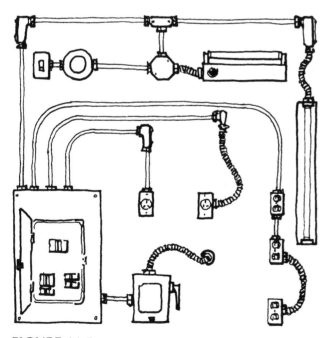

FIGURE 11.5

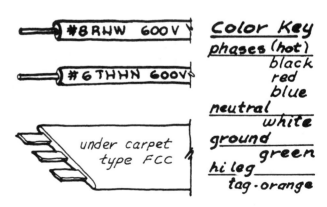

FIGURE 11.6

Installing Conductors

A fish tape is a flexible metal strip used to pull conductors into conduit. It is first pushed into the conduit, and then pulled back with appropriate conductors attached.

Compressed air and vacuum are also used to push or draw fish line through conduit, and for long pulls a lubricant is applied to the conductors for easier installation.

Conductor Installation Practice

+ A maximum of four 90° bends are permitted between pull-boxes.
+ Do *not* mix high- and low-voltage conductors in the same conduit (high = over 600 volts).
+ Do *not* mix control and power conductors in the same conduit.
+ Do *not* mix phone and power conductors in the same conduit.
+ *Do* place all three phases in the same conduit (single-phase conductors can induce current flow in the conduit).

Special Conduits

Round conduit is not the only option for protecting and rewiring commercial installations. *Cable trays* and *busways* replace conduit where large currents must be distributed. Laboratory and manufacturing buildings substitute surface-mounted *raceways* for conduit, where many outlets are required in a small area. Office buildings use *under-floor ducts* to serve floor outlets (see Figure 11.7).

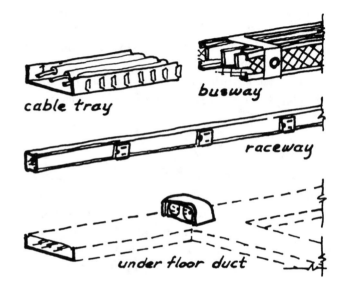

FIGURE 11.7

11.1 CIRCUITS

LIGHTING CIRCUITS

Commercial lighting circuits differ from their residential counterparts as follows:

Shared neutral
More amperes
Higher voltage

Also, duplex outlets are not connected on lighting circuits in commercial work.

Shared Neutral

Commercial lighting circuits often use a common neutral wire. With three-phase power, three hot wires can share a single neutral wire as they serve three circuits. A shared neutral reduces wiring costs.

More Amperes

When heavy-duty lamp holders are used, lighting circuits up to 50 amperes are allowed. However, most lighting circuits are protected with 20 ampere circuit breakers, and are loaded to 80% of capacity (16 amperes). Circuit breakers are sometimes used to switch a group of light fixtures. When this is done, SWD (switch duty) breakers are specified.

Higher Voltage

In large buildings, fluorescent lighting ballasts are specified at 277 volts (347 volts in Canada) instead of 120 volts. This cuts electrical construction costs because each lighting circuit serves more fixtures. When 277 volt power is used for lighting, dry transformers are installed to carry the 120 volt loads.

POWER CIRCUITS

Commercial buildings use three-phase power for all but the smallest motors. Three hot wires carry motor loads, and grounding is provided by the conduit system, or by placing an individual ground at each motor. Large motors are equipped with *starters* to control starting current and protect from overloads.

Motors can be enclosed to minimize arcing danger in explosive environments. When enclosed, a ducted air supply is connected to each motor for cooling.

DEDICATED CIRCUITS AND UPS

In homes, separate circuits are used for appliances like ranges and air conditioners. In commercial buildings, similar separate circuits are *dedicated* for most motors, refrigeration equipment, and emergency power.

Building electrical equipment can produce harmonic currents that may overload common neutral conductors. Separate circuit neutrals or an oversized common neutral abate this problem.

Computers and computer-related equipment are sensitive to harmonic currents that distort power quality. Computers and stored data can be protected using dedicated UPS (uninterrupted power supply) circuits. UPS systems use batteries, isolating transformers, and control circuitry to ensure a clean, reliable power supply for computers and related accessories.

11.2 PANELS

LIGHTING AND POWER PANELS

Large commercial buildings use many panels to subdivide current and protect individual circuits. Separate panels are used for lighting, power, and emergency loads.

Lighting panels contain many single-pole circuit breakers, and designers *balance* lighting loads by allocating lighting watts equally among three phases. When power panels include single-pole loads, they are also balanced. Codes require separate panels, conductors, and conduit for all emergency circuits (see Figure 11.8).

PANEL CAPACITY

Panels of 100, 200, 225, or 400 ampere capacity are typical in commercial installations. Larger panels—up to 1,200 amperes—are called *switchboards*. When a building's total electrical load exceeds 1,200 amperes, electrical designers consider a high-voltage power supply. If a building service calculation totals 2,000 amperes at 240 volts, construction and utility costs can be reduced by taking 1,000 amperes at 480 volts or 125 amperes at 4,160 volts instead. Extra costs for transformers and switchgear may be offset by reduced power costs and smaller service components.

SWITCHGEAR

Switchgear is a term for large electrical load centers that allocate power to transformers, motors, and panels (see Figure 11.9). Switchgear usually includes overcurrent protection so downstream panels are installed without main circuit breakers. The ampere capacity of a panel without main circuit breakers is designated MLO (main lugs only).

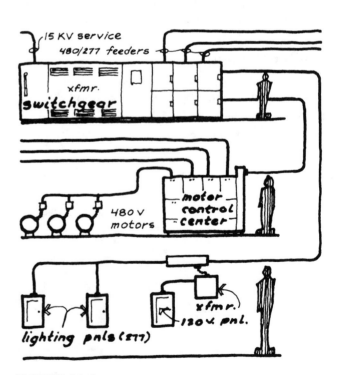

FIGURE 11.9

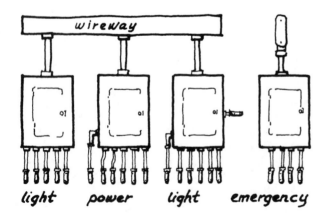

FIGURE 11.8

11.3 SERVICES

THREE-PHASE SERVICES (3Ø)

Three-phase services usually include three hot phase conductors and a neutral. The neutral conductor is usually smaller than the phase conductors because the neutral only carries unbalanced current (see Figure 11.10).

When two or three hot wires serve a piece of equipment they provide the circuit loop, and a neutral conductor is not required. Neutral current occurs only in single-phase (one-pole) circuits that serve loads like lighting or duplex outlets.

DELTA OR WYE

One of two electrical geometries can be used for building services. *Delta* geometry is usual in industrial applications and *wye* geometry is typical for office buildings and shopping centers. The term *geometry* here refers to the relationship between the three-phase conductors and the neutral.

In delta systems the neutral conductor is centered between two-phase conductors, and phase-to-phase voltage is double the phase-to-neutral voltage. Delta geometry's high leg conductor serves only three-phase loads and cannot be used with the neutral (see Figure 11.11).

In wye or star systems the neutral conductor is connected between all three-phase conductors. This allows each phase conductor to serve single-phase loads. In wye systems, phase-to-phase voltage is 1.73 times the phase-to-neutral voltage (see Figure 11.12).

In delta installations, utilities balance loads by alternating the high leg in adjacent buildings. In wye systems, each building is designed for balanced electrical load on all three phases.

You can identify service geometry by observing service conductor size (see Figure 11.13). Each of the three-phase conductors is equal in wye systems, but in delta systems two conductors are large and one is small.

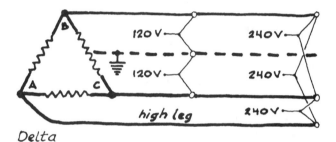

Delta

FIGURE 11.11

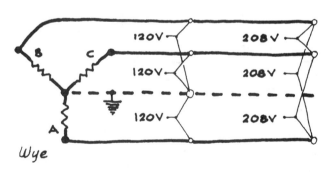

Wye

FIGURE 11.12

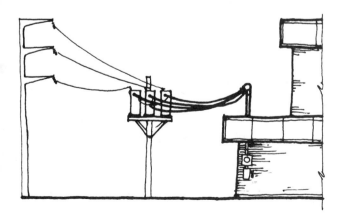

FIGURE 11.10

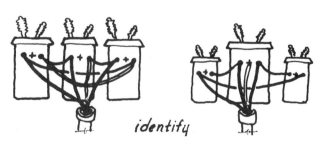

identify

FIGURE 11.13

INCREASED SERVICE VOLTAGE

Lighting is often the largest consumer of electrical energy in commercial buildings. Typically 1,920 watts is the maximum load connected to a 20 ampere, 120 volt circuit. When lighting is operated at higher voltage, each circuit carries more fixtures, reducing electrical construction costs. A single 277 volt lighting circuit easily serves more fixtures than two 120 volt circuits.

Motor loads for fans, pumps, elevators, refrigeration, and cooling towers may equal or exceed lighting energy in commercial buildings. Electric motors are designed for operation at a specific voltage, *but* higher voltage means less amperes and smaller conductors for a given motor horsepower. In larger commercial buildings, 480 or 600 volt motors are typical.

In the United States 277/480 volt, three-phase electrical systems are considered to serve building loads from 300 kVA to 1,600 kVA (see Figure 11.14). This service uses 480 volt, three-phase power for motors and 277 volt, single-phase power for most lighting. Small transformers throughout the building reduce 277 to 120 volts for other electrical loads. Canada uses 347/600 volt services in larger commercial buildings.

Very large buildings cut electrical costs by taking power at high voltage (5 to 15 kV). Utilities charge less for high-voltage power because the building owner installs and maintains transformers and switchgear.

TRANSFORMERS

Transformers are rated in kVA. If total building load is 600 amperes at 480 volts, find the transformer size required to serve the building.

$$(600)(480)(1.73) = +/- 500,000 \text{ or } 500 \text{ kVA}$$

Three-phase transformers are available, but for maintenance purposes, three single-phase transformers are usually specified.

Typical Building Services

Service	Amps	Building Type
120/240 1ø 120/208 1ø	Up to 200	Home or apartment
120/240 3ø 120/208 3ø	200 to 800	Small commercial or manufacturer
240/480 3ø 277/480 3ø 347/600 3ø*	400 to 2,000	Large commercial or manufacturer
5–15 kV	Low	Very large

*Large commercial buildings in Canada.

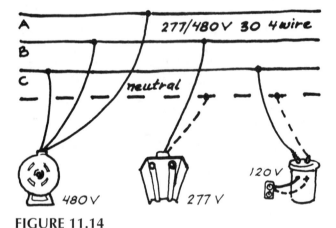

FIGURE 11.14

EMERGENCY POWER

As building size and occupancy increase, emergency power requirements increase. A small, one-story building may need just a few exit lights and several battery powered light fixtures to permit safe egress in a power outage.

Emergency lighting and night security lighting are frequently combined. One or two fluorescent fixtures in each room or space are connected to a circuit that is not switched. These lights stay on 24 hours a day and they include a battery pack that will light one fluorescent lamp for about an hour in the event of a power outage.

In larger buildings an emergency generator with automatic start is usually installed to ensure occupant safety. The generator is sized to carry items like fire pumps, emergency lighting, the fire alarm system, communications equipment, and smoke-control fans. Most codes also require emergency power sufficient to operate at least one elevator in multi-story buildings.

Hospitals require more emergency power circuits because of the life-threatening implications of a power outage. Surgeries, intensive care units, and many medical instruments require a continuous power supply for safe operation. Emergency power for specific locations and devices is run in separate conduit and is isolated from the electrical system components used in normal building operations (see Figure 11.15).

Emergency circuits served by utility power are usually connected ahead of the building's main disconnect so firefighters have the option of keeping emergency power on.

LOW VOLTAGE

Most phone, sound, TV, thermostat, security, and control wiring is operated at low voltage supplied through small transformers. Low voltage (often 24 volts) can be run in open cable trays or in plastic conduit, but it *cannot* be run in power or lighting conduit.

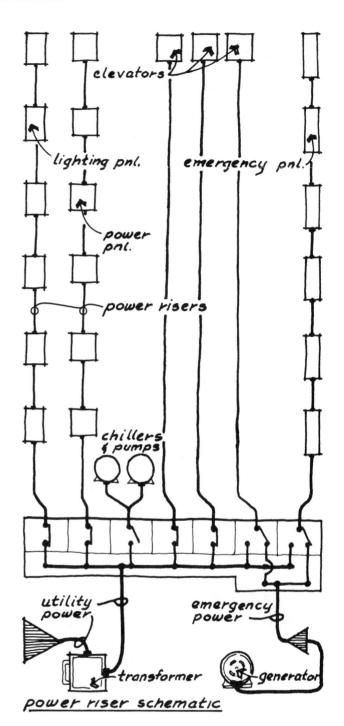

power riser schematic

FIGURE 11.15

11.4 SERVICE CAPACITY

SERVICE SIZE

The ampacity of an electrical service reflects the construction budget and anticipated future expansion plans. Sizing the service to meet the design load produces the lowest initial cost, but as time passes, building electrical loads tend to increase and it's difficult and expensive to increase the size of an existing service. Many building owners invest in added electrical capacity by oversizing the service and installing additional panels, conduit, and wiring to accommodate future growth without disrupting operations.

SERVICE DISCONNECTS

The power supply to a building can be turned off (disconnected) by a main circuit breaker or a fused switch (see Figure 11.16). Disconnecting building electrical power is an important first step in a fire emergency. Fuses have a better interrupting capacity than circuit breakers so fused disconnects are often used to protect and disconnect the building service. The National Electric Code allows a maximum of six disconnects on a building service, but most local codes require *one* switch or breaker that will completely disconnect all building power.

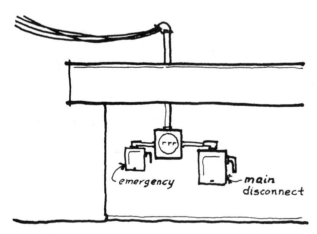

FIGURE 11.16

NEMA, the National Electrical Manufacturers Association, sets standards for disconnects. For example, NEMA 1 is the indoor standard, and NEMA 3R is the rainproof standard.

ELECTRICAL COSTS

The kWh graph in Figure 11.17 shows decreasing real costs for electrical energy, but utilities bill commercial customers for energy (kWh) *and* peak demand (kW). A home might be billed 7¢ per kWh, while a nearby commercial building pays 2¢ per kWh *plus* $12 per kW of demand.

Because peak charges are substantial, commercial building owners are most interested in reducing demand, while home owners try to cut consumption. As a result, commercial building owners invest in peak limiting controls and thermal storage, while home owners can cut bills by improving the thermal performance of their walls, roof, and windows.

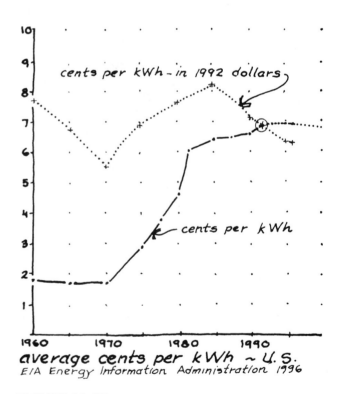

FIGURE 11.17

REVIEW QUESTIONS

1. Name three advantages of conduit vs. romex.
2. Aluminum conduit must *not* be installed in contact with _____.
3. Select a steel conduit type to connect the starter to an electric motor.
4. What steel conduit type joins with compression fittings?
5. Select a conduit material for underground landscape lighting circuits.
6. Select a steel conduit type for surface mounting in a large warehouse.
7. Which of the following is the largest conductor?
   250 MCM RHW   #4/0 TW   #14 THHN
8. Which of the following should be used in wet locations?
   R   TW   THHN   THWN
9. Which of the following conductors has the highest safe operating temperature?
   250 MCM RHW   #4/0 TW   #14 THHN
10. Which of the following conductors will safely carry the largest current?
    #12 RHW   #12 THW   #12 THHN
11. Which of the following conductors has the thickest insulation?
    #12 RHW   #12 THW   #12 THHN
12. When very large currents are distributed, what is used to replace conduit?
13. How can three separate lighting circuits be served with only four wires?
14. Why do commercial lighting circuits use 277 or 347 volt power?
15. UPS is used for ___ power.
16. The designation 225 A - MLO means ___.
17. Is a 347/600 volt service delta or wye?
18. Which 3ø geometry includes a "high leg" that can't serve single-pole loads?
19. Which 3ø geometry is balanced by the utility?
20. Which 3ø geometry is typical in large commercial buildings?
21. Why do very large buildings take power at high voltage?
22. A new office building owner asks designers to oversize the electrical service by 50%. Why?
23. Peak demand for a 20,000-square-foot commercial building is 140 kW. Monthly consumption is 40,000 kWh. Calculate the monthly utility bill if rates are $10 per kW plus 3¢ per kWh.

ANSWERS

1. protect, change, ground
2. concrete
3. BX or Green Field
4. EMT
5. plastic
6. rigid or IMT
7. 250 MCM RHW
8. TW or THWN
9. #14 THHN
10. #12 THHN
11. #12 RHW
12. busways or cable trays
13. three individually protected phase conductors and a single common neutral
14. more fixtures per circuit = fewer circuits = lower electrical construction cost
15. computer
16. 225 amperes, main lugs only
17. wye
18. delta
19. delta
20. wye
21. reduced life cycle costs
22. Anticipated load growth. (50% was within the historical 10-year load growth range for office buildings during the 1960s.)
23. $2,600

CHAPTER 12

Example Office Building

Architecture is 90% business and 10% art.

Albert Kahn

————◦◦◦————

Tables and example questions begin this chapter. They illustrate circuit breaker, conductor, conduit, panel, and transformer selection. Complete each example and check your answers so you will understand the following electrical plans and panel schedules.

The example office building* is used to illustrate electrical design and component selection. Drawings and panels are developed for the lobby and an office area. Then lighting, duplex, and power loads are estimated for the entire building and an electrical service is designed. Study this chapter by reading the text, and then reinforce each text entry by identifying it on the accompanying drawing or diagram. Trace each circuit from plan to panel, and then follow the panel feeders to the building service.

———

*Lobby lighting design is covered in Chapter 6. More information about the building's HVAC systems is provided in Efficient Building Design Series, Volume 2: Heating, Ventilating, and Air Conditioning. Here, the example office is assumed to be an "all electric" building to illustrate as many electrical loads as possible.

————◦◦◦————

12.0 TABLES

Use Tables 12.1 through 12.3 and the following instructions to select circuit breakers, conductors, and conduit for the example questions.

Select conductors with an ampere rating that equals or exceeds the circuit breaker trip amperes.

- Select copper conductors unless the local code authority specifically permits aluminum.
- Allow voltage drop for individual circuits. For example, 120 = 115, 208 = 200, 277 = 265.
- Use design voltage for transformers and feeders, that is, 120, 208, 240, 277, 480.
- Amps = watts ÷ volts (or volt-amperes ÷ volts) for single-phase loads.
- Amps = watts ÷ volts√3 (or volt-amperes ÷ volts√3) for three-phase loads.
- Add 25% to calculated amps for lighting loads or loads that operate continuously for 3 hours or more.
- Select circuit breaker amps next above calculated amps, and select circuit conductors with ampacity equal to or greater than their breakers.

Example Questions

1. Select a conductor to carry 45 amperes.
2. Select a copper conductor to carry 80 amperes. How many of these conductors are required for a 115 volt circuit?
3. A 115 volt lighting circuit totals 1,900 watts. Select circuit breaker, conductors, and conduit.
4. A 115 volt duplex circuit totals 1,080 watts. Select circuit breaker, conductors, and conduit.
5. Three 115 volt, 20 ampere lighting circuits will be run in a single conduit. How many #12 copper wires and what size conduit?

TABLE 12.1

Circuit Breakers (standard trip amperes)

15–50 by 5s

15	20	25*	30	35*	40	45*	50

(*25, 35, and 45 for motor circuits)

60–110 by 10s

60	70	80	90	100	110

125–250 by 25s

125	150	175	200	225	250

300–500 by 50s

300	350	400	450	500

600–1,000 by 100s

600	700	800	900	1,000

1,200–2,000 by 200s

1,200	1,400	1,600	1,800	2,000

TABLE 12.2

Conductors (sized by amperes)

Allowable amperes for three THWN (75°C) insulated conductors in a raceway based on an ambient temperature of 30°C.

Amperes	Aluminum*	Copper
15	#12*	#14
20	#10*	#12
25	#10*	#10
30	#8*	#10
35	#8*	#8
40	#8*	#8
45	#6*	#8
50	#6*	#8
60	#4*	#6
70	#3*	#4
80	#2*	#4
90	#2*	#3
100	#1*	#3
110	#1/0*	#2
125	#2/0*	#1
150	#3/0*	#1/0
175	#4/0*	#2/0
200	250 MCM*	#3/0
225	300 MCM*	#4/0
250	350 MCM*	250 MCM
300	500 MCM*	350 MCM
350	700 MCM*	400 MCM
400	900 MCM*	600 MCM

*Many local codes prohibit aluminum conductors inside buildings.
Conductors in air with insulation rated for higher temperature can carry more current.

6. Find the maximum lighting watts allowable on a 20 ampere, 265 volt circuit.

7. A single-phase transformer rated at 15 kVA converts 277 volts to 120 volts. Find the aluminum conductor and conduit size for primary and secondary circuits. Allow 125% over current capacity for continuous operation.

8. A separate circuit will be run for a 230 volt water heater rated at 4,500 watts. Select circuit breaker, conductors, and conduit.

9. A separate circuit will be run for a 200 volt heater rated at 9,600 watts. Select a circuit breaker, conductors, and conduit.

10. Select circuit breaker, conductors, and conduit for a three-phase (3ø), 200 volt heater rated at 9,600 watts.

11. Select aluminum feeders and conduit for a single-phase 225 ampere panel.

12. Select aluminum feeders and conduit for a three-phase 400 ampere panel.

13. Select aluminum feeders and conduit for a three-phase 208 volt service if the total load is 287 kVA.

14. Select circuit breaker, conductors, and conduit for a three-phase, 575 volt, 25 horsepower motor.

Answers

1. #6 THWN aluminum or #8 THWN copper
2. #4 THWN, two (one hot and one neutral)
3. 20 ampere, one-pole CB, 2 #12 THWN copper wires, in 1/2″ conduit
4. 15 ampere, one-pole CB, 2 #14 THWN copper wires, in 1/2″ conduit, *but* 20 ampere circuits are recommended for all duplex and lighting loads.
5. With a three-phase Y system, four wires (three hot and a common neutral) in a 1/2″ conduit. The three hot wires *must* be connected to three separate panel busses.
6. 4,240 watts. For continuous loads like lighting, circuit loading is limited to 80% or $(265)(20)(80\%) = 4,240$ watts.
7. 2 #3 aluminum THWN, in 1″ conduit for the primary, 2 #4/0 aluminum THWN, in 1½″ conduit for the secondary.
8. 30 ampere, two-pole CB, 2 #10 THWN copper wires, in 1/2″ conduit. Calculates 19.6 amps, but allow 125% (24.5 A) for circuits subject to continuous operation.

TABLE 12.3

Conduit

Maximum number of type THWN or THHN conductors in conduit or tubing

Wire Size	Conduit Size 1/2″	3/4″	1″	1 1/4″
14	13	24	39	69
12	10	18	29	51
10	6	11	18	32
8	3	5	9	16
6	1	4	6	11
4	1	2	4	7
3	1	1	3	6
2	1	1	3	5
1		1	1	3
0		1	1	3
00		1	1	2

Wire Size	Conduit Size 1 1/2″	2″	2 1/2″	3″
8	22	36	51	79
6	15	26	37	57
4	9	16	22	35
3	8	13	19	29
2	7	11	16	25
1	5	8	12	18
0	4	7	10	15
00	3	6	8	13
000	3	5	7	11
0000	2	4	6	9
250	1	3	4	7
300	1	3	4	6
350	1	2	3	5

Wire Size	Conduit Size 3 1/2″	4″	5″	6″
2	33	43	67	97
1	25	32	50	72
0	21	27	42	61
00	17	22	35	51
000	14	18	29	42
0000	12	15	24	35
250	10	12	20	28
300	8	11	17	24
350	7	9	15	21
400	6	8	13	19
500	5	7	11	16
600	4	5	9	13
700	4	5	8	11
750	3	4	7	11

9. 60 ampere, two-pole CB, 2 #6 THWN copper wires, in 3/4″ conduit (allow 125%)

10. 40 ampere, three-pole CB, 3 #8 THWN copper wires, in 1/2″ conduit (allow 125%)

11. Three 300 MCM THWN aluminum wires, in 2″ conduit. This answer assumes neutral current is equal to the phase conductor current.

12. Seven 250 MCM THWN aluminum wires, in 3 1/2″ conduit. This answer assumes the neutral wire carries only half as much current as the phase conductors.

13. Fourteen 250 MCM THWN aluminum wires, in 5″ conduit. Each phase must carry almost 800 amperes, and this answer assumes a calculated maximum neutral current of 400 amperes. Twelve phase conductors and two neutral conductors.

14. 60 amperes, three-pole CB, 3 #8 THWN copper wires, in 1/2″ conduit. Check this answer in Table 12.6 on page 164.

MOTORS

Use Tables 12.4 through 12.6 and the following notes to select motor circuit breakers and conductors. Check conduit sizes in Table 12.3.

- ♦ Amps = VA ÷ volts, for single-phase loads.
- ♦ Amps = VA ÷ volts√3, for three-phase loads.
- ♦ Use volt-amperes instead of watts for motor loads.
- ♦ Copper conductors are used in the tables, but aluminum conductors can be used for large motor circuits.
- ♦ Verify circuit breaker amps and wire size with motor manufacturer.
- ♦ To properly start and further protect electric motors a starter must be installed nearby (see Figure 12.1).

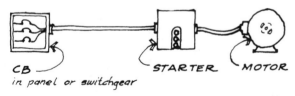

CB
in panel or switchgear   **STARTER**   **MOTOR**

FIGURE 12.1

Example Questions

1. Find the circuit breaker, wire, conduit, and load in volt-amperes for a 3 horsepower, single-phase, 115 volt motor.

2. Find the circuit breaker, wire, conduit, and load in volt-amperes for a 3 horsepower, single-phase, 200 volt motor.

3. Find the circuit breaker, wire, conduit, and load in volt-amperes for a 3 horsepower, single-phase, 230 volt motor.

4. Find the circuit breaker, wire, conduit, and load in volt-amperes for a 3 horsepower, three-phase, 230 volt motor.

5. Find the circuit breaker, wire, conduit, and load in volt-amperes for a 3 horsepower, three-phase, 460 volt motor.

6. Find the circuit breaker, wire, conduit, and load in volt-amperes for a 30 horsepower, three-phase, 575 volt motor.

7. Find the circuit breaker, wire, conduit, and load in volt-amperes for a 30 horsepower, three-phase, 200 volt motor.

8. Find the circuit breaker, wire, conduit, and load in volt-amperes for a 30 horsepower, three-phase, 230 volt motor.

Answers

	Breaker	Conductors	Conduit	Load
1.	70 A, one-pole	2 #8	1/2″	3,910 VA
2.	40 A, two-pole	2 #10	1/2″	3,920 VA

Load is carried by two hot wires, half on each.

3.	35 A, two-pole	2 #10	1/2″	3,910 VA
4.	20 A, three-pole	3 #14	1/2″	3,824 VA

Load is carried by three wires, 1,275 VA on each.

5.	15 A, three-pole	3 #14	1/2″	3,824 VA
6.	60 A, three-pole	3 #8	1/2″	31,870 VA
7.	125 A, three-pole	3 #2	1″	31,870 VA
8.	110 A, three-pole	3 #3	1″	31,870 VA

TABLE 12.4

Single-Phase Motors—115, 200, and 230 Volts

Horsepower, full load amperes (FLA), dual element time delay fuse amperes, circuit breaker amperes, minimum THWN copper wire size.

Single-Phase 115-Volts (120)

HP	FLA	Fuse	CB	Wire
1/4	5.8	9	15	#14
1/3	7.2	12	15	#14
1/2	9.8	15	20	#14
3/4	13.8	20	25	#12
1	16	25	30	#12
1 1/2	20	30	40	#10
2	24	30	50	#10
3	34	50	70	#8
5	56	80	90	#4

Single-Phase 200 Volts (208)

HP	FLA	Fuse	CB	Wire
1/4	3.3	5	15	#14
1/3	4.1	6.25	15	#14
1/2	5.6	10	15	#14
3/4	7.9	12	15	#14
1	9.2	15	15	#14
1 1/2	11.5	17.5	20	#14
2	13.8	20	25	#12
3	19.6	30	40	#10
5	32.2	50	60	#8
7 1/2	46.0	60	90	#6

Single-Phase 230 Volts (240)

HP	FLA	Fuse	CB	Wire
1/4	2.9	4.5	15	#14
1/3	3.6	5.6	15	#14
1/2	4.9	8	15	#14
3/4	6.9	10	15	#14
1	8	12	15	#14
1 1/2	10	15	20	#14
2	12	17.5	25	#14
3	17	25	35	#10
5	28	40	60	#8
7 1/2	40	60	80	#8

TABLE 12.5

Three-Phase Motors—200 and 230 Volts

Horsepower, full load amperes (FLA), dual element time delay fuse amperes, circuit breaker amperes, minimum THWN copper wire size.

Three-Phase 200 Volts (208)

HP	FLA	Fuse	CB	Wire
1/2	2.3	3.5	15	#14
3/4	3.2	5	15	#14
1	4.1	6.25	15	#14
1 1/2	6.0	10	15	#14
2	7.8	12	15	#14
3	11.0	17.5	20	#14
5	17.5	25	35	#10
7 1/2	25.3	40	50	#8
10	32.2	50	60	#8
15	48.3	60	90	#6
20	62.1	90	100	#4
25	78.2	100	110	#3
30	92	125	125	#2
40	120	175	175	#1/0
50	150	200	200	#3/0
100	285	400	400	500

Three-Phase 230 Volts (240)

HP	FLA	Fuse	CB	Wire
1/2	2.0	3.2	15	#14
3/4	2.8	4.5	15	#14
1	3.6	5.6	15	#14
1 1/2	5.2	8	15	#14
2	6.8	10	15	#14
3	9.6	15	20	#14
5	15.2	25	30	#12
7 1/2	22	30	45	#10
10	28	40	60	#8
15	42	60	80	#6
20	54	80	90	#4
25	68	100	100	#4
30	80	100	110	#3
40	104	150	150	#1
50	130	200	200	#2/0
100	248	350	350	350

TABLE 12.6

Three-Phase Motors—460 and 575 Volts

Horsepower, full load amperes (FLA), dual element time delay fuse amperes, circuit breaker amperes, minimum THWN copper wire size.

Three-Phase 460 Volts (480)

HP	FLA	Fuse	CB	Wire
1/2	1.0	1.6	15	#14
3/4	1.4	2.25	15	#14
1	1.8	2.8	15	#14
1 1/2	2.6	4	15	#14
2	3.4	5.6	15	#14
3	4.8	8	15	#14
5	7.6	12	15	#14
7 1/2	11	17.5	20	#14
10	14	20	25	#12
15	21	30	40	#10
20	27	40	60	#8
25	34	50	70	#8
30	40	60	80	#8
40	52	80	90	#6
50	65	100	100	#4
100	124	175	200	#2/0

Three-Phase 575 Volts (600)

HP	FLA	Fuse	CB	Wire
1/2	0.8	1.25	15	#14
3/4	1.1	1.8	15	#14
1	1.4	2.25	15	#14
1 1/2	2.1	3.2	15	#14
2	2.7	4.5	15	#14
3	3.9	6.25	15	#14
5	6.1	10	15	#14
7 1/2	9	15	15	#14
10	11	17.5	20	#14
15	17	25	35	#10
20	22	30	45	#10
25	27	40	60	#8
30	32	50	60	#8
40	41	60	80	#6
50	52	80	90	#6
100	99	150	150	#1

Time delay fuses are much used as motor circuit protectors. They are oversized by at least 125% of motor full load amperes to pass the starting current surge.

Circuit breakers protecting motors are oversized more than time delay fuses to pass the starting current surge. Motor circuits are an exception to the rule that circuit breaker trip amperes set circuit wire size. Some wires listed in the motor tables are rated for less amperes than the circuit breaker trip setting.

PANELS AND SWITCHBOARDS

Try to locate panels near the center of the electrical loads they serve to minimize voltage drop. Standard Panel capacities are given in Table 12.7. Tabulate all electrical loads on panel form(s) and calculate amperes. Then select panel capacity to accommodate loads. Panels are ordered with or without main circuit breakers. Specify MCB if a main breaker is required, or MLO (main lugs only) when the panel has remote protection.

TABLE 12.7

Panels and Switchboards

Capacity in amperes for mains and mugs (MLO), and number of spaces or poles.

Single-Phase 120/208 or 120/240

Capacity	Spaces/Poles
40 or 70	2 or 4
100	8-12-16-20-24
125	2-4-6-8-12-16-20-24
150	12-16-20-24-30
200	4-8-12-16-20-24-30-40-42
225	24-30-42
400	24-30-42
600	24-30-42

Three-Phase 120/240 or 120/208

Capacity	Spaces/Poles
60	3
100	12-18-24-30
125	12-20-30
150	18-24-30-40-4220012-18-24-30-40-42
225	30-40-42
400	24-30-42
600	24-30-42

Three-Phase 277/480

Capacity	Spaces/Poles
125	12-18-30
225	30-42
400	30-42
600	42

Switchboard Amperes

480 volts	400	600	800	
600 volts	1,000	1,200	1,600	2,000
2,500				

This is a partial listing of manufactured panels and switchboards. Verify availability and check capacity when multi-pole breakers are installed.

Compact *tandem* breakers are available. They pack two single-pole breakers in the space of a standard single-pole breaker.

Panels are manufactured 14" or 20" wide, depths range from 3" to 6", and heights vary with capacity up to 60".

TRANSFORMERS

Transformer size varies with capacity (see Fig. 12.2). Because they hum and heat, location and ventilation are important considerations. Small transformers on each floor serve 120-volt loads in buildings with 277/480 volt services, but large transformers are located with switch gear in buildings with 5 or 15 kV services. Table 12.8 lists standard transformer capacities.

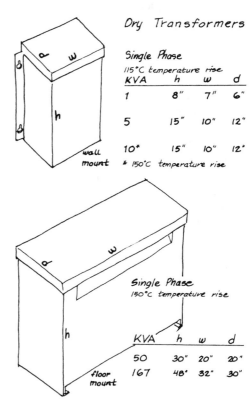

FIGURE 12.2

TABLE 12.8

Standard Transformer kVA

Single-Phase, kVA

1 - 3 - 5 - 7 1/2 - 10 - 15 - 25 - 37 1/2 - 50 - 67 1/2 - 100 - 125 - 167 1/2 - 200 - 250 - 333 - 500

Three-Phase, kVA

3 - 6 - 9 - 15 - 30 - 45 - 75 - 100 - 150 - 225 - 300 - 500 - 750 - 1,000 - 1,500 - 2,000 - 5,000 - 7,500 - 10,000

12.1 BUILDING SERVICE EXAMPLE

Select all the keyed components in the electrical service diagram in Figure 12.3 using the preceding tables; then check your selections with the answers that follow.

Select all panels, switches, fuses, lugs, conductors, conduit, and the transformer. Begin with panel D and work back to the main switch.

Given:

+ **D** panel (duplex).
  3ø, 120/208 volts, serves duplex and other loads. Phase total 60,000 volt-amperes, neutral maximum 14,000 volt-amperes. Total poles = 30.
+ **X** transformer.
  3ø, 277/480 to 120/208 volts.
+ **L** panel (lighting).
  3ø, 277/480 volt lighting panel. Phase total 65,000 volt-amperes, neutral maximum 22,000 volt-amperes. 16 single-pole circuits.
+ **P** panel (power).
  3ø, 277/480 volt power panel. Phase total 165,000 volt-amperes, no neutral load. 11 three-pole circuits.

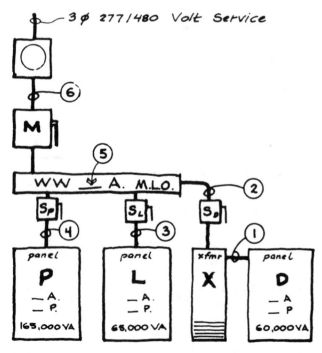

FIGURE 12.3

+ S_P S_L S_D switches.
  Fuse each for protected panel load.
+ **WW** wireway.
  Size lugs for total load.
+ **M** main switch.
  Fuse for service capacity.

Answers

+ **D** Panel. Select:
  200 A, MLO with 40 pole spaces.
  $(60,000) \div (208)(\sqrt{3}) = 167$ A.
  Neutral current is $(14,000) \div (120) = 117$ A.
+ **1.** Select:
  Three 250 MCM and one #2/0 aluminum THWN in 2 1/2″ conduit. Phase conductors sized for 200 A. Could have sized for 175 A, but limits expansion potential. Neutral sized for 117 A.
+ **X** Transformer. Select:
  75 kVA $(200)(208)(\sqrt{3}) = 72,000$
+ S_D Switch. Select:
  100 A, three-pole fused switch
+ **2.** Select:
  Three #1 and one #6 aluminum THWN in 1 1/2″ conduit. $(200)(208) \div (480) = 86$ A. Could size for 90 A, but 100 A fuse same price.
+ **L** Panel. Select:
  100 A, MLO with 20 pole spaces.
  $(65,000) \div (480)(\sqrt{3}) = 78$ A. Could use 80 A.
  Neutral current is $(22,000) \div (277) = 79$ A.
+ S_L Switch. Select:
  100 A, three-pole fused switch
+ **3.** Select:
  Three #1 and one #2 aluminum THWN in 1 1/2″ conduit.
+ **P** Panel. Select:
  225 A, MLO with 42 pole spaces.
  $(165,000) \div (480)(H\sqrt{3}) = 198$ A. Could use 200 A to cut conductor cost.
+ S_P Switch. Select:
  225 A, three-pole fused switch
+ **4.** Select:
  Three 300 MCM aluminum THWN in 2″ conduit.
+ **5.** Wireway lugs. Select:
  400 A, MLO. Total connected load is 349 A. 400 allows almost 15% expansion. Many owners would specify a 600 A service.
+ **M** Main disconnect. Select:
  400 A, three-pole fused switch
+ **6.** Select:
  Six 250 MCM and one #3/0 neutral aluminum THWN in 3″ conduit. Neutral current is 130 A.

PLAN

This electrical installation example uses the building shell shown in Figure 12.4. Detailed electrical plans are illustrated for a rental office space on the north east side of the ground floor, and for the central two-story lobby.

The building's panels, feeders, and service are sized to serve the estimated electrical requirements for both floors, even though detailed drawings for the office and lobby account for only about 15% of the total building area. Utility service is three-phase, 120/208 volts.

ELECTRICAL LOADS

Lighting, duplex, and selected power outlets are shown on the detail plans, and inferred for the remaining spaces. The following HVAC and elevator loads will be used to calculate the building service.

Cooling 66 kW

Nine air handlers serve eight rental office zones and the two-story lobby. Nine DX, split system, air-cooled condensing units are located on the building roof.

Calculated heat gain of 630,172 BTUH or 52.5 tons, is met by five 5-ton and four 7.5-ton units. Larger units serve the four large office spaces. Second-floor air handlers circulate more air to carry roof heat gain. Electrical load is estimated at 1.2 kW per ton including the air handlers.

Heating 100 kW

Resistance heating elements are installed in each of nine air handlers.* Calculated heat loss for the example building is 406,850 BTUH, so 120 kW should be installed ($406 \div 3.4 = 120$). By reducing night ventilation rates, and taking a partial credit for heat from lights, resistance heating capacity was reduced to 100 kW.

Ventilation

Two 1/2 horsepower exhaust fans serve the building rest rooms.

Elevator Power

Two 30 horsepower motors power the elevators.

---

*Electric resistance heating is *not* energy-efficient, but it is used in the example to illustrate circuiting and load calculations.

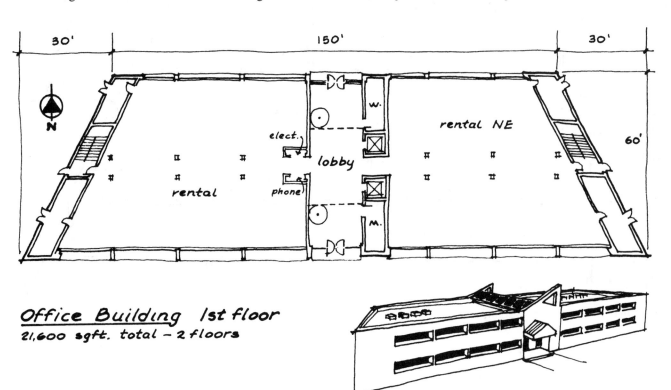

Office Building 1st floor
21,600 sqft. total – 2 floors

FIGURE 12.4

NORTHEAST OFFICES

The office area shown in Figure 12.5 is leased by a small graphic design firm specializing in computer generated video product. Staff members include the owner, an office manager, two designers, and a receptionist.

Interior office spaces include the following:

1. Waiting area
2. Reception
3. Print room
4. Lunch room
5. Graphic designer workstations
6. Office manager
7. Owner
8. Conference and presentation
9. Library with two workstations
10. Mechanical and storage
11. Corridor

The firm's work is accomplished on an interconnected computer network supported by UPS (uninterrupted power supply). The reception-waiting area is used to display recent commissions, and the library maintains an extensive CD reference collection.

Each designer has two workstations, one with a window view, and a second in the windowless library. The conference room is a focal point for client proposals and presentations.

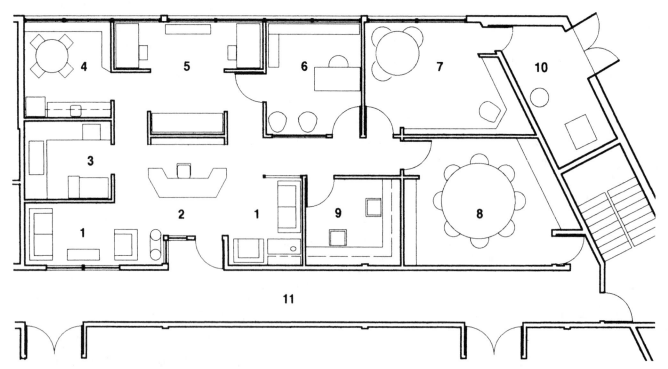

FIGURE 12.5 Northeast Offices

12.2 EXAMPLE OFFICE ELECTRICAL PLANS

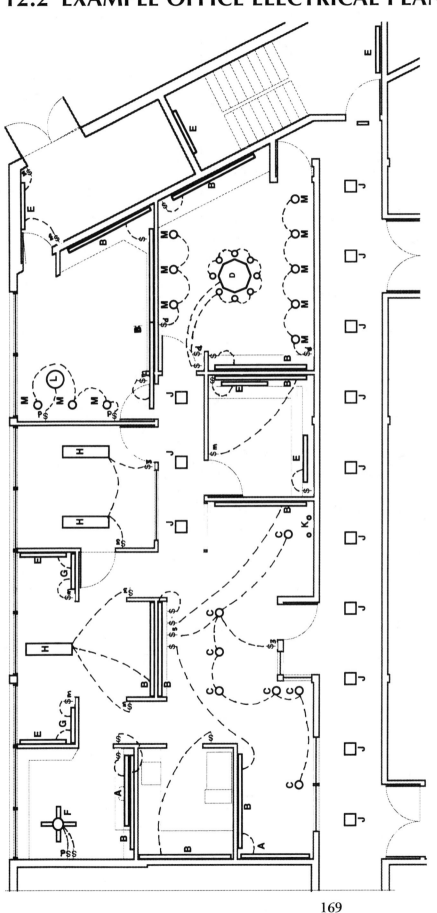

SWITCHING LIGHTS

Fixture design, selection, and layout were covered in previous chapters. This drawing shows fixtures and switching for the northeast office.

Switch Key

$	Single-pole switch
$_3$	Three-way switch (two locations)
$_d$	Dimmer
$_k$	Key activated
$_m$	Motion activated
$_{pc}$	Photocell (light activated)
$_t$	Timer activated

Study the drawing and notice the unswitched fixtures in halls and stairways. These fixtures operate 24 hours a day for safety and security reasons; they are controlled by a switch duty circuit breaker located in an emergency panel. Also notice there is no switch shown for fixture K. Two lamps designated K are installed in a wall-mounted display case which has a built-in switch.

Three-way switches are shown when fixtures must be controlled from two locations. Three-way designation indicates three wires connected to the switch; when more than two control locations are required four-way switches must be used.

Dimmer switches are shown controlling some fixtures; dimmers are economical for incandescent lamps but expensive when used to control fluorescent lamps.

Motion activated switches are used to save energy in unoccupied spaces. They are shown at switch locations, but they can be mounted in the fixture.

Key switches (rest rooms), photocell switches (exterior and perimeter), and timer switches are not shown on this drawing.

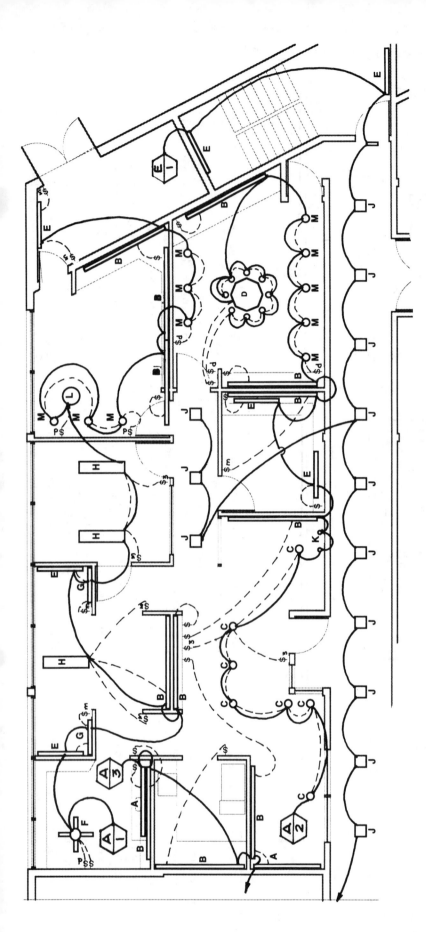

LIGHTING CIRCUITS

Curved solid lines are used to show circuits serving lighting fixtures. Begin circuit runs at a distant fixture and work toward the panel along a single path. The following rules guide circuiting:

1. When a group of fixtures is controlled by a switch they must be connected to a single circuit.

2. Maximum circuit load is 1,920 watts. Try to connect at least 1,800 watts on all but the last circuit.

3. Use Table 12.9 to add lighting watts, then total and describe each circuit in the panel schedule as shown in Table 12.10.

A hexagon key is used to designate the panel and circuit; locate this key at either end of circuit path.

TABLE 12.9

Fixture Schedule

Key	Watts	Fixture
A	110	Fluorescent strip
B	130	Fluorescent strip
C	50	Incandescent can
D	500	Incandescent, custom
E	72	Fluorescent strip
F	200	Fan and light
G	55	Fluorescent strip
H	72	Recessed fluorescent
J	28	Recessed fluorescent
K	70	In display case
L	250	Incandescent pendant
M	50	Incandescent eyeball
=	18	Exit

TABLE 12.10

Circuit Tabulation for Panel A

Circuit	Watts	Description
1	1,942	Ltg. perimeter—NE
2	1,834	Ltg. recept. & conf.—NE

Check circuit wattage tabulations for accuracy before going on to the following drawings. See Table 12.10.

Two additional circuits shown on the drawing are not tabulated in panel A. An emergency circuit shows 526 watts, but additional lighting will be connected before this circuit is run to the emergency panel. Circuit A-3 serves 610 watts in the reception, print, and lunch rooms. It continues into the rest room to serve additional lighting loads.

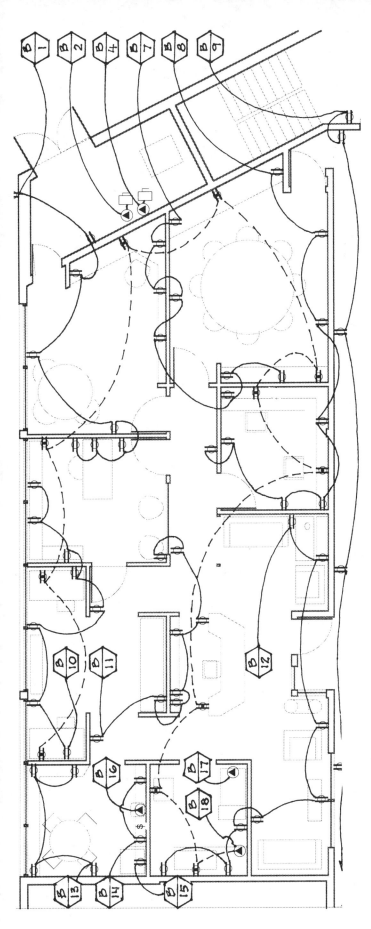

DUPLEX AND POWER CIRCUITS

Study the duplex circuits first. Codes allow a maximum of 13 duplex outlets on a single 20 ampere circuit, but usual commercial practice counts circuits 8. Each duplex is counted as 180 watts unless it serves a specific appliance.

Duplex and Power Key
- Standard duplex outlet (15 A, 125 V)
- Computer network duplex outlet
- ▲ Power outlet

This drawing is too small for a complete key. When preparing contract drawings use a larger scale and add needed information at each duplex, for example:

42" Outlets above counters

GFI Outlets in wet locations

Also add a Δ key for each phone outlet.

Curved solid lines show circuits, and hexagons indicate the panel and circuit number. Trace several duplex circuits and verify watts tabulated in the panel. One circuit is used for the refrigerator, and the lunch room has two circuits to accommodate appliances like microwaves and toasters.

UPS. Dashed lines are used to show computer network outlets served by an uninterrupted power supply.

Power outlets Include 120 volt, 208 volt, and 208 volt, three-phase loads. Usually three-phase loads like strip heat are connected in large panels with elevator motors and condensing units. Here, strip heat is included in panel B for example purposes.

Table 12.11 tabulates each circuit shown on the plan and Panel B (Figures 12.10 and 12.13) notes protection and conductors required for each circuit.

Review and verify these panel loads. They will be used to size panels and the building service in following text.

TABLE 12.11

Circuit Tabulation for Panel B

Circuit	Watts	Description
1	1,440	Duplex—owner & manager
2	1,580	Air handler fan - 3/4 hp
4	10,000	Strip heat - 3 phase
7	1,440	Duplex - owner & conf.
8	1,440	Duplex - library & conf.
9	1,440	Duplex - hall
10	1,440	Duplex - manager & work
11	1,440	Duplex - manager & recept.
12	1,440	Duplex - waiting & print
13	720	Duplex - lunch
14	360	Duplex - lunch
15	300	Duplex - refrigerator
16	830	Duplex - garbage disposer
17	1,800	Duplex - copy machine
18	5,000	UPS (power supply)

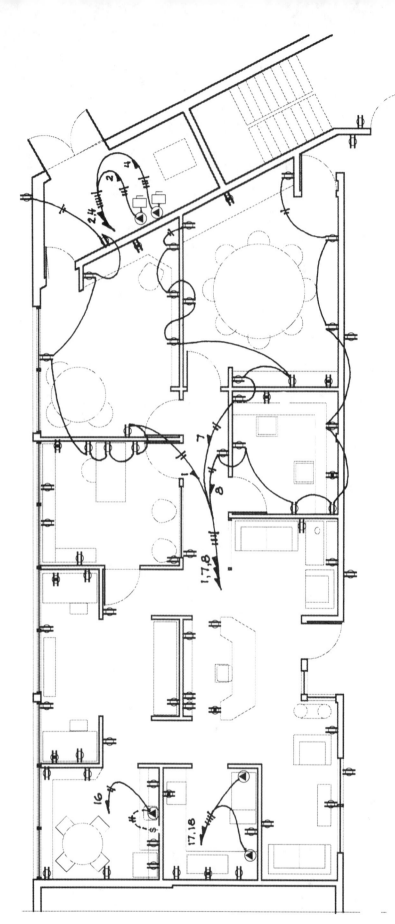

CIRCUITING AND SYMBOLS

Hexagon panel keys, and dotted lines for switches or special circuits, communicate effectively for a project like the example office. Another set of circuiting keys and symbols is illustrated above for information.

Drawings for government projects frequently detail each junction box and conduit run to encourage competitive bidding.

The plan shown here repeats selected circuits shown in the preceding figure to illustrate alternate circuit keys and symbols. Arrows replace hexagons and locate home runs for fully loaded circuits. Circuit numbers above the arrows designate the panel space assigned to each circuit. Slash marks show the number of conductors in a conduit. A small

slash is used for a hot wire, and a larger slash designates a neutral wire. Circuits 2 and 4 require several hot wires but share a common neutral. These 208 volt circuits don't cause neutral current, and the neutral is used as a ground conductor. When a grounded conduit system is connected to such loads the neutral may be omitted. Even more detail, specifying and locating each junction box and conduit run, is required on some government work.

Lighting and duplex circuits in three-phase systems can use a common neutral to reduce wiring costs. Circuits 1, 7, and 8 require separate hot wires, but they share a single neutral conductor.

A 1/2" conduit can hold ten 20 ampere conductors, so seven 120 volt circuits can be run in just one 1/2" conduit (seven hot and three neutral wires).

Selected Symbols

1,2,3 ╱╱╱╱ #12 - ½"C.	home run to panel LP-3, ckts. #1-2-3. # 12 wires - 1/2"C.
╱╱╱ ½"	two hot wires, one neutral and one switch leg (S) in a 1/2" C.
(black triangle)	phone outlet (never run with AC - use separate conduit)
(circle target)	duplex outlet in floor
⊖ gfi 42"	ground fault duplex outlet 42" above finished floor
LP-3 (black bar)	lighting panel LP-3

LOBBY

The lobby is a first experience for guests and tenants that sets "building image." Planters and display cases flank the entry doors, and two large decorative vertical tapestries are suspended below a stained glass ceiling.

A bridge, accessed by elevators and a decorative circular stair, carries second-floor tenant and guest traffic between the east and west office spaces. A reception desk, building directory, and small waiting area share space beneath the bridge (see Figure 12.6).

Lobby Lighting

Scene controller dimmers set light intensity for seven lobby lighting circuits (see Table 12.12). Six scenes are preset and a photocell override changes scene settings in response to changing daylight conditions. A-4 lights the stair, bridge, and building directory. A-5 and A-6 illuminate decorative tapestries and plants. A-7 and A-8 control backlights for the stained glass lobby ceiling 20 feet above the floor. The backlights are fluorescent fixtures equipped with electronic dimming ballasts. A-9 and A-10 light the entrances, display cases, and reception spaces below the bridge.

Six lighting scenes are preset: morning, daylight winter, daylight summer, daylight overcast, evening, and midnight to sunrise.

TABLE 12.12

Scene Circuit Summary

Key	Watts	Fixtures Illuminate
A-4	1,138	Stair, bridge, and directory
A-5	1,200	Tapestry (two at 600 each)
A-6	1,750	Plants (seven at 250 each)
A-7	1,440	Stained glass backlights
A-8	1,440	Stained glass backlights
A-9	1,750	Display cases and under bridge
A-10	1,000	Exterior (ten at 100 each)

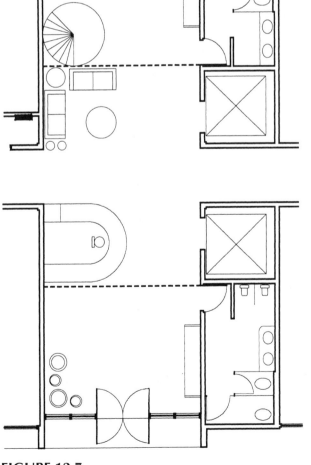

FIGURE 12.7

FIGURE 12.6

TABLE 12.13

Lobby Fixture Schedule

Key	Watts	Fixture
B	130	Fluorescent strip
C	50	Incandescent can
E	72	Fluorescent—wall mount
N	240	Industrial fluorescent (locate between the skylight and the stained glass ceiling)
O	600	Incandescent (a circle of twelve 50 watt MR-16 spots illuminates each tapestry)
P	460	Multi-vapor cylinder
R	100	Incandescent can
S	500	Incandescent—display case
T	250	Incandescent can
U	56	Fluorescent recessed
V	100	Incandescent wall mount
W	288	Fluorescent directory sign
	18	Exit lamp with battery

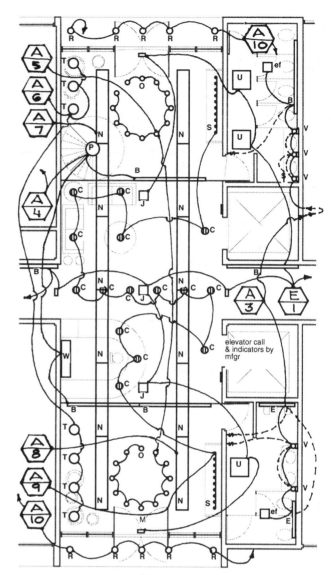

FIGURE 12.8 Lobby Lighting Plan

Watts are noted for each fixture so readers can verify panel load calculations that follow (see Table 12.13). Fixture selection and placement for lighting design is covered in Chapters 4 and 6.

LOBBY FIXTURES

Light fixtures B, C, and E from the northeast offices, and N through W will be used to illuminate the lobby (see Figure 12.7).

LOBBY LIGHTING

Panel A serves building lighting loads. Seven lobby lighting circuits are regulated by a scene controller that dims or brightens selected circuits as sunlight intensity varies. Read the descriptions that follow, and trace each circuit on Figure 12.8 or swap for lighting plan.

Emergency Lighting

Circuit E-1 serves exit lights and a few fixtures in the rest rooms and under the bridge. These lights will operate on emergency power in the event of a utility power failure. E-1 extends to ground-floor corridors and stairway lighting.

Rest Room Lighting

Circuit A-3 (1,884 watts) serves rest room lighting and also several fixtures in the northeast offices.

12.3 EXAMPLE OFFICE PANELS

OVERVIEW

Preparation of electrical plans is a four-step process:

1. Select and locate fixtures and switches.
2. Locate duplex and power outlets.
3. Circuit loads and size panels.
4. Size and detail the electrical service.

Plans illustrate steps 1 and 2 for the northeast offices and the lobby. Lighting and power loads for the other building tenants are inferred from the northeast offices.

Plans also show circuiting (step 3) for the northeast offices and the lobby. Look back and confirm the loads noted in the panel A schedule (see Figure 12.9).

LIGHTING PANEL A

Panels apportion electrical power among individual circuits. Single-pole, 20 ampere circuits are used for most building lighting, and connected loads are limited to 80% of circuit rating. This means a 20 ampere circuit can carry a maximum load of 16 amperes or 1,920 watts at 120 volts.

Each single-pole circuit breaker occupies one space in the panel, and #12 copper conductors are selected to safely carry 20 amperes.

PANEL SCHEDULE

The three-phase panel schedule shown in Figure 12.9 will be used for all examples. Start by filling in the panel key and voltage entries at the top of the form. Values for amperes, spaces, and feeders will be set after all panel circuits are tabulated.

Field entries on the form are divided into five vertical columns as follows:

Key is the number assigned to a given circuit on the plan drawing. Each key digit also represents a space in the panel, and each space can hold a single-pole circuit breaker. Usual lighting panel capacity choices are 20, 30, 40, or 42 spaces.

Description identifies the circuit location on the plan drawing.

PANEL [A]   *Lighting*

| 120/208 volts | | amps MCB or MLO | | spaces or poles |

feeders __ # ___ and __ # ___ _____ in ___ " C. or _____

Key	Description		CB A-P	wire	Load (watts or volt-amps)		
1	NE Offices		20-1	#12	1,942		
2	NE Offices		20-1	#12		1,834	
3	NE Offices & R.R.		20-1	#12			1,884
4	Lobby Scene	stair bridge	20-1	#12	1,138		
5	Lobby Scene	tapestry	20-1	#12		1,200	
6	Lobby Scene	tapestry	20-1	#12			1,750
7	Lobby Scene	ceiling	20-1	#12	1,440		
8	Lobby Scene	ceiling	20-1	#12		1,440	
9	Lobby Scene	display	20-1	#12			1,750
10	Lobby Scene	exterior	20-1	#12	1,000		
11							
12							
13							

FIGURE 12.9

CB A-P is the column where circuit breaker amps and poles are entered for each circuit.
Wire notes conductor size for each circuit.
Load entries tabulate total connected watts or volt-amperes. Three entry columns alternate under the load heading. Each column represents one of the three busses in a three-phase panel.

RECEPTACLE (AND HVAC) PANEL B

Refer back to the northeast office Duplex and Power Circuits to check circuit loads. Then read the key summary in Figure 12.10 and verify each circuit in the panel schedule.

Duplex Circuits B-1 and B-7 through B-15

Commercial electrical installations connect up to eight duplex outlets on a 20 ampere circuit. Recall that each duplex outlet is counted as a 180 watt load, so a typical duplex circuit load is 1,440 watts.

Lunch room circuits B-13 and B-14 serve less than eight duplex outlets so toasters, coffee pots, and microwaves are less likely to overload them. Circuit B-15 serves just the refrigerator.

HVAC CIRCUITS

Air handlers and resistance heat strips are included in this panel to illustrate two- and three-pole loads. A typical office building would serve such loads in a separate power panel instead of mixing duplex and HVAC.

Circuit B-2

A single-phase, 3/4 horsepower, 208 volt air handler motor is protected by a two-pole circuit breaker that takes two spaces in the panel. Motor loads are tabulated in volt-amperes and this motor draws 7.9 amps. A 15 ampere circuit is specified to pass the motor's starting current surge.*

---

*The 3/4 hp motor load is shared equally by two panel busses so each carries 790 volt-amperes ($200 \times 7.9 \div 2 = 790$). Calculate with 200 volts instead of 208 volts to allow for voltage drop in the circuit conductors between the panel and the motor.

PANEL B — Power

Key	Description	CB A-P	wire	Load (watts or volt-amps)		
1	duplex NE Offices	20-1	#12	1,440		
2	air handler NE (¾ hp)	15-2	#14		790	
3	↓					790
4	strip heat NE (10 kW)	40-3	#8	3,333		
5	↓				3,333	
6	↓					3,333
7	duplex NE Offices	20-1	#12	1,440		
8	duplex NE Offices	↓	↓		1,440	
9	duplex Hall	↓	↓			1,440
10	duplex NE Offices	↓	↓	1,440		
11	duplex NE Offices	↓	↓		1,440	
12	duplex NE Offices	↓	↓			1,440
13	duplex - lunch room NE	↓	↓	720		
14	duplex - lunch room NE	↓	↓		360	
15	duplex - refrigerator	↓	↓			300
16	garbage disposer (⅓ hp)	15-1	#14	830		
17	copy machine	20-1	#12		1,800	
18	UPS (5 kVA)	30-2	#10			2,500
19				2,500		

FIGURE 12.10

Circuit B-4

Inefficient resistance heat strips are used to illustrate circuiting. The northeast offices need 34,000 BTUH or 10 kW for space heating. A three-phase strip heater has three internal resistance wire loops, and each loop is connected across two hot wires. Three two-pole circuit breakers could serve the heater, but using a single three-pole circuit breaker saves panel space and wiring.

Calculate circuit amperes = 28.9 (10,000 ÷ 200× $\sqrt{3}$). Minimum circuit ampacity is 125% of the calculated value or 36.1 amperes, so a 40 ampere circuit breaker is selected. The 10,000 watt load is divided equally across the three panel busses.

Circuits B-16 and B-17

A dedicated circuit is usually provided for larger equipment or appliances.

Circuit B-18

The 5 kVA UPS (uninterrupted power supply) is served by a two-pole breaker. Calculated circuit amperes = 25, and the manufacturer specifies 30 ampere circuit protection. Conduit for UPS conductors is isolated from all other electrical conduit.

SCHEDULE PANEL A (LIGHTING)

The form in Figure 12.11 is a completed panel schedule. It describes each circuit and calculates loads to size the feeders. The northeast office's lighting load is about 2 watts per square foot of floor area, so two times floor area should provide a reasonable estimate of lighting load for all other office areas. The lobby and northeast office lighting totals about 15 kW. If the other offices add 45 kW the lighting panel(s) should have a capacity of about 60 kW.

Lighting circuits for the lobby and the northeast offices fill 10 panel spaces. The 45 kW lighting load of the other offices will require 25* panel spaces or poles, so the panel should have at least 35 spaces.

Lighting circuits 11 through 36 are filled allowing 2 watts per square foot. Designers work to balance the total watts connected to each panel bus so feeder loads are equal.

A 40 space lighting panel is specified. Typical installations include open spaces in panels for future expansion; this example reserves 10%. Consider including spare breakers in the open panel spaces and rough in wiring to an accessible junction box above the ceiling to ease future expansion (see Figure 12.12).

Calculate Panel Amperes

Add the watts connected to each panel bus, and then add three busses to find total panel load. This load is shared by three feeders. Each feeder carries about 169 amperes ($60,778 \div (208)(\sqrt{3}) = 169$).

The neutral feeder provides a return path for current serving 120 volt loads. Current flows in the neutral when panel loads are not balanced, and maximum unbalance occurs when all lights connected to one bus are operating, but all other lights are off.

To calculate maximum neutral current, total the 120 volt loads for each bus and then divide the largest by 120. The panel has a maximum neutral current of 169 amperes ($20,320 \div 120 = 169$).

Select Panel

Standard panel capacities are 100, 125, 150, 200, 225, 400, and 600 amperes. Select a 200 ampere panel to carry the 169 ampere load and accommodate future expansion. In a smaller building the panel would include a three-pole main circuit breaker. For this example, panel protection will be located at the service entry. Specify 200 amperes MLO (main lugs only) for panel A. The panel lugs and busses are sized for 200 amperes but the panel does not have a main circuit breaker. Complete the second line in the panel schedule accordingly.

Size Panel Feeders and Conduit

Select four #3/0 copper panel feeders or four 250 MCM aluminum feeders to carry 200 amperes. Aluminum panel feeders are used in the example, but *many local codes prohibit aluminum* conductors inside buildings. Verify THWN feeder sizes on page 160. THWN is rated at 75°C. THHN rated at 90°C allows higher current for a given conductor size.

The neutral conductor could be #4/0 at 169 amps, but to allow for expansion, neutral ampacity serving a lighting panel is usually specified equal to the phase conductor ampacity. Use 2" conduit for copper feeders or 2 1/2" conduit for aluminum feeders.*

---

*45 kW at about 1,800 watts per circuit = 25.

*Verify conductor ampacity, conduit size, and panel poles (or spaces) on pages 160–165.

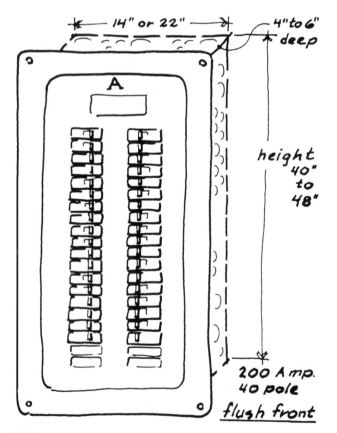

FIGURE 12.12

14" or 22"

4" to 6" deep

A

height 40" to 48"

200 Amp. 40 pole flush front

PANEL A   *Lighting*

120/208 volts   200   amps ~~MCB or~~ (MLO)   40   spaces or poles

feeders 4 # 250 and __ # ___ THWN in 2½" C. or _____
            MCM-AL

Key	Description		CB A-P	wire	Load (watts or volt-amps)		
1	NE Offices	1st floor	20-1	#12	1 942 *		
2	NE Offices	1st floor	20-1	#12		1 834	
3	NE Offices	1st floor	20-1	#12			1 884
4	Lobby scene	stair-bridge	20-1	#12	1 138		
5	Lobby scene	tapestry	20-1	#12		1 200	
6	Lobby scene	tapestry	20-1	#12			1 750
7	Lobby scene	ceiling	20-1	#12	1 440		
8	Lobby scene	ceiling	20-1	#12		1 440	
9	Lobby scene	display	20-1	#12			1 750
10	Lobby scene	exterior	20-1	#12	1 000		
11	SE Offices	1st floor	20-1	#12		1 800	
12							1 700
13					1 900		
14						1 700	
15	NW Offices	1st floor					1 600
16					1 800		
17						1 700	
18	SW Offices	1st floor					1 700
19					1 900		
20						1 800	
21							1 600
22	NE Offices	2nd floor			1 800		
23						1 700	
24							1 700
25	SE Offices	2nd floor			1 900		
26						1 800	
27							1 600
28					1 800		
29	NW Offices	2nd floor				1 700	
30							1 700
31					1 900		
32	SW Offices	2nd floor				1 800	
33							1 600
34					1 800		
35						1 700	
36							1 700
37							
38							
39							
40							
41							
42							

* cut ckt. 1 to 1920 - why?

$\dfrac{60778}{208\sqrt{3}}$

connected load amps 169

phase totals | 20,320 | 20,174 | 20,284

$\dfrac{20,320}{120}$

panel total 60,778

max. neutral amps 169 by GJM date 9·1·99

FIGURE 12.11

SCHEDULE PANEL B

The form in Figure 12.13 is a completed panel schedule. It describes each circuit and calculates loads to size the feeders. Duplex, air handler, and strip heat loads in the northeast offices use 18 panel spaces and total about 30 kW. Panel B will serve the northeast *and southeast* offices in 36 spaces with a total load of about 60 kW.

The northeast and southeast offices occupy about 25% of the building area, so when you calculate the building service allow for three more panels, each equal to panel B. Designated B_2, B_3, and B_4, they will serve duplex, air handler, and strip heat loads for the west offices and the second-floor offices.

A typical office building of this size would use separate panels for duplex loads and HVAC equipment. Panel B includes strip heat and air handlers with the duplex circuits *only* to illustrate two- and three-pole loads and the neutral current calculation (see Figure 12.14).

Calculate Panel Amperes

Add the watts connected to each panel bus, and then add three busses to find total panel load. This load is shared by three feeders and *each* feeder must carry 168 amperes.
$(60,349 \div (208)(\sqrt{3}) = 168)$.

Select Panel

Standard panel capacities are 100, 125, 150, 200, 225, 400, and 600 amperes. Select a 200 ampere panel to carry the 168 ampere load and accommodate future expansion. In a smaller building the panel would include a three-pole main circuit breaker, but for this example panel protection is located at the service entry. Specify 200 amperes MLO (main lugs only) for panel B. The panel lugs and busses are sized for 200 amperes but the panel does not have a main circuit breaker. Complete the second line in the panel schedule accordingly.

Size Panel Feeders and Conduit

Select three #3/0 copper panel feeders or three 250 MCM aluminum feeders to carry 200 amperes. Aluminum panel feeders are used in the example because they're lighter and easier to install than copper, but *many local codes prohibit aluminum* conductors in buildings.

The neutral conductor provides a return path for current serving 120 volt loads, but 208 volt equipment does *not* cause neutral current. To calculate maximum neutral current total *only* the 120 volt loads for each bus and then divide the largest by 120. The maximum neutral watts is 11,520 (line 42) so the maximum neutral current is 96 amperes (11,520 ÷ 120 = 96). Select a #3 copper or a #1 aluminum neutral to carry 100 amperes. Select 2″ conduit for copper feeders or 2 1/2″ conduit for aluminum feeders.*

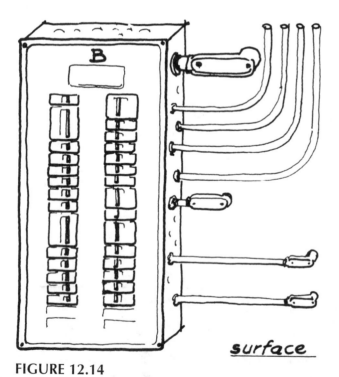

surface

FIGURE 12.14

---

*Verify conductor ampacity, conduit size, and panel poles (or spaces) on pages 160–165.

PANEL B, Power

120/208 volts | 200 amps MCB or ⟨MLO⟩ | 40 spaces or poles

feeders 3 #250 MCM AL and 1 # 3 AL THWN in 2" C. or _____

Key	Description	CB A-P	wire	Load (watts or volt-amps)		
1	duplex NE Offices	20-1	#12	1,440		
2	air handler NE (¾ hp)	15-2	#14		790	
3						790
4	strip heat NE (10 kW)	40-3	#8	3,333		
5					3,333	
6						3,333
7	duplex NE Offices	20-1	#12	1,440		
8	duplex NE Offices				1,440	
9	duplex Hall					1,440
10	duplex NE Offices			1,440		
11	duplex NE Offices				1,440	
12	duplex NE Offices					1,440
13	duplex - lunch room NE			720		
14	duplex - lunch room NE				360	
15	duplex - refrigerator					300
16	garbage disposer (⅓ hp)	15-1	#14	830		
17	copy machine	20-1	#12		1,800	
18	UPS (5 kVA)	30-2	#10			2,500
19				2,500		
20	duplex Lobby (not shown)	20-1	#12		1,440	
21	air handler SE (1hp)	15-2	#14			920
22				920		
23	strip heat SE (12 kW)	50-3	#8		4,000	
24						4,000
25				4,000		
26	duplex SE Offices	20-1	#12		1,440	
27						1,440
28				1,440		
29					1,440	
30						1,440
31				1,440		
32					1,440	
33						1,440
34				1,440		
35					720	
36						720
37						
38						
39						
40						
41						
42		(neutral	totals)	(10,190)	(11,520)	(8,220)

phase totals | 20,943 | 19,643 | 19,763

$$\frac{60,349}{208\sqrt{3}}$$

connected load amps 168

$$\frac{11,520}{120}$$

panel total 60,349

max. neutral amps 96 by JOG date 9-9-99

SCHEDULE PANEL C (POWER)

The form in Figure 12.15 is a completed panel schedule. It describes each circuit and calculates loads to size the feeders. Panel C supplies condensing units and elevators. Five 5-ton condensers serve the lobby and smaller offices, while four 7.5-ton units carry the larger offices. Second-floor air handlers circulate a bit more air than first-floor air handlers, to carry the added cooling load caused by roof heat gain.

Condenser circuits (poles 1–27). Panel loads are estimated in volt-amperes based on each condenser's full load ampere (FLA) rating. The 7.5-ton units in panel C require 26 FLA or 9,000 volt-amperes at 200 volts ($26 \times 200 \sqrt{3} = 9,000$). This electrical load is shared equally by the panel feeders.

Circuit protection is specified by condenser manufacturers to accommodate the starting current surge. The rule of thumb for estimating motor circuit protection is 125% of FLA, but manufacturers frequently specify 150% or more.

Elevators (poles 28–35). The 30 horsepower elevator motors demand nearly 92 FLA so 125 ampere circuit breakers are specified. Motors are an exception to the general rule that circuit wire ampacity must equal the circuit breaker trip rating. The #2 copper wire used in these circuits is rated for only 115 amperes.

Spaces. A 40 space panel is selected. Three single-pole circuits fill spaces 34–36 and the remaining empty spaces allow for expansion or omissions (forgotten electrical loads).

Note: A typical office building of this size would include the HVAC strip heat and air handler circuits from panel B in panel C. These loads were included in panel B only to illustrate two- and three-pole loads and the neutral current calculation.

Calculate Panel Amperes

Add the volt-amperes connected to each panel bus, and then add three busses to find total panel load. This load is shared by three feeders and *each* feeder will carry 370 amperes ($133{,}170 \div (208)(\sqrt{3}) = 370$).

Select Panel

Standard panel capacities are 100, 125, 150, 200, 225, 400, and 600 amperes. Select a 400 ampere panel allowing 30 amperes for expansion. In a smaller building the panel would include a three-pole main circuit breaker, but for this example panel protection is located at the service entry. Specify 400 amperes MLO (main lugs only) for panel C. The panel lugs and busses are sized for 400 amperes but the panel does not have a main circuit breaker. Complete the second line in the panel schedule accordingly.

Size Panel Feeders

600 MCM copper or 900 MCM aluminum feeders will carry 400 amperes, but installation is difficult. Two #3/0 copper or two 250 MCM aluminum feeders for each phase allow easier installation. Aluminum panel feeders are used in the example, but *many local codes prohibit aluminum* conductors in buildings. Neutral current is less than 20 amperes so a #10 aluminum neutral is specified.

Danger! Some code authorities require a full size equipment ground conductor. Others allow the conduit system to serve as a ground for three-phase equipment.

Select 2 1/2″ conduit for copper or 3″ conduit for aluminum feeders.*

---

*Verify conductor ampacity, conduit size, and panel poles (or spaces) on pages 160–165.

PANEL [C] *Power (a.c. & elevator)*

[120/208] volts   [400] amps ~~MCB or~~ (MLO)   [40] spaces or poles

feeders 3-900 MCM and 1 # 12 AL THWN in 3½" C. or 6-250 MCM & 1#12 in 3"C
            ↳ AL   Aluminum #feeders

Key	Description	CB A-P	wire	Load (watts or volt-amps)		
1	a.c. NE 1st floor↓ 5T	40 - 3	# 8	2,000		
2					2,000	
3						2,000
4	a.c. SE 7½T	50 - 3	# 8	3,000		
5					3,000	
6						3,000
7	a.c. NW 5T	40 - 3	# 8	2,000		
8					2,000	
9						2,000
10	a.c. SW 7½ T	50 - 3	# 8	3,000		
11					3,000	
12						3,000
13	a.c. Lobby	40 - 3	# 8	2,000		
14					2,000	
15						2,000
16	a.c. NE 2nd floor↓ 5T	40 - 3	# 8	2,000		
17					2,000	
18						2,000
19	a.c. SE 7½T	50 - 3	# 8	3,000		
20					3,000	
21						3,000
22	a.c. NW 5T	40 - 3	# 8	2,000		
23					2,000	
24						2,000
25	a.c. SW 7½T	50 - 3	# 8	3,000		
26					3,000	
27						3,000
28	elevator N 30hp	125-3	# 2	10,600		
29					10,600	
30						10,600
31	elevator S 30hp	125-3	# 2	10,600		
32					10,600	
33						10,600
34	elevator controls	20 -1	#12	1,200		
35	elevator controls	20 -1	#12		1,200	
36	security system	20 -1	#12			1,130
37						
38						
39						
40						
41						
42						

phase totals | 44,400 | 44,400 | 44,370 |

panel total 133,170

133,170/208√3 ~

connected load amps __370__   1200/120 allow→ max. neutral amps __20__   by __cb__   date __9-9-99__

FIGURE 12.15

OTHER ELECTRICAL LOADS

Two tasks remain before sizing the building service and completing this long example:

* Select and size the emergency panel.
* Check for errors and omissions on all electrical plans and circuits.

Emergency and omissions loads are estimated, lest faithful readers grow weary studying panel forms.

Panel E (Emergency)

A 60 ampere, three-pole panel will be used for three emergency circuits that total 5,000 watts. The emergency panel carries the building fire alarm system, exit signs, stair lighting, hallway lighting, and some lighting in each office. Emergency lighting operates 24 hours a day, and selected light fixtures also include a battery pack to provide an hour of illumination during a power failure.

In small buildings with few emergency power requirements, battery packs can replace the emergency panel. However, in high-rise offices or hospitals, extensive emergency loads require panels, generators, and a separate distribution system for emergency circuits.

Panel O (Omissions)

What's missing? For this example, panel O is estimated at 28,000 watts and a 100 ampere, 24-pole panel will be used. Good electrical designers don't need an omissions panel because they anticipate all electrical loads and allow expansion capacity in each panel. Panel O is used here, so careful readers can review the preceding pages and identify forgotten loads. Visualize the building *site* and think about electrical loads. Then, before you look at the following list, look back to panels B and C and see if you can identify two missing HVAC circuits.

Forgotten loads in panel O include:

* Air handlers and strip heat*
* Water heater
* Rest room exhaust fans
* Parking lot lighting
* Landscape lighting
* Christmas lights
* Site fountain (pump and lighting)
* Pumps for site drainage

---

*12 kW of strip heat and an air handler for the lobby.

SERVICE DIAGRAMS

An electrical service diagram is a schematic drawing identifying major components of a building's electrical service. Electrical subcontractors use this diagram and the electrical floor plans to price project labor and material.

Before sizing the service for the example building consider a hypothetical *smaller building* where the total building electrical load is carried by two panels. Assume these two panels are identical to example panels A and B, and that all electrical loads draw current simultaneously.

Smaller Building Service

The hypothetical smaller building has two 200 ampere panels. The building service will be sized for 400 amperes and each panel will be protected by a 200 ampere circuit breaker located below a wireway. The wireway is an enclosure with 400 ampere lugs where the service is split (see Figure 12.16).

Single Main Disconnect

Many localities require a single switch to shut off all electrical power in the event of a fire. Fused disconnects are indicated in Figure 12.17 instead of circuit breakers; both work, and selection is usually based on cost.

1,200 amperes?

Some office buildings install separate electrical services for each tenant, but the example building will be detailed with a single service.

The actual load on panels A and B totals 336 amperes. A 350 ampere service would reduce conductor cost but limit future expansion.

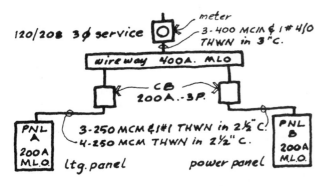

FIGURE 12.16

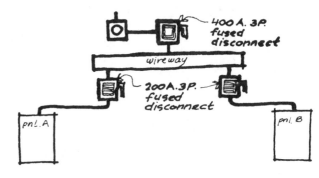

FIGURE 12.17

12.4 EXAMPLE OFFICE SERVICE

EXAMPLE BUILDING ELECTRICAL SERVICE

Using 120/208 volt power, the smallest possible standard service for the example building is 1,200 amperes. Review the following discussion and the illustrations until you understand and can explain this service ampacity.

Total capacity of eight panels in the example is 1,560 amperes. That's a lot of amperes and the building electrical service will be large and expensive (see Figure 12.18).

To reduce service size and cost use the actual connected amperes instead of the panel capacity (this reduces the potential for future expansion). Actual connected amperes total 1,304.

When all building electrical loads operate simultaneously the service must be sized to meet the total connected load. In the example building, heating and cooling are noncoincident loads so the service size can be reduced to serve only the largest of these. Resistance heating totals

100 kW or 278 amps and condensing units total 66 kVA or 183 amps. Subtract 183 amperes from the connected total, because simultaneous heating and cooling is not anticipated, and the minimum service is 1,121 amperes.

Manufacturers' standard ratings for panels and lugs are 400, 600, 800, 1,200, 1,600, and 2,000 amperes. Select a 1,200 ampere service, allowing 79 amperes (28 kW) of expansion capacity (see Figure 12.19). Verify conductor and conduit sizes for the 1,200 ampere service and for the building neutral.

The meter shown is "schematic" because it is not actually connected across the main feeders. The emergency panel is located ahead of the main switch so firefighters have the option of leaving emergency power on during a fire.

FIGURE 12.18

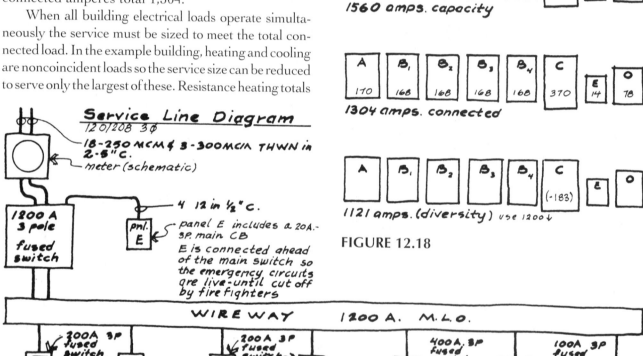

FIGURE 12.19

12.5 SERVICE OPTIONS
A BETTER WAY? SWITCHBOARD

In a building of this size with a single electrical service, a switchboard could replace the main switch, wireway, and seven fused switches. Wireways and disconnects are specified when each tenant is metered separately.

Switchboards act as large panels. They draw power from the service and apportion current to individual panels. The conductors, conduit, and panels shown in Figure 12.20 are identical to those in the preceding service diagram. Each fused switch has been replaced with a circuit breaker located in the switchboard.

277/480 VOLT SERVICE

Experienced electrical designers would consider increased service voltage for the example building. The diagram in Figure 12.21 illustrates a 277/480 volt service. Increasing service voltage reduces service size and cost.

The example building's service capacity is 432 kVA ($1,200 \times 208 \sqrt{3} = 432,000$).

Operating elevator motors, condensing units, and resistance heat strips at 480 volts cut current required by more than half. Ballasts designed for 277 volt operation reduce lighting current and the number of lighting circuits. Transformers that provide power for 120 volt loads are an added cost for the 277/480 volt system.

Calculations used for the 120/208 volt service are easily revised for a 277/480 volt installation (or for the 347/600 volt system of choice in Canada). The building's 432 kVA load requires 520 amperes at 480 volts. A 600 ampere service would be specified. Panels would be revised to serve motor, heating, and ballasted lighting at 277/480 volts. Duplex panels are served by 277 120-volt or 480 120/208-volt transformers.

Very large buildings cut electrical costs by taking power at high voltage (5 to 15 kV). Utilities charge less for high-voltage power because the building owner installs and maintains transformers and switchgear.

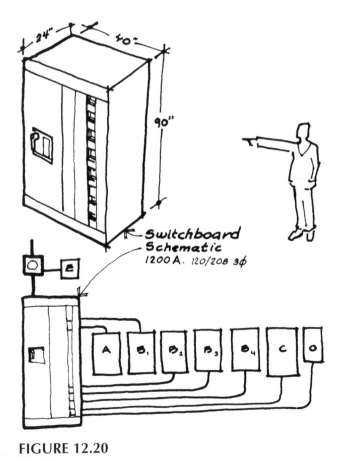

FIGURE 12.20

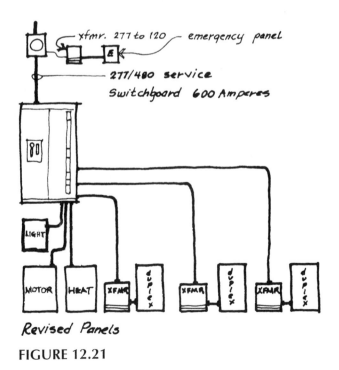

FIGURE 12.21

LOAD GROWTH

It's easy to calculate a building's electrical service capacity, but experience and judgment are necessary when oversizing to accommodate future loads. Historical 10-year load growth for office buildings has been in the 40 to 80% range, but recent lighting retrofits and HVAC improvements have cut electrical demand and consumption substantially. Because it's common practice to select the next largest standard size service equipment, some expansion capacity is usually available.

Because new panels and a larger electrical service are difficult and expensive renovations in an existing building, knowledgeable owners are willing to spend construction dollars on increased service capacity to ease future expansion. Some owners will also install extra panels and conduit stubs. However, low-budget projects rarely commit construction dollars for future expansion.

SMALLER SERVICE?

Resistance heating specified for the example building is *not* energy-efficient. Experienced designers would specify gas or oil-fired heating or heat pumps instead. Efficient HVAC equipment can reduce annual heating costs and reduce the size of the electrical service.

The example also totals more than 5 watts per square foot for duplex loads. This allowance is at the very high end of the office building range. A minimum electrical service for the building using gas heat and allowing 2.5 watts per square foot for duplex loads could cut service size (cost and electric bills) by one third (or 33%).

RIGHT SERVICE?

Two electrical services have been proposed for the example building and more follow. The right service is the one that best meets the construction budget and anticipated operating requirements.

Low-budget speculative rental office #1.
> 1,000 ampere, 120/208* volt service. Use gas heat and cut duplex load to 2.5 watts per square foot.

Low-budget speculative rental office #2.
> Five 200 ampere (or ten 100 ampere), 120/208* volt metered services. Use gas heat and cut duplex load to 2.5 watts per square foot. Individual meters pass utility costs to the tenants, but the number of services divides the building into 5 or 10 rental areas which may not suit some potential tenants.

Medium-quality office for four tenants #1.
> 600 ampere, 277/480 volt service. With gas heat and 5 watts per square foot duplex load, this service allows for 25% load growth.

Medium-quality office for four tenants #2.
> Four metered 150 ampere, 277/480 volt services. Allows 25% load growth as above but limits building occupancy to four equal area tenants.

Medium-quality office for one owner.
> 800 ampere, 277/480 volt service. With gas heat and 5 watts per square foot duplex load, this service allows for almost 100% load growth.

High-quality office for one owner.
> 1,000 ampere, 277/480 volt service. With gas heat and 5 watts per square foot duplex load, this service would include electrical rough-in for future load growth.

---

*Or 120/240 delta depending on the utility.

12.6 TABLES AND PANEL FORMS

TABLE 12.14

Circuit Breakers (trip amperes)

15–50 by 5s

15	20	25*	30	35*	40	45*	50

(*25, 35, and 45 for motor circuits)

60–110 by 10s

60	70	80	90	100	110

125–250 by 25s

125	150	175	200	225	250

300–500 by 50s

300	350	400	450	500

600–1,000 by 100s

600	700	800	900	1,000

1,200–2,000 by 200s

1,200	1,400	1,600	1,800	2,000

Select conductors with an ampere rating that equals or exceeds the circuit breaker trip amperes.

TABLE 12.15

Conductors (sized by amperes)

Allowable amperes for three THWN (75°C) insulated conductors in a raceway based on an ambient temperature of 30°C.

Amperes	Aluminum	Copper
15	#12	#14
20	#10	#12
25	#10	#10
30	#8	#10
35	#8	#8
40	#8	#8
45	#6	#8
50	#6	#8
60	#4	#6
70	#3	#4
80	#2	#4
90	#2	#3
100	#1	#3
110	#1/0	#2
125	#2/0	#1
150	#3/0	#1/0
175	#4/0	#2/0
200	250 MCM	#3/0
225	300 MCM	#4/0
250	350 MCM	250 MCM
300	500 MCM	350 MCM
350	700 MCM	400 MCM
400	900 MCM	600 MCM

TABLE 12.16

Conduit

Maximum number of type THWN or THHN conductors in conduit or tubing

Wire Size	Conduit Size			
	1/2″	3/4″	1″	1 1/4″
14	13	24	39	69
12	10	18	29	51
10	6	11	18	32
8	3	5	9	16
6	1	4	6	11
4	1	2	4	7
3	1	1	3	6
2	1	1	3	5
1		1	1	3
0		1	1	3
00		1	1	2

Wire Size	Conduit Size			
	1 1/2″	2″	2 1/2″	3″
8	22	36	51	79
6	15	26	37	57
4	9	16	22	35
3	8	13	19	29
2	7	11	16	25
1	5	8	12	18
0	4	7	10	15
00	3	6	8	13
000	3	5	7	11
0000	2	4	6	9
250	1	3	4	7
300	1	3	4	6
350	1	2	3	5

Wire Size	Conduit Size			
	3 1/2″	4″	5″	6″
2	33	43	67	97
1	25	32	50	72
0	21	27	42	61
00	17	22	35	51
000	14	18	29	42
0000	12	15	24	35
250	10	12	20	28
300	8	11	17	24
350	7	9	15	21
400	6	8	13	19
500	5	7	11	16
600	4	5	9	13
700	4	5	8	11
750	3	4	7	11

Conductors in air or with insulation rated for higher temperature operation can carry more current.

SINGLE PHASE

PANEL ☐ _____

☐ volts ☐ amps <u>MCB or MLO</u> ☐ spaces or poles

feeders __ # ___ and __ # ___ _____ in ___" C. or _____

Key	Description	CB A-P	wire	Load (watts or volt-amps)
1				
2				
3				
4				
5				
6				
7				
8				
9				
10				
11				
12				
13				
14				
15				
16				
17				
18				
19				
20				
21				
22				
23				
24				
25				
26				
27				
28				
29				
30				
31				
32				
33				
34				
35				
36				
37				
38				
39				
40				
41				
42				

phase totals ☐ ☐ ☐

panel total _____

connected load amps _____ max. neutral amps _____ by _____ date _____

THREE-PHASE

PANEL ☐ _____

☐ volts   ☐ amps <u>MCB or MLO</u>   ☐ spaces or poles

feeders __ # ___ and __ # ___ _____ in ___" C. or _____

Key	Description	CB A-P	wire	Load (watts or volt-amps)
1				
2				
3				
4				
5				
6				
7				
8				
9				
10				
11				
12				
13				
14				
15				
16				
17				
18				
19				
20				
21				
22				
23				
24				
25				
26				
27				
28				
29				
30				
31				
32				
33				
34				
35				
36				
37				
38				
39				
40				
41				
42				

phase totals ☐ ☐ ☐

panel total _____

connected load amps _____   max. neutral amps _____   by _____   date _____

CHAPTER

13

Energy Profiles

". . . . how can the brute 'causes' of finance be translated into the lasting stuff of profound aesthetic symbolism."

Louis Sullivan

Architects, engineers, and constructors aspire to create beautiful, functional, comfortable, economical, efficient buildings. Designers seek "profound aesthetic symbolism," and design development is a series of choices about orientation, fenestration, lighting, HVAC, and electrical systems that can support the symbolism. Responsible designers and constructors consider energy-conserving opportunities with leisurely paybacks, because a building will consume energy for 50 years or more.

This short chapter begins with a discussion of electrical energy use in buildings, and an attempt to quantify lighting, duplex, and HVAC loads. Electric bill profiles for existing buildings are analyzed to explain probable energy consumption by new buildings.

After reading the chapter and answering the review questions, test your skills by obtaining, plotting, and analyzing a year's utility bills for a commercial building of your choice. Attempt to quantify electrical energy consumption by end use, and explain variations in annual consumption.

13.0 ESTIMATING ENERGY USE

Load density and operating hours set building energy consumption. Three end uses—lighting, duplex, and HVAC—can account for more than 80% of commercial building electrical energy costs. "Watts per square foot" is a convenient load index and operating hours are easily estimated.

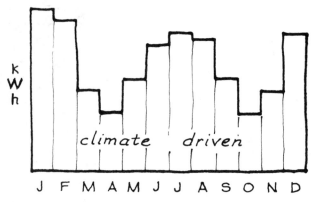

Monthly Electrical Consumption

Watts per Square Foot*

Building Type	Lights	Duplex	HVAC
Office	1–2	3–5	4–7
Hospital	1–4	1–2	5–9
Hotel	1–2	1	3–7
Retail	3–5	1	5–8
School	1–2	1–2	3–5

*Very approximate ranges. Use actual watts ÷ floor area.

Electric bills can guide conservation strategies. Two bill profiles, climate driven or people driven, are typical in commercial buildings. Climate-driven buildings use significant amounts of energy for winter heating and summer cooling. People-driven buildings use nearly equal amounts of energy each month of the year irrespective of outdoor conditions (see Figure 13.1).

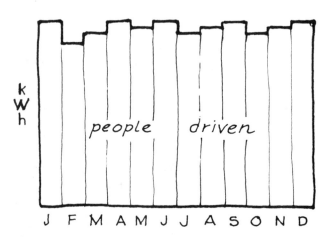

Monthly Electrical Consumption

FIGURE 13.1

ESTIMATING LIGHTING & HVAC

Estimating lighting energy is easy. Total the connected lighting watts, multiply by expected hours of operation, and divide by 1,000 to get kWh. Remember to count 24 hours daily for stair, hallway, and exit lighting. Allow extra lighting hours for cleaning and night or weekend overtime. Dollars are easier to understand than kWh, so determine an average cost per kWh based on past billing data, and prepare estimates in dollars.

Begin by converting peak BTU of building heat gain or loss into kW. Then develop monthly heating and cooling hours based on local climate and proceed as with lighting.*

---

*Chapter 6 of *Efficient Buildings 2* provides more detailed HVAC cost estimates including heat pumps, boilers, and furnaces.

Dollar Estimate Example See Figure 13.2

Lighting

Total connected lighting	40,000 watts
Monthly operating time	250 hours
Average $ per kWh*	$0.08
Monthly lighting cost	$800

Heating (HVAC)

Peak heat loss	136,000 BTU
Resistance heating capacity	40 kW
January heating hours	400 hours
Average $ per kWh*	$0.07
January heating cost	$1,120

Cooling (HVAC)

Peak heat gain	120,000 BTU
Cooling energy at 1 kW per ton	12 kW
July cooling hours	420 hours
Average $ per kWh*	$0.06
July cooling cost	$302

* $ per kWh arbitrary here. Use actual local utility costs.

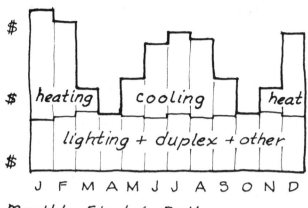

Monthly Electric Dollars

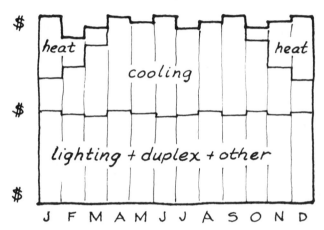

Monthly Electric Dollars

FIGURE 13.2

OTHER ENERGY USES

Lighting, duplex, and HVAC loads are large electrical energy end uses in many commercial buildings, but refrigeration, food preparation, and water heating can be substantial in selected occupancies.

Refrigeration

Supermarkets use more than half of their electrical energy for refrigeration. The good news is refrigeration replaces lots of HVAC load. Air lost from food coolers aids summer cooling, and heat rejected by refrigeration condensers can be recycled for winter heating.

Refrigeration equipment typically operates for at least 16 hours a day. Capacity is rated in horsepower and 1 horsepower produces about 1 ton (12,000 BTUH) of cooling.

When preparing an energy estimate for a new building with lots of refrigeration, verify actual operating hours for similar existing buildings in the same climate.

Food Preparation

Restaurants use substantial amounts of energy for cooking and refrigeration. Moreover, kitchen ventilation requirements increase HVAC loads. Consult restaurant operators and kitchen equipment suppliers before developing energy estimates for these occupancies.

Water Heating

Hotels use lots of hot water between 6 and 8 AM for showers. Estimate water heating BTU for each shower at 1,200 BTU per minute of shower operation. Laundries also use a great deal of hot water. Washer manufacturers can provide water quantity and temperature requirements.

Electric water heating is usually expensive and inefficient. Use it *only* where gas, oil, or propane is not available.

Duplex Loads

Efficient lamps and ballasts have reduced building lighting loads, but increased duplex loads like computers, monitors, scanners, and printers eliminate lighting savings and increase total energy use.

13.1 BUILDING ENERGY PROFILES

Studying energy consumption in existing buildings will enhance your ability to develop valid estimates for new buildings. Electric bills for the past 12 months are easily available for most buildings, and historical bills are accessible without great difficulty. Bills tabulate energy consumption, and they reveal energy use patterns that suggest effective energy-conserving strategies.

A monthly graph of annual energy use is the ideal starting point for studying energy consumption. Two example "all electric" buildings are used to illustrate utility bill analysis.

BUILDING A

Building A is climate driven. The winter and summer graph mountains are heating and cooling energy (see Figure 13.3). Lighting-duplex energy is estimated using watts per square foot and operating hours. Other energy can include elevators, water heating, refrigeration, pumps, food preparation, landscape lighting, security systems, and so on.

Strategies for reducing energy consumption in building A should focus first on heating and cooling loads. Cost-effective energy-conserving renovations may include double glazing, added insulation, more efficient heating-cooling equipment, and reduced ventilation rates.

BUILDING B

Building B is occupant driven. The internal heat from people, lights, and equipment conceals heating and cooling requirements (see Figure 13.4). Actually, building B uses more cooling energy than building A, but it's hidden by the nearly uniform monthly totals. During cold weather the heating system is warming the building perimeter while the cooling system cools the "heat rich" interior. Many large buildings meter heating and cooling loads separately. On the graph they're estimated as explained previously.

Strategies for reducing energy consumption in building B should focus first on internal loads. Cost-effective energy-conserving renovations will include new lighting, heating and cooling, and ventilation equipment. Renovations that upgrade the building envelope will not be cost-effective until the internal loads are minimized.

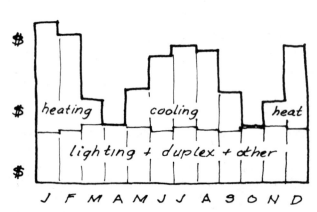

FIGURE 13.3

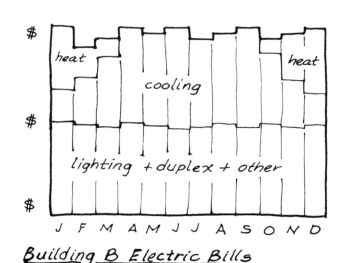

FIGURE 13.4

13.2 DEMAND CHARGES

The preceding examples are based on consumption, but don't despair as you read the following paragraphs about demand charges. An average cost per kWh for consumption is a valid analysis tool, even when demand charges are a large part of a customer's bill.

UTILITY DEMAND

Most electric utilities in the United States experience peak demand between 4 and 8 PM on a hot summer day (see Figure 13.5). Demand billing allocates the costs of generating capacity, and charges are usually based on the maximum kW demand metered in any 15-minute period during a billing month.

An ideal utility customer would impose a constant electrical demand 24 hours a day. With a constant load, utilities could operate plant and distribution lines at full capacity, maximizing operating efficiency. However, electrical demand varies on a daily, weekly, monthly, and annual basis. Utilities offer discount rates for customers who take power during "off peak" periods.

DEMAND COSTS

Commercial buildings are billed for demand plus consumption while residential buildings are billed a higher rate for consumption only (see Figure 13.6). The following example illustrates commercial and residential billing.

Demand can be reduced by many of the same techniques that reduce energy consumption. However, if existing lighting, HVAC equipment, and controls are not upgraded, envelope improvements will probably *not* reduce electrical demand.

Billing Example

Commercial rate— 3¢ per kWh plus $20 per kW demand. Store uses 15,000 kWh per month and has a peak demand of 35 kW.

monthly bill = $1,150

Residential rate—8¢ per kWh. Residence uses 1,500 kWh per month.

monthly bill = $120

Note: The average cost per kWh is nearly equal for these two customers. Envelope upgrades will be most effective in cutting utility costs for the home; while lighting and electrical upgrades will be most effective for the store.

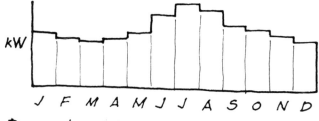

Demand ~ utility year

Demand ~ peak week

Demand ~ peak day

FIGURE 13.5

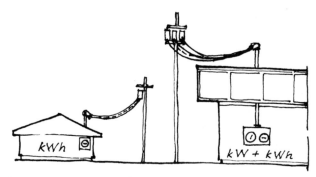

FIGURE 13.6

13.3 REDUCE DEMAND kW

Utilities offer discounts to customers who reduce electrical demand during the peak load period. Programmed controls can cycle intermittent loads like refrigeration or water heating to prevent coincident operation. Thermal storage equipment makes ice at night and uses it to cool building air between noon and 8 PM the following day. Replacing inefficient equipment will also cut electrical demand.

- *Sequencing.* A control system can reduce demand in a cold storage warehouse with 10 refrigeration units serving 10 storerooms. When controls are set so that only eight units operate concurrently, refrigeration demand will be cut by 20%. Sequencing may increase the temperature swing in individual storerooms, but with a design storage temperature of -20°F the temperature swing caused by sequencing will be less than the temperature swing experienced during a typical storeroom loading cycle.
- *Delay.* Air conditioning is a large component of utility peak demand, and thermal storage can delay AC loads until off-peak night hours. Many utilities will pay for thermal storage equipment and discount electrical rates, because thermal storage is cheaper than new generating capacity. Bid proposals from sequencing control and thermal storage equipment suppliers frequently guarantee utility demand savings.
- *Equipment.* Replacing chillers, cooling towers, motors, lamps, and other equipment with more efficient units can reduce demand kW and consumption kWh.

DEMAND SAVINGS

With a current rate schedule and an accurate estimate of kW saved, estimating dollar savings resulting from reduced demand is easy . Review the following example and notice that demand savings can be used to recalculate the *average* cost per kWh.

Billing Example

Lighting	120 kW
Heating (gas)	0 kW
Chiller with pumps, and tower	80 kW
Air handler fans	40 kW
Miscellaneous power	60 kW
Total demand	300 kW
Estimated consumption	100,000 kWh

Rate—3¢ per kWh plus $20 per kW

Monthly bill:

Demand	$6,000
Consumption	3,000
Monthly total	$9,000

Find monthly savings if peak demand is cut 50 kW by sequencing controls (consumption is unchanged).

50 kW at $20 saves $1,000

Update your energy analysis for this building by changing the average cost per kWh from 9¢ to 8¢.

13.4 REDUCE CONSUMPTION kWh

Reducing demand cuts utility costs, but sequencing and thermal storage don't cut energy consumption. Efforts in the following four opportunity areas can reduce energy demand AND consumption.

Efficient equipment. Motors, and HVAC equipment including fans, chillers, cooling towers, compressors, pumps, and controls.

Efficient lighting. Improved lamps and ballasts and reduced illuminance (the eye does not see illuminance, it adapts to field luminance.)

Daylighting. Fenestration sized and located to maximize interior daylight with:

* Shading to exclude direct sun in summer
* Insulating covers or shades to minimize winter night heat losses

Efficient building envelope. Fenestration sized and located to minimize heat gains and losses, and maximize interior daylight. Sealing the envelope to minimize infiltration. Insulating the envelope to reduce heat gains and losses.

OTHER FORMS OF CONSERVATION

Cogeneration

Cogeneration is a term used to describe customers selling power to their supplying utility. A law dating from the 1970s requires such purchases. The law's intent was increased efficiency of electrical generation through on-site use of waste heat. Its effect has been to encourage private investment in new generating capacity.

Cogeneration systems for institutional buildings have been used for many years. Building complexes such as colleges and prisons install generating equipment and use waste heat from the generation process for building heating and cooling. Efficient dual cycle gas fired generating plants and utility deregulation make cogeneration less attractive when natural gas prices are low. Many schools installed similar generation and waste heat utilization equipment in the 1960s, calling their installations "total energy systems."

Photovoltaics

Converting sunlight to electrical energy with photovoltaic cells is a viable way to provide small amounts of power in remote locations (railroad signals or sailboat battery charging). Photovoltaics are not yet economically competitive with traditional building electrical power sources, but some future low-power applications are likely. Peak clear-day solar energy is about 1 kW per square meter, and peak efficiency for cells marketed in the 1990s was about 10%.

Motor Speed Control

Most electric motors operate at a constant speed called *synchronous speed*. With 60 Hz power the synchronous speed of an electric motor is determined by the number of pairs of motor poles as follows:

$$SS \text{ (rpm)} = 3{,}600 \div \text{\# of pole pairs}$$

A motor with two poles will turn at 3,600 rpm and one with six poles at 1,200 rpm.

When a motor is loaded its speed decreases a bit, but motors try to run at synchronous speed. Two- and three-speed motors are made by using only part of the motor windings but these motors are less efficient when operating at reduced speed.

Electronic motor speed control is expensive, but it will conserve energy when motor load varies.

REVIEW PROBLEMS

Use the following rate schedule to solve the following review problems.

Residential at 8¢ per kWh
Commercial at 3¢ per kWh plus $16 per kW

1. In March, a 1,500-square-foot home uses 1,000 kWh. Estimate the electric bill.
2. In July, the home in problem 1 uses 2,000 kWh. Estimate the electric bill and the probable cause of the increase over May.
3. A home has a 240 volt, 100 ampere service. Find the home's potential peak demand (and the required transformer capacity).
4. A 15,000-square-foot commercial office building uses 35,000 kWh per month, and has a peak demand of 150 kW. Estimate the monthly electric bill and the annual electric cost.
5. Find the average cost per kWh for the building in problem 4.
6. The example office building used in the preceding chapter had a three-phase 120/208 volt, 1,200 ampere service. Estimate the monthly demand bill.
7. If the building service for the example office building in problem 6 was changed to three-phase 277/480 volts, how many kW of demand would be saved?
8. The floor area of the example office building in problem 6 is 21,600 sq. ft. Why is its demand charge so much higher than the building in problem 4?
9. Get a 12-month utility bill summary for a building you are familiar with. Plot monthly dollars and then break out annual costs for lighting, HVAC, and other large electrical uses.
   * If a lighting retrofit will cut the lighting load by 1 watt per square foot, calculate annual savings.
   * If an HVAC retrofit cuts 20% (peak kW and kWh), calculate annual savings.

ANSWERS

1. $80
2. $160, probably air conditioning
3. Demand of 24 kW requires a 25 kVA transformer, but utilities allow 5 kW per home because of diversity so a 25 kVA transformer can serve five homes.
4. $3,450 per month, $41,400 per year
5. 9.9¢
6. $6,912 (1,200)(208)($\sqrt{3}$)($16$)
7. None. Service amperes would be cut but demand is unchanged.
8. Larger building, resistance heat, and high duplex load causes higher demand (432 kW instead of 150 kW).